# Building Engines for Growth and Competitiveness in China

# Building Engines for Growth and Competitiveness in China

*Experience with Special Economic Zones
and Industrial Clusters*

Douglas Zhihua Zeng
Editor

THE WORLD BANK
Washington, D.C.

ISBN: 978-0-8213-8432-9
eISBN: 978-0-8213-8433-6
DOI: 10.1596/978-0-8213-8432-9

**Cover photo:** Tianjin Economic–Technological Development Area (TEDA) Archives/Jiao Yongpu
**Cover design:** Quantum Think

**Library of Congress Cataloging-in-Publication Data**
Building engines for growth and competitiveness in China : experience with special economic zones and industrial clusters / edited by Douglas Zhihua Zeng.
    p. cm.
  Includes bibliographical references and index.
  ISBN 978-0-8213-8432-9 — ISBN 978-0-8213-8433-6 (electronic)
1. Industrial clusters—China. 2. Enterprise zones—China. 3. Industrial policy—China. 4. Economic development—China. 5. China—Economic policy. I. Zeng, Douglas Zhihua.
  HC430.D5B85 2010
  338.8'7—dc22

2010017085

# Contents

**Figures**

## Maps

## Tables

# Foreword

In the past 30 years, China has achieved phenomenal economic growth, an unprecedented development "miracle" in human history. Since the institution of its reforms and Open Door policy in 1978, China's gross domestic product (GDP) has been growing at an average annual rate of more than 9 percent. In 2010, it is poised to surpass that of Japan and become the world's second-largest economy.

How did China achieve this rapid growth? What have been its key drivers? And, most important, what can be learned from China's success? Policy makers, business people, and scholars all over the world continue to debate these topics, but one thing is clear: the numerous special economic zones (SEZs) and industrial clusters that emerged after the country's reforms are without doubt two important engines of China's remarkable development.

The SEZs and industrial clusters have made crucial contributions to China's economic success. Foremost, the SEZs (especially the first several) successfully tested the market economy and new institutions and became role models for the rest of the country to follow. Together with the numerous industrial clusters, the SEZs have contributed significantly to national GDP, employment, exports, and attraction of foreign investment. The SEZs have also played important roles in bringing new technologies to China and in adopting modern management practices.

The key experiences of China's SEZs and industrial clusters can best be summarized as gradualism with an experimental approach; a strong commitment; and the active, pragmatic facilitation of the state. Some of the specific lessons include the importance of strong commitment and pragmatism from the top leadership; preferential policies and broad institutional autonomy; staunch support and proactive participation of governments, especially in the areas of public goods and externalities; public-private partnerships; foreign direct investment and investment from the Chinese diaspora; business value chains and social networks; and continuous technology learning and upgrading.

Given the vast number of SEZs and clusters in China, it is impossible to cover all of them. For the purpose of illustration, this volume focuses on three SEZs (Shenzhen, Tianjin, and Kunshan) and on two industrial clusters (the Wenzhou footwear cluster in Zhejiang Province and the Xiqiao textile cluster in Guangdong Province).

The volume begins with a summary piece that briefly reviews the development experiences of China's SEZs and industrial clusters and then follows with the five case studies. Together, they are intended to benefit developing countries in particular and the global development community in general. There is, however, no silver bullet for development: what is important is that each country must find the model best suited to its own unique situation.

**Justin Yifu Lin**
Senior Vice President and Chief Economist
Development Economics
World Bank

**Sanjay Pradhan**
Vice President
World Bank Institute
World Bank

# Acknowledgments

This book was prepared by Douglas Zhihua Zeng, senior economist at the World Bank, and was financed through the generous support of the U.K. Department for International Development (DFID) China–Africa Trust Fund, the Korea–World Bank Institute (WBI) Skills and Innovation Program Trust Fund, and the Multi-Donor Trust Fund (MDTF) for Trade and Development.

The editor wishes to thank Janamitra Devan (vice president and head of network, Financial and Private Sector Development, World Bank Group) for his valuable comments. Ardo Hansson and Vincent Palmade were peer reviewers. The editor is grateful to Marilou Jane Uy, Klaus Rohland, Bruno Laporte, Raj Nallari, and Kurt Larsen for their management support. Special thanks go to Frank Sader, Ganesh Rasagam, William Martin, Philip Karp, Thomas Farole, Yan Wang, Xiaobo Zhang, William Kingsmill, Gokhan Akinci, and Justine White for their strong support and valuable input. This book also benefited from discussions with Michael J. Enright (professor, University of Hong Kong) and Christian Ketels (principal associate, Institute for Strategy and Competitiveness, Harvard Business School). Bintao Wang provided excellent analytical support.

The cases studies in this book were originally produced for the multiyear high-level China–Africa South–South Development Experience-Sharing

Program sponsored by the Chinese government and facilitated by the World Bank, which took place in May 2008 and July 2009 (with the third program scheduled for September 2010) and the Africa–East Asia South–South Exchange Program on Special Economic Zones and Competitive Clusters, sponsored by the Finance and Private Sector Development Unit of the Africa Region of the World Bank, in partnership with the WBI, which took place in May 2009. Most of the case studies in this book have been presented at various South-South learning events, including two Global Development Learning Network (GDLN) events between China and African countries in 2008 and 2009.

# Abbreviations

| | |
|---|---|
| AD | anno domini |
| CAD | computer-aided design |
| CAGR | compound annual growth rate |
| CAM | computer-aided manufacturing |
| CCP | Chinese Communist Party |
| CCPCC | Chinese Communist Party Central Committee |
| CIMS | computer-integrated manufacturing system |
| EPZ | export-processing zone |
| ERP | enterprise resources planning |
| ETDZ | economic and technological development zone |
| EuP | energy-using products |
| FDI | foreign direct investment |
| FSMC | Fabrics Sample–Manufacturing Corporation |
| FTZ | free trade zone |
| GDP | gross domestic product |
| GIP | gross industrial product |
| HIDZ | high-tech industrial development zone |
| IC | integrated circuit |
| IPR | intellectual property rights |
| IT | information technology |
| KEPZ | Kunshan Export-Processing Zone |

| | |
|---|---|
| KETD | Kunshan Economic-Technological Development Zone |
| LCD | liquid crystal display |
| Ltd. | limited |
| MIS | management information system |
| MNC | multinational corporation |
| MOFCOM | Ministry of Commerce |
| MOST | Ministry of Science and Technology |
| OEM | original equipment manufacturer |
| OTC | over the counter |
| PDM | product data management |
| PPP | public-private partnership |
| PSU | public service unit |
| R&D | research and development |
| REACH | Registration, Evaluation, and Authorization of Chemicals |
| RoHS | Restrictions on the Use of Certain Hazardous Substances |
| S&T | science and technology |
| SATRA | Shoe and Allied Trade Association |
| SEZ | special economic zone |
| SME | small and medium enterprise |
| SOE | state-owned enterprise |
| SSTEC | Sino-Singapore Tianjin Eco-City |
| TEDA | Tianjin Economic–Technological Development Area |
| TIAC | Textile Industry Association of China |
| TIC | technology innovation center |
| TSO | technology service organization |
| VAT | value-added tax |
| WCSC | Wenzhou China Shoe Capital |
| WEEE | Waste Electrical and Electronic Equipment |
| WHEZ | Wenzhou Headquarters Economy Zone |
| WTO | World Trade Organization |

*Note:* Hong Kong and Macao are the two Special Administrative Regions in China. China regained sovereignty of Hong Kong from the United Kingdom on July 1, 1997, and of Macao from Portugal on December 1, 1999.

**Currency**
$ = U.S. dollar
RMB = Chinese renminbi; the currency unit is yuan
Exchange Rate Effective June 1, 2010
$1 = RMB 6.8302
RMB 1 = 0.1464

# CHAPTER 1

# How Do Special Economic Zones and Industrial Clusters Drive China's Rapid Development?

## Douglas Zhihua Zeng

China's meteoric economic rise over the past three decades is an unprecedented "growth miracle" in human history. Since the Open Door policy and reforms that began in 1978, China's gross domestic product (GDP) has been growing at an average annual rate of more than 9 percent, with its global share increasing from 1 percent in 1980 to almost 6.5 percent in 2008 (see figure 1.1) and its per capita GDP increasing from US$193 to US$3,263 (see figure 1.2). Total exports have been growing at an average annual rate of 13 percent (21.5 percent from 1998 to 2007), with China's share of total exports increasing from 1.7 percent in 1980 to 9.5 percent

The author is a senior economist at the World Bank and has worked on countries in the regions of Africa, East Asia and Pacific, Latin America and the Caribbean, and Europe and Central Asia. He has written intensively on innovation, clusters, private sector development, competitiveness, skills, and the knowledge economy. Recent publications (including those co-authored) include *Knowledge, Technology, and Cluster-Based Growth in Africa; Promoting Enterprise-Led Innovation in China; Innovation for Development and the Role of Government;* and *Enhancing China's Competitiveness through Lifelong Learning,* among others. He can be reached at Zzeng@worldbank.org.

**Figure 1.1    China's GDP Growth, 1980–2008**

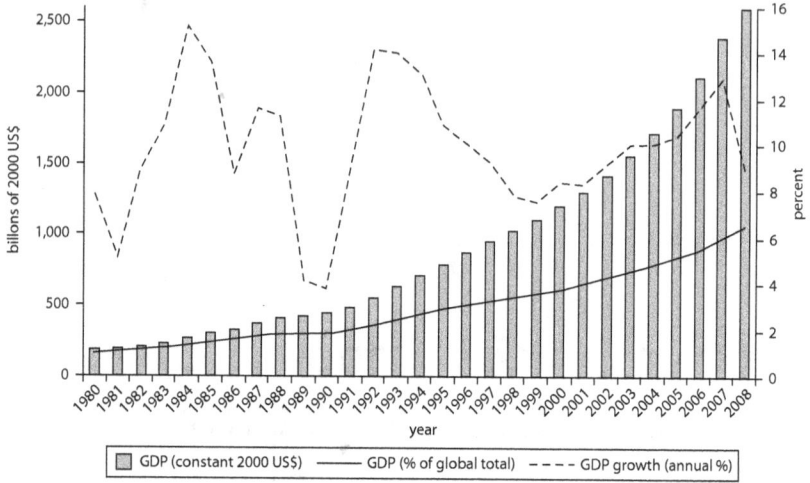

Sources: World Bank Global Development Finance and World Development Indicators central database, September 2009.

**Figure 1.2    China's Per Capita GDP, 1980–2008**

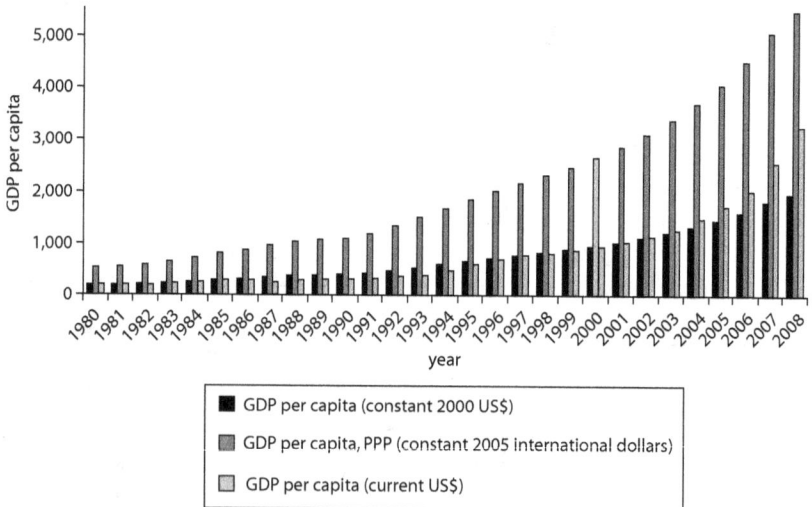

Sources: World Bank Global Development Finance and World Development Indicators central database, September 2009.
Note: PPP = purchasing power parity.

in 2008 (see figure 1.3). In 2007, China's incremental growth in real GDP actually exceeded its entire real GDP in 1979. In 2010, China is set to outpace Japan and become the world's second-largest economy. China has indisputably become an important growth engine of the global economy and a leader in international trade and investment. Rapid growth in the past decades has helped lift more than 400 million people out of poverty. These results are truly impressive.

While China's rapid rise has become a hot topic for development debate among policy makers, business people, and scholars all over the world, the numerous special economic zones (SEZs) and industrial clusters that have sprung up since the reforms are undoubtedly two important engines for driving the country's growth. This chapter will briefly summarize the development experiences of China's SEZs and industrial clusters, based on case studies, interviews, field visits, and extensive reviews of the existing literature in an attempt to benefit other developing countries as well as the broader development community.

**Figure 1.3    China's Exports of Goods and Services, 1980–2008**

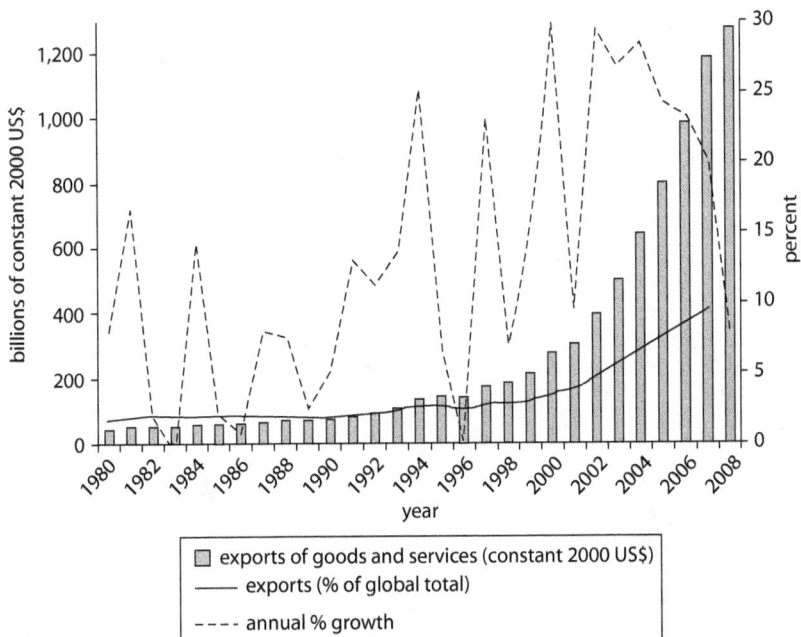

*Sources:* World Bank Global Development Finance and World Development Indicators central database, September 2009.

## Terms and Definitions

As we begin our discussion, some clarifications on the terms and definitions would be helpful. In particular, we need to differentiate between the various types of economic zones and industrial clusters.

### Special Economic Zones

*Special economic zone* is a generic term that covers recent variants of the traditional commercial zones. The basic concept of a special economic zone includes several specific characteristics: (a) it is a geographically delimited area, usually physically secured; (b) it has a single management or administration; (c) it offers benefits based on physical location within the zone; and (d) it has a separate customs area (duty-free benefits) and streamlined procedures (World Bank 2009). In addition, an SEZ normally operates under more liberal economic laws than those typically prevailing in the country. SEZs confer two main types of benefit, which explain in part their popularity: "direct" economic benefits such as employment generation and foreign exchange earnings; and the more elusive "indirect" economic benefits, which are summarized in table 1.1.

The term *SEZ* covers a broad range of zones, such as free trade zones, export-processing zones, industrial parks, free ports, enterprise zones, and others. As used in China, however, the term *SEZ* refers to a complex of related economic activities and services rather than to a unifunctional entity (Wong 1987). As a result, Chinese SEZs are more functionally diverse and cover much larger land areas than other types of economic

**Table 1.1    Potential Benefits Derived from Special Economic Zones**

|  | Direct benefits | Indirect benefits |
|---|:---:|:---:|
| Foreign exchange earnings | ■ |  |
| Foreign direct investment | ■ |  |
| Government revenue | ■ |  |
| Export growth | ■ |  |
| Skills upgrading |  | ■ |
| Testing field for wider economic reform |  | ■ |
| Technology transfer |  | ■ |
| Demonstration effect |  | ■ |
| Export diversification |  | ■ |
| Enhancing trade efficiency of domestic firms |  | ■ |

*Source:* World Bank staff.

zones. In China, *SEZ* normally refers to seven specific zones: Shenzhen, Zhuhai, Shantou, Xiamen, Hainan, Shanghai Pudong New Area, and Tianjin Binhai New Area, which will be discussed later. In this book, however, the term is used in a broad sense; that is, it refers not only to the seven special economic zones (hereafter referred to as comprehensive SEZs) but also to China's economic and technological development zones (ETDZs), free trade zones (FTZs), export-processing zones (EPZs), high-tech industrial development zones (HIDZs), and the like.

## Industrial Clusters

An industrial cluster is generally defined as a geographic concentration of interconnected firms in a particular field with links to related institutions. Often included in this category are financial providers, educational institutions, and various levels of government. These entities are linked by externalities and complementarities of different types and are usually located near each other (World Bank 2009). Increasingly, both developed and developing countries use cluster initiatives to promote economic development, a concept supported by the development community at large. Popularized through such works as *The Competitive Advantage of Nations* (Porter 1990, 1998) and others (Schmitz 1992, for example), clusters have been viewed as a mechanism for enabling firms to join their efforts and resources and work with government toward greater regional, national, and international competitiveness (World Bank 2010). Do clusters foster innovation? Nadvi's collective efficiency model (1999) highlights four key variables that determine competitiveness in enterprise clusters: market access, labor-market pooling, intermediate input effects, and technological spillovers. Nadvi (1997, 1999) and Meyer-Stamer (1998) recognize that clustering offers unique opportunities for firms to take advantage of a wide array of domestic links between users and producers and between the economy's knowledge sector and its business sector. Such linkages have the potential for stimulating learning and innovation.

Clusters, however, are not necessarily innovation systems (McCormick and Oyelaran-Oyeyinka 2007), and innovative clusters are not necessarily high-technology clusters. Mytelka (2004) also emphasizes the role of clusters in promoting the kind of interactivity that stimulates innovation but cautions that the geographic proximity of actors does not automatically lead to learning and innovation. However, there is a growing recognition that cluster initiatives could be an effective means for producing an environment conducive to innovation (Andersson et al. 2004). All these arguments can find their roots in different cluster examples.

Although clusters come in several different forms and various scholars have tried different typologies, all clusters share one commonality: each comprises a multitude of firms of different sizes belonging to one branch of industry. Markusen (1996) has classified clusters into four categories: Marshallian, hub and spoke, satellite platform, and state anchored (see table 1.2). Others have described them by development stage, such as agglomeration, emerging, potential, and mature.

## SEZs and Clusters: "Top-Down" versus "Bottom-Up"?

While SEZs are normally constructed through a "top-down" approach by government policies, most clusters are formed in an organic way through a "bottom-up" process. Some clusters, however, have emerged from or within industrial parks or export-processing zones over time but rarely in developing countries. A study of 11 African clusters across several countries reveals that most of them formed spontaneously, with the exception of the Mauritian textile cluster, which evolved from an export-processing zone (Zeng 2008).

Because the formation of clusters takes time and needs an ecosystem based on market forces, the purely top-down approach to cluster creation

**Table 1.2    Markusen's Typology of Industrial Clusters**

| Cluster type | Characteristics of member firms | Intracluster interdependencies | Prospects for employment |
|---|---|---|---|
| Marshallian | Small and medium locally owned firms | Substantial interfirm trade and collaboration | Dependent on synergies and economies provided by cluster |
| Hub and spoke | One or several large firms with numerous smaller supplier and service firms | Cooperation between large firms and smaller suppliers on terms of the large firms (hub firms) | Dependent on growth prospects of large firms |
| Satellite platform | Medium and large branch plants | Minimum interfirm trade and networking | Dependent on ability to recruit and retain branch plants |
| State anchored | Large public or nonprofit entity and related supplier and service firms | Restriction of purchase-sale relationships between public entity and suppliers | Dependent on region's ability to expand political support for public facility |

*Source:* Markusen 1996.

should be exercised with caution, especially in low-capacity countries, where many such efforts have failed. The challenges, however, should not necessarily prevent governments from facilitating the formation, growth, or scale-up of emerging clusters, especially through improving the business environment and making appropriate interventions in the public-goods or quasi–public-goods areas of clusters. Inevitably, it is easier to devise policies for a functioning cluster and devilishly hard to call a cluster into existence, especially when the essential industrial nuclei are difficult to identify (Yusuf, Nabeshima, and Yamashita 2008). In this sense, a mixture of bottom-up and top-down approaches to cluster development are possible, but initially clusters in developing countries are formed mainly through market forces or for "accidental reasons" (Krugman and Venables 1996). (An exception is those that "naturally" or "accidentally" derive from policy-induced SEZs or industrial parks, along with a few special cases, such as specialized industrial parks in certain countries.) Such a "mixed" approach applies perfectly to the case of China as discussed in this volume.

Despite the fact that government can have more control over SEZ development than over that of industrial clusters, an SEZ is not necessarily easier to develop, and many SEZ initiatives have failed. The success of SEZs requires a very capable government and a well-functioning market system, at least inside the zone or park. To design an SEZ using a purely cluster approach might be possible but can also increase the risk of failure unless the market signals are clear and the government has a perfect understanding of the domestic comparative advantages and market situations (both domestic and international), which is often beyond the government's capacity.

In China, while market forces are usually responsible for initially producing industrial clusters, the government supports or facilitates them in various ways, including setting up an industrial park on the basis of an existing cluster (a process discussed in later sections). Meanwhile, after decades of development, some clusters have begun to grow out of certain SEZs, such as the information and communication technology clusters in Zhongguancun (Beijing) and Shenzhen, the electronics and biotech clusters in Pudong (Shanghai), the software cluster in Dalian, and the optoelectronics cluster in Wuhan. The emergence of these clusters actually hinges on the success of these SEZs, which serve as their "greenhouse," and on market forces over time. Furthermore, in recent years, some cities have begun to set up cluster-type industrial parks, or "specialized industrial parks," such as the liquid crystal display (LCD) high-tech park in

Kunshan and the Wuxi Wind Power Science and Technology Park and the Photovoltaic Industry Park in Jiangsu Province. In these examples, two different models are tending to converge. However, despite the fact that in recent years SEZs and clusters in China have overlapped to some extent, in most cases their origins, development trajectories, market segments, industry compositions, level of operations, and success factors are quite different. Because of those differences, we will treat them differently in this volume.

In China, generally speaking, SEZs operate in more technology- and capital-intensive formal sectors and enjoy greater government support, more foreign direct investment (FDI), and stronger links to the global market. Clusters, in contrast—with the exception of the few emerging from the existing SEZs—usually operate in the low-technology and labor-intensive sectors with less government support. Many of them are in informal sectors and consist of numerous small and medium enterprises, although some of them are gradually upgrading and moving up the value chains.

The following sections provide an overview of the formation of the SEZs and industrial clusters, their contributions to the national economy, their success factors, and the challenges they face for sustainability, as well as some possible areas or measures for policy intervention, so that policy makers, development practitioners, and researchers all over the world (especially those in developing countries) can benefit from the unprecedented "China miracle."

## Special Economic Zones in China: A Testing Lab for the Market Economy

China launched its Open Door reforms in 1978 as a social experiment—one that was designed to test the efficacy of market-oriented economic reforms in a controlled environment. Not knowing what to expect from the reforms, Chinese authorities decided not to open the entire economy all at once but just certain segments: in Deng Xiaoping's words, "crossing the river by touching the stones." Therefore, besides the usual objectives of an SEZ—such as attracting foreign investment and technologies, promoting exports, and generating employment and spillovers to the local economy—one important mission of the first Chinese SEZs was to test the new policies and new institutions for a market-oriented economy. Such an approach was a sharp departure from the country's then totally centrally planned economy.

### The Establishment of SEZs in China

In the late 1970s—after the decade-long debacle of the Cultural Revolution, which left the economy dormant and the people physically and emotionally drained—China was in dire need of systemic change. To answer this urgent call, Deng Xiaoping, chief architect of China's Open Door policy, launched economic reform in 1978—a drastic measure at that time. In November 1978, farmers in Xiaogang, a small village in Anhui Province, pioneered the "contract responsibility system," which was subsequently recognized as the initial impetus for far-reaching and ultimately successful rural reforms in China (*South China Morning Post* 2008). The following month, the central government adopted the Open Door policy, and in July 1979, it decided that Guangdong and Fujian provinces should take the lead in opening up to the outside world and implement "special policies and flexible measures" (Yeung, Lee, and Kee 2009).

By August 1980, Shenzhen, Zhuhai, and Shantou in Guangdong Province were designated as special economic zones, followed by Xiamen in Fujian Province in October 1980. The four SEZs were quite similar in that they comprised large areas within which the objective was to facilitate broadly based, comprehensive economic development, and they all enjoyed special financial, investment, and trade privileges. They were deliberately located far from the center of political power in Beijing to minimize both potential risks and political interference. They were encouraged to pursue pragmatic and open economic policies that would serve as a test for innovative policies that, if proven successful, would be implemented more widely across the country. The four SEZs were located in coastal areas of Guangdong and Fujian, which had a long history of contact with the outside world and were near Hong Kong,[1] Macao,[2] and Taiwan, China. The choice of Shenzhen was especially strategic because of its location across a narrow river from Hong Kong, the principal area from which China could learn capitalist modes of economic growth and modern management technologies (Yeung, Lee, and Kee 2009).

Because China had just reopened to foreign trade and investment, the SEZs had an almost immediate impact. In 1981, the four zones accounted for 59.8 percent of total FDI in China, with Shenzhen accounting for the lion's share at 50.6 percent. Three years later, the four SEZs still accounted for 26 percent of China's total FDI. By the end of 1985, realized FDI in the four zones totaled US$1.17 billion, about 20 percent of the national total (Wong 1987). The combination of favorable policies and the right mixture of production factors in the

SEZs resulted in unprecedented rates of growth in China. Against a national average annual GDP growth of roughly 10 percent from 1980 to 1984, Shenzhen grew at a phenomenal 58 percent annual rate, followed by Zhuhai (32 percent), Xiamen (13 percent), and Shantou (9 percent). By 1986, Shenzhen had already developed rudimentary markets in capital, labor, land, technology, communication, and other factors of production (Yeung, Lee, and Kee 2009).

The initial opening to trade and investment having proved successful, China resolved to open its economy further. In 1984, the central authorities created a variant of SEZs, which they dubbed economic and technological development zones, informally known as China's national industrial parks. The difference between the comprehensive SEZs and the ETDZs is one of scale. A comprehensive SEZ often consists of a much larger area (sometimes an entire city or province). From 1984 to 1988, 14 ETDZs were established in additional coastal cities[3] and in the following years in cities in the Pearl River Delta, the Yangtze River Delta, and the Min Delta in Fujian. Meanwhile, in 1988, the entire province of Hainan was designated as the fifth comprehensive SEZ, and in 1989 and 2006, Shanghai Pudong New Area and Tianjin Binhai New Area were granted such status as well.

Subsequently, in 1992, the State Council created another 35 ETDZs. In doing so, they sought (a) to extend the ETDZs from the coastline to inland regions and (b) to focus less on fundamental industries and more on technology-intensive industries. By the end of 2008, there were 54 state-level ETDZs. By April 2010, this number increased to 69: 18 in the Yangtze River Delta, 10 in the Pearl River Delta, 15 in the central region, 11 in the Bohai Bay region, 2 in the northeast region, and 13 in the western region (see map 1.1). ETDZs are typically located in the suburban regions of a major city. Within the ETDZ, an administrative committee, commonly selected by the local government, oversees the economic and social management of the zone on behalf of the local administration (China Knowledge Online 2009).

In addition to the special economic zones mentioned above, other types of SEZs in China include high-tech industrial development zones (HIDZs), free trade zones (FTZs), export-processing zones (EPZs), and others. Each has a different focus.

***High-tech industrial development zones.*** The establishment of high-tech industrial development zones was to implement the Torch Program initiated by the Ministry of Science and Technology in the late 1980s. The

**Map 1.1   Economic and Technological Development Zones, 2010**

*Source:* Author's research.

main objective of the program was to use the technological capacity and resources of research institutes, universities, and large and medium enterprises to develop new and high-tech products and to expedite the commercialization of research and development (R&D).

In 1988, the first HIDZ was established in Zhongguancun (Beijing). As of today, there are 54 state-level HIDZs in China—25 in the coastal and 29 in the inland regions (see annex A for a list of the state-level HIDZs). Although these HIDZs have played important roles in promoting China's high-tech industries overall, their performances differ; some function similarly to ETDZs, and the line between these two types of zones has blurred in these cases (China Knowledge Online 2009). In 2006, the five top performers in terms of value added were Beijing Zhongguancun, Shanghai Zhangjiang, Nanjing, Wuxi, and Shenzhen.

***Free trade zones.*** Free trade zones were set up to experiment with free trade before China's accession to the World Trade Organization (WTO).

FTZs had three targeted functions: export processing, foreign trade, and logistics and bonded warehousing. The first state-level FTZ, Shanghai Waigaoqiao FTZ, was set up in 1990. These FTZs may be viewed as enclaves within China. Although they are physically inside China's border, they function outside China's customs regulations. Companies in FTZs are eligible for tax refunds on exports, import duty exemption, and concessionary value-added tax.

Currently, there are 15 FTZs in 13 coastal cities (see annex B for a list of the FTZs). Upon China's entry into the WTO, the original unique advantages of FTZs faded. To maintain their competitive edge, China has been linking FTZs with nearby ports since 2004. This process has expanded the size of FTZs and strengthened their logistics and warehousing functions in international trading (China Knowledge Online 2009).

*Export-processing zones.* Export-processing zones (EPZs) were created to develop export-oriented industries and enhance foreign exchange earnings. The first EPZ was inaugurated in Kunshan in 2000. So far, 61 EPZs have been set up in China; 44 of them are located in the coastal region, while the other 17 are inland. EPZs are similar to FTZs but are solely for the purpose of managing export processing. FTZs are the preferred locations for companies involved in export-trading and processing, while EPZs are more advantageous locations for manufacturing companies that export most, if not all, their goods to locations outside China (ProLogis 2008).

The success of state-level SEZs spurred the speedy development of new ones by different levels of governments. By 2004, there were nearly 7,000 industrial parks in China. To curb the blind expansion of industrial parks, China stepped up its efforts to clean up unqualified industrial parks. By the end of 2006, the number of industrial parks had been reduced to 1,568, among which 222 are state-level zones. The total planned area had been reduced from 38,600 square kilometers to 9,900 square kilometers (74.4 percent less) (China Knowledge Online 2009).

### Contributions of SEZs to China's Development

The SEZs have made crucial contributions to China's success. Most of all, they—especially the first ones—successfully tested the market economy and new institutions and established role models for the rest of the country to follow. By 1992, the concept of openness had been extended to the entire coastal region and to all capital cities of provinces and autonomous regions in the interior, and various types of SEZs had begun to spring up throughout the country. Thus, when Deng Xiaoping made his famous southern tour that year, the mission that had started with the creation of the first five SEZs had in many respects been accomplished: the "special" economic zones by that time were no longer so special (Yeung, Lee, and Kee 2009).

***Contribution to GDP.*** Economically, SEZs have contributed significantly to national GDP, employment, exports, and attraction of foreign investment and new technologies, as well as adoption of modern management practices, among others. In 2006, the five initial SEZs accounted for 5 percent of China's total real GDP, 22 percent of total merchandise exports, and 9 percent of total FDI inflows. At the same time, the 54 national ETDZs accounted for 5 percent of total GDP, 15 percent of exports, and 22 percent of total FDI inflows (see table 1.3).

Because of the large number of SEZs of various types and the difficulty of obtaining recent data (especially from those at the subnational level), it is hard to paint an overall picture of the contributions of the SEZs, but some estimated aggregations could be obtained based on available data for 2006 and 2007. In 2006, the 54 state-level ETDZs, 53 state-level HIDZs,[4] and 15 FTZs accounted for a combined 11.1 percent of China's

**Table 1.3    Performance of Initial Five Special Economic Zones and National Economic and Technological Development Zones, 2006**

| Indicator | SEZs | National ETDZs | China |
|---|---|---|---|
| Total employment | | | |
| (millions) | 15 | 4 | 758 |
| as % of China total | 2.0 | 0.5 | 100 |
| Real GDP | | | |
| (RMB 100 millions) | 9,101 | 8,195 | 183,085 |
| as % of China total | 5.0 | 4.5 | 100 |
| Utilized FDI | | | |
| (US$100 millions) | 55 | 130 | 603 |
| as % of China total | 9.1 | 21.6 | 100 |
| Merchandise exports | | | |
| (US$100 millions) | 1,686 | 1,138 | 7,620 |
| as % of China total | 22.1 | 14.9 | 100 |
| Total population | | | |
| (millions) | 25 | — | 1,308 |
| as % of China total | 1.9 | — | 100 |

*Source:* National Statistics Bureau 2006.
*Note:* — = not available.

total GDP and 29.8 percent of exports (China Knowledge Online 2009). The same year, the total GDP for Shanghai Pudong and Tianjin Binhai was RMB 236.53 billion and RMB 196.05 billion, respectively; and their exports were US$44.5 billion and US$18.5 billion (Shanghai Statistics Bureau 2008; Tianjin Statistics Bureau 2008). If the figures cited in table 1.3 are added, then the total GDP of the majority of the state-level SEZs (including the seven comprehensive SEZs, ETDZs, HIDZs, and FTZs) would account for about 18.5 percent of China's total GDP and about 60 percent of total exports. In 2007, the five initial SEZs produced a total GDP of RMB 1,110.7 billion, and Shanghai Pudong and Tianjin Binhai produced a total GDP of RMB 511.5 billion (Zhong et al. 2009). The total GDP of the state-level ETDZs was RMB 1,269.6 billion (Hefei ETDZ 2009). The contribution of HIDZs to the national GDP was 7.1 percent (Qian 2008). The total value added for the 15 FTZs was RMB 180.1 billion (Zhong et al. 2009), and the total industrial value added of 38 EPZs was RMB 562.6 billion (MOFCOM 2008a). Based on these figures, we can estimate that in 2007 the total GDP of the major state-level SEZs accounted for roughly 21.8 percent of national GDP. If other subnational-level SEZs were added, the figure could be higher.

*Contribution to foreign investment.* The SEZs are also a major platform for attracting foreign investment. In 2007, the actual utilized FDI of the five initial SEZs was about US$7.3 billion.[5] The number for Shanghai Pudong and Tianjin Binhai was about US$7.2 billion (Zhong et al. 2009), for the ETDZs about US$17.3 billion (MOFCOM 2008b), and for the FTZs about US$2.6 billion (Zhong et al. 2009). The total FDI figures for the HIDZs were not available. In 2007, China's total utilized FDI was US$74.8 billion. Based on these figures, we can estimate that the total utilized FDI from the major national-level SEZs (excluding HIDZs) accounted for about 46 percent of the national total in 2007.

*Contribution to employment.* The contribution of SEZs to national employment is also very significant. In 2006, the total employment of the initial five SEZs was about 15 million, accounting for 2 percent of national employment (see table 1.3). In 2007–08, total employment was about 1.47 million in the Shanghai Pudong area (Shanghai Pudong Government 2008), accounting for about 17 percent of the total employment of the municipality of Shanghai. In 2007, the figure for Tianjin Binhai was about 0.33 million, accounting for about 5.4 percent of the total Tianjin municipality employment.[6] In 2007, total employment of the 54 ETDZs and the 54 HIDZs was about 5.35 million and 6.5 million, respectively (MOST 2009). Added together, the total employment of the seven SEZs, the ETDZs, and the HIDZs accounted for about 4 percent of total national employment (770 million). Of course, this picture is still incomplete, because many subnational SEZs were not included, and if we account for only the share of SEZs in urban employment, that number should be more than 10 percent. Currently, about half of China's laborers are still employed in rural areas. SEZs absorbed mostly the high-end, skilled workers in China.

***Contribution to high technology.*** The SEZs are also the hotbed of China's new and high-technology firms. In 2007, the 54 HIDZs hosted about half the national high-tech firms and science and technology incubators. They registered some 50,000 invention patents in total, more than 70 percent of which were registered by domestic firms (Zhong et al. 2009). They also hosted 1.2 million R&D personnel (18.5 percent of HIDZ employees) and accounted for 33 percent of the national high-tech output (Qian 2008). Over the 15 years since the formation of HIDZs, they have accounted for half of China's high-tech gross industrial output and one-third of China's high-tech exports. In addition, the ETDZs are also responsible for another one-third of China's high-tech industrial output and exports (rising from 31.3 percent in 2004 to 35.5 percent in 2005). HIDZs are also quite R&D intensive: their expenditure on R&D in 2002 was RMB 31.4 billion and accounted for 24.4 percent of China's total R&D expenditure. Within the following four years, their R&D expenditure tripled to RMB 105.4 billion, and the share rose to 35.1 in 2006 (Fu and Gao 2007).

Although figures are not available, the seven comprehensive SEZs have also undoubtedly contributed to the development of China's technology-intensive sectors. For example, by 1998 with high-tech industries accounting for almost 40 percent of industrial output, the Shenzhen SEZ set the pace for moving toward a more technology-intensive, higher–value-added stage of development, a goal since the late 1980s. Many Chinese-patented products have a large share of the international market, for example, Huawei, ZTE, and Great Wall computers. In 2008, Shenzhen ranked first among all Chinese cities, registering 2,480 new patents (Yeung, Lee, and Kee 2009). As this evidence shows, the various types of SEZs, especially the HIDZs and ETDZs, are in fact the engines of China's high-tech industries and contribute greatly to its technology upgrade.

By every account, most of the SEZs in China, though differing in performance and speed, are quite successful. Together, they have formed a powerful engine to drive China's reform process and economic growth. Let us now examine how these SEZs grew out of a then severely constraining regime and succeeded beyond the most optimistic expectations.

## Major Factors for Success and Lessons Learned

Many factors contributed to the success of China's SEZs, and in every case, the situations and factors might be different. However, their success draws on some common key elements and points to some common lessons.

### Strong commitment to reform and pragmatism from top leadership.

Despite the high uncertainty at the beginning, the top leaders were determined to make changes, through a gradualist approach. Such a determination ensured a stable and supportive macroenvironment for reform and for the new Open Door policies to prevent political opposition and temporary setbacks from undermining the economic experiment with the special economic zones. Deng's southern tour in 1992 clearly demonstrated his determination to reassert the government's commitment to market-oriented reforms in the face of much opposition.

Meanwhile, China did not simply copy ready-made models for reform but instead explored its own way toward a market economy, incorporating characteristics that fit China's unique situation as a country with a civilization more than five thousand years old. At a time when the ideological wars were prevalent, China decisively abandoned such debates and embraced a practical path toward development. This sentiment is vividly captured in Deng's famous saying: "No matter if it is a white cat or a black cat, as long as it can catch mice, it is a good cat." Such pragmatism is crucial for achieving any successful reform.

### Preferential policies and institutional autonomy.

To encourage firms to invest in the zones, the SEZs had in place various preferential policies, including inexpensive land, tax breaks, rapid customs clearance, the ability to repatriate profits and capital investments, duty-free imports of raw materials and intermediate goods destined for incorporation into exported products, export tax exemption, and a limited license to sell into the domestic market, among others (Enright, Scott, and Chung 2005). Favorable policies were also in place to attract skilled labor, including the overseas diaspora, such as the provision of housing, research funding, subsidies for children's education, and assistance in "Hukou"[7] transfer, among others.[8]

In addition, the SEZs (especially the comprehensive SEZs and ETDZs) were given greater political and economic autonomy. They had the legislative authority to develop municipal laws and regulations along the basic lines of national laws and regulations, including local tax rates and structures, and to govern and administer these zones. At that time, in addition to the National People's Congress and its Standing Committee, only the provincial-level People's Congress and its Standing Committee had such legislative power.[9] That discretion allowed them more freedom in pursuing the new policies and the development measures deemed necessary to vitalize the economy. For instance, SEZs were the first to establish a labor market. Companies operating inside the zones could enter into enforceable labor contracts with specific term limits, could dismiss unqualified or underperforming employees, and could adjust wage and compensation rates to reflect the market situation (ProLogis 2008). These factors were critical to attracting the right talent.

In Shenzhen, the government was very pragmatic, and its policy innovations were especially successful. In 1981, the Guangdong Province granted Shenzhen the same political status as Guangzhou, the provincial capital; in 1988, Shenzhen was upgraded to the level of a province; and in 1992, the central government granted legislative power.[10] With that autonomy, Shenzhen carried out many institutional innovations that played a very important role in its remarkable success. For example, Shenzhen was the first to adopt wage reform, in which compensation was based on three elements: base pay, occupational pay, and a variable allowance. It also adopted a minimum wage and a social insurance package superior to anything previously available in China (Sklair 1991). Such a "free" labor market attracted many skilled workers. Shenzhen was also the first city to establish the system of government approval within 24 hours, which greatly improved administrative efficiency.[11] In the Tianjin Economic–Technological Development Area (TEDA), an ETDZ, the government also had the legislative power to experiment with various pioneering reforms. One of the innovations of TEDA was to invite renowned universities to establish campuses in the zone to conduct vocational education and industry-related research.[12] This was an effective way to build university-industry links.

***Strong support and proactive participation of governments.*** The central government had tried to decentralize its power and help create an open and conducive legal and policy environment for the SEZs. At the same time, the local governments made a great effort to build a sound business environment. They not only put in place an efficient regulatory and administrative system but also good infrastructure, such as roads, water, electricity, gas, sewerage, telephone, and ports, which in most cases involve heavy government direct investments, especially in the initial stages. In the case of Kunshan, before it was approved as a state-level ETDZ in 1992, all infrastructure in the park had been built by the local government on a self-financing basis.[13]

Beyond the basic infrastructure, local governments also provide various business services to many SEZs, especially to the HIDZs and ETDZs; these include, among others, accounting, legal, business planning, marketing, import-export assistance, skills training, and management consulting. For example, in Suzhou Technology Park, the government offers seed money, information services, laboratories, product testing centers, technology trading rooms, and the like for start-ups (Zeng 2001).

In addition, the SEZ governments are able to make timely adjustments to relevant policies and regulations based on business needs and market conditions, as well as on development stage. For example, after the zones were successful, the governments began to put more emphasis on the technology-intensive or high–value-added sectors and to adjust their FDI policies to create a level playing field for both foreign and domestic firms. In 2007, China established a common effective tax rate of 25 percent for both foreign and domestic companies.

***Foreign Direct Investment and the Chinese diaspora.*** FDI and the Chinese diaspora have played important roles in the success of the SEZs by attracting capital investment, technologies, and management skills; generating learning and spillovers; and ultimately helping to build local manufacturing capacity. At the same time that the SEZs were opening up in the 1980s, Hong Kong, Macao, and Taiwan, China, were also beginning to upgrade their industrial structure and transfer out their labor-intensive manufacturing sectors. The cheap labor and good infrastructure in the SEZs, as well as the Open Door policies coupled with generous incentives, provided a great opportunity for FDI to flow into China from the diaspora. Given the culture, language, and location advantages, such investments were dominant in the beginning stage, especially for the early SEZs (see table 1.4 for the FDI inflows to these SEZs).

The measures for attracting FDI included streamlined administrative control; concessionary tax rates, breaks, and exemptions; preferential fees for land or facility use; reduced duties on imports; free or low-rent business accommodation; flexibility in hiring and firing workers; depreciation

**Table 1.4    FDI Inflows in Five Comprehensive Special Economic Zones, 1978–2008**

| Year | Shenzhen | Zhuhai | Shantou | Xiamen | Hainan |
|------|----------|--------|---------|--------|--------|
| | | *Exports (billion current US$)* | | | |
| 1978 | 0.009[a] | 0.009[a] | 0.251[b] | 0.082 | — |
| 1990 | 8.152 | 0.489 | 0.84 | 0.781 | 0.471 |
| 2000 | 34.564 | 3.646 | 2.595 | 5.880 | 0.803 |
| 2006 | 135.959 | 14.843 | 3.484 | 20.508 | 1.376 |
| 2007 | 168.542 | 18.477 | 3.912 | 25.555[c] | 1.838[c] |
| 2008[d] | 163.780 | 19.730 | 3.278[e] | 26.970 | — |
| | | *Utilized FDI (million current US$)* | | | |
| 1978 | 5.48[a] | n.a. | 1.61[b] | — | 0.10[b] |
| 1990 | 389.94 | 69.1 | 98.09 | 72.37 | 100.55 |
| 2000 | 1961.45 | 815.18 | 165.61 | 1031.50 | 430.8 |
| 2006 | 3268.47 | 824.22 | 139.60 | 954.61 | 748.78 |
| 2007 | 3662.17 | 1028.83 | 171.62 | 1272[c] | 1120[c] |
| 2008[d] | 3929.58 | 1138.49 | — | 1955.63 | — |

*Sources:* Yeung et al. 2008; Yeung, Lee, and Kee 2009.
*Note:* — = not available.
a. 1979.
b. 1980.
c. Preliminary figures.
d. January–November.
e. January–September.

allowances; and favorable arrangements pertaining to project duration, size, location and ownership (Ge 1999). For FDI, the corporate tax rate was especially generous—15 percent as opposed to 30 percent for domestic firms—plus exemption from local income tax.[14]

Empirical evidence shows that FDI inflow is indeed positively linked with the expansion of output, employment, and labor productivity in the SEZs. Several figures based on the Shenzhen case illustrate this relationship. Figures 1.4 and 1.5 show that the trend of foreign investment in the secondary and tertiary sectors (where most of the FDI goes) appears to be closely correlated to the changing pattern of production, with some time lags.

Figure 1.6 shows that the rapid expansion in labor employment, especially in the nonstate sector, where the foreign enterprises account for an overwhelmingly large proportion, is closely associated with the upward trend of foreign investment in Shenzhen.

Also a study based on the 1993 data indicates that, in the Shenzhen SEZ, foreign firms, as well as those Hong Kong, Macao, and Taiwan, China invested firms, are generally more efficient than their domestic counterparts (Ge 1999). The data on sector output after 1993 were no longer

**Figure 1.4    Output and Foreign Investment in Shenzhen's Secondary Sector, 1979–2006**

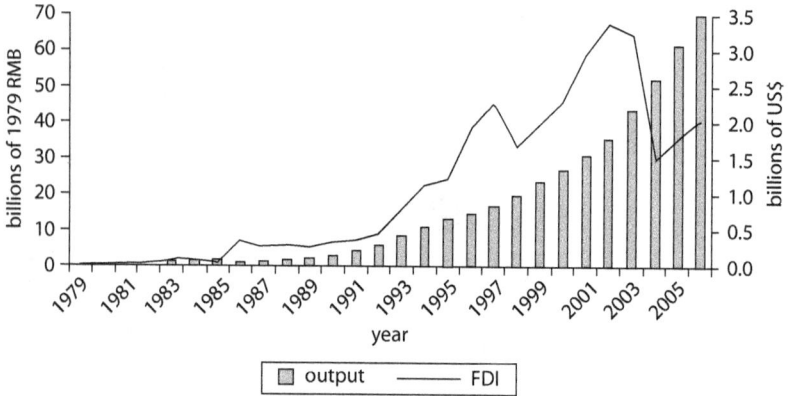

*Source:* Shenzhen Statistics Bureau, various years.
*Note:* FDI = foreign direct investment.

**Figure 1.5    Output and Foreign Investment in Shenzhen's Tertiary Sector, 1979–2006**

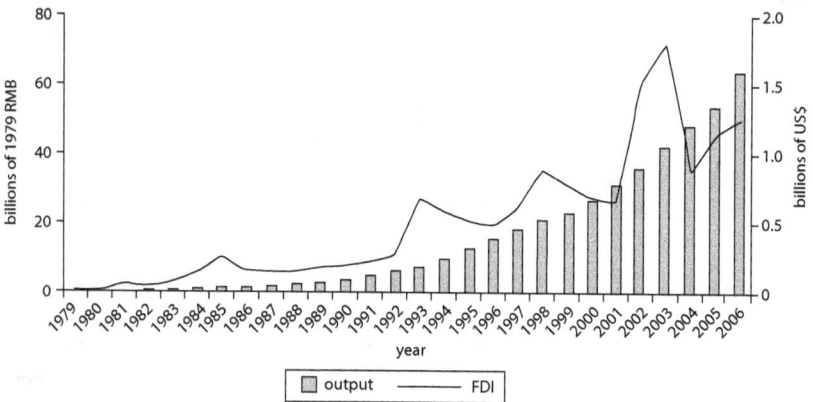

*Source:* Shenzhen Statistics Bureau, various years.

segregated by type of enterprise ownership, so it is difficult to conduct a similar type of analysis; but a comparison of productivity growth between two sectors—the primary sector with very little FDI and the transportation, postal, and telecom sector where FDI is very heavy—shows that FDI is still very positively linked to the sectoral productivity improvement after 1993 (see figure 1.7).

**Figure 1.6    Employment and Foreign Investment in Shenzhen, 1979–2006**

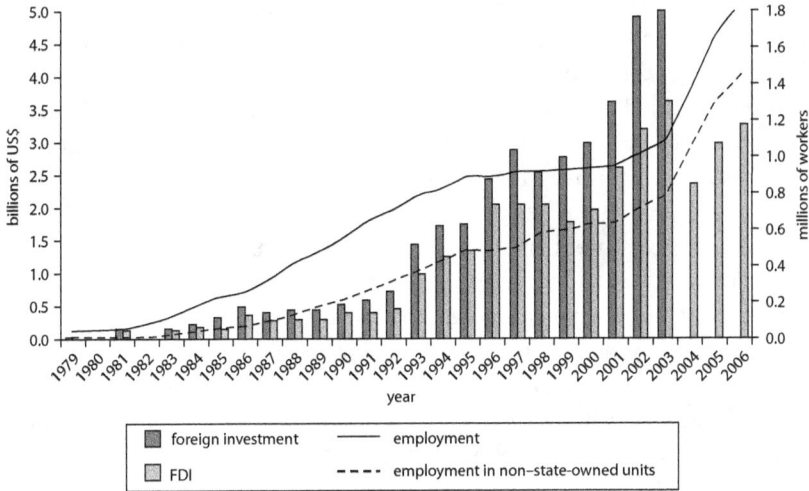

*Source:* Shenzhen Statistics Bureau, various years.

**Figure 1.7    Productivity of Selected Sectors in Shenzhen, 1993–2004**

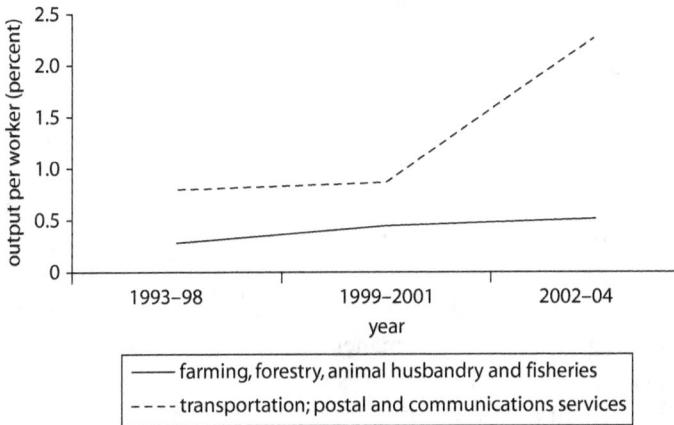

*Source:* Author's calculations based on data from the Shenzhen Statistics Bureau, 1994, 1999, 2002, 2005, 2006, 2007.

*Technology learning, innovation, upgrading, and strong links with the domestic economy.* One of the key strengths of the SEZs is that they have a high concentration of very skilled people, including many R&D personnel, especially in the HIDZs and ETDZs. As a result, they have become centers of knowledge and technology generation, adaptation, diffusion, and innovation. The abundance of FDI provides a good opportunity for technology learning. Governments also put strong emphasis on technology learning and innovation, as well as on technology-intensive industries. For example, the Shenzhen government set up an intellectual property office and issued a number of policies and regulations to protect intellectual property rights. It also implemented many preferential tax policies and financial incentives to encourage high-tech industries, such as the software and integrated circuits (IC) industries, R&D spending, and venture capital investment and to attract technology talents.[15] By 2010, R&D spending is expected to reach 4 percent of Shenzhen's GDP, and the high-tech sector is expected to grow at an average rate of 20 percent over the next few years (Asian Development Bank 2007). In the Tianjin Economic–Technological Development Area, great emphasis has also been placed on technology innovation. Within the zone, the government has built major technology innovation platforms, such as an innovation park, an R&D center, and industrialization bases.[16]

In addition, the SEZs are closely linked to domestic enterprises and industrial clusters through supply chains or value chains. This connection not only helps achieve economies of scale and business efficiency, but also stimulates synergistic learning and enhances industrial competitiveness.

*Innovative cultures.* In addition to institutional flexibility, the composition of people in the SEZs also helped nurture innovation and entrepreneurship. Because most SEZs were built in new areas or suburbs of cities and were open to all qualified workers, they have attracted a large number of immigrants from across the country and, recently, from overseas, who hope for better jobs and new opportunities. Such a strongly motivated migrant community tends to generate an innovative and entrepreneurial culture. For example, in Shenzhen, migrants account for 83 percent of the total population. Among its permanent citizens, 21 percent are under 16, and 62 percent are between the ages of 17 and 44 (Asian Development Bank 2007). Such a young and innovative culture makes Shenzhen one of the most dynamic SEZs in China. Besides the many innovative policies mentioned above, Shenzhen was the first city in China to set up a center to monitor currency exchange rates, to privatize a portion of its state-owned enterprises through stock-sharing plans, to permit the entry of foreign banks, and, in 1990, to establish a stock exchange (Asian Development Bank 2007).

***Clear objectives, benchmarks, and intense competition.*** In China, SEZs were normally set up in batches—initially four—and then the number increased rapidly. Despite the large number of these zones, they all have clear goals and targets in GDP growth, exports, employment, revenues, FDI generation, and the like. These expectations put a great deal of pressure and responsibility on the shoulders of the government. Meanwhile, the hundreds of SEZs are highly competitive among themselves. Each SEZ strives to distinguish itself in service, quality of infrastructure, and appearance to attract new enterprises and reach the targeted development goals. Such competition helps make them more efficient and competitive.

*Location advantages.* Most SEZs in China are located in the coastal region or near major cities with a history or tradition of foreign trading or business and thus are better linked to the international market. They also have good access to major infrastructure, such as ports, airports, and railways. The location advantage is especially obvious for the SEZs in the Pearl River Delta region (close to Hong Kong, China) and the Min Delta region (close to Taiwan, China). Hong Kong, China has provided capital, logistical support, access to world markets, management know-how, technology, and management skills. The Pearl River Delta region has provided labor, land, and natural resources. It is this interaction that has allowed the Greater Pearl River Delta region to emerge relatively quickly as one of the world's major manufacturing bases (Enright, Scott, and Chung 2005).

It is worth noting that, despite the overall success of China's SEZs, they have great disparities in performance and speed of growth. Given the numerous SEZs, a broad assessment is difficult, but a preliminary comparison among the three initial SEZs in Guangdong Province could yield some interesting lessons. Although all three were given the same privileged status at almost the same time, Shenzhen has been growing much faster and is much more innovative than the other two. This superiority could be attributed to many factors, but one could be the capacity of an SEZ to identify its comparative advantages and bottlenecks accurately and implement the right strategy to remove problems as well as to build a conducive business environment.

While Shenzhen was quick in identifying its industrial position and to build a good enabling environment, Zhuhai and Shantou seemed a step behind. With the intense competition for FDI, the first-mover advantage is always important. Zhuhai actually overbuilt its infrastructure beyond sustainable demand, and the symbolic relationship with Macao, China has not blossomed (Yeung, Lee, and Kee 2009). Its oversized airport exhausted its initial capital and became a drag on its economy (Zhong et al. 2009). Shantou has reached average rates of economic growth, but at various times that growth has been stalled by scandals traced to corruption, customs irregularities, smuggling, and the like. It also suffers from poor social credit and trust. In addition, the urban and zone management is not well planned, and there have been some institutional conflicts (Zhong et al. 2009).

In addition, although all SEZs enjoy a flexible policy environment, Shenzhen seems to be more innovative in designing many probusiness policies and institutions, perhaps because of its immigrant culture, where investors feel more accepted and have a sense of ownership. In comparison, Zhuhai and Shantou are historic cities with strong local customs and culture, as well as their own languages. Such an environment might sometimes deter foreign investors and innovative approaches. This could be an exogenous factor for the performance gap among them, although it is hard to prove.

## Industrial Clusters in China:
## A Competitive Engine for the Local Economy

The advantages of industrial clusters have been well documented in different literatures. Since the seminal work of Alfred Marshall (*Principles of Economics* 1920), three major advantages of industrial clusters have conventionally been recognized: information spillovers, the specialization and division of labor among enterprises, and the development of skilled labor markets. Sonobe and Otsuka (2006) further defined them into two: first, the development of markets, which facilitates the transactions of parts, final goods, and skilled workers among parts suppliers, assemblers, and merchants; and second, the promotion of innovation through attracting useful human resources.

In general, the colocation of numerous firms can generate substantial employment and achieve significant benefits through economies of scale. Clusters also enhance industrial competitiveness through product specialization and improve the collective efficiency through business value chains and lowered transaction costs. In addition, clustered firms also foster a high degree of networking and interconnections that encourage knowledge and technology spillovers, thus stimulating productivity and innovation. Such enterprises can acquire a self-sustaining dynamic arising from a resilient comparative advantage in a specific range of products and services. Furthermore, innovative clusters are able to diversify and transition to a fresh line of products if demand for the existing product mix declines (Yusuf, Nabeshima, and Yamashita 2008).

Without a doubt, one of the reasons for China's spectacular industrial dynamics in the past decades is the agglomeration of specialized enterprises that sprang up since the reforms in extremely varied forms and deeply affected the development of certain regions (Ganne and Lecler 2009). These agglomerations of enterprises make up an important part of the competitive power of the country, especially in the traditional industries, although some of them are also operating or are gradually upgrading into technology-intensive sectors. They are an important driver of China's rapid export-led growth.

Given the large magnitude of industrial clusters in China, it is virtually impossible to examine all of them. Here we intend to give a brief overview of their formation, success factors, challenges, and lessons learned through several case studies.

### A Brief Overview of China's Industrial Clusters

As in many other countries, most of the industrial clusters in China have emerged spontaneously, but government (especially local governments) has given all kinds of support to their development process.[17] These clusters operate mainly in the labor-intensive manufacturing sectors, that is, at the lower end of the global value chain. In recent years, some high-end clusters have also grown out of SEZs, such as those in Beijing, Shanghai, and Shenzhen, whose success is inseparable from the success of the SEZs studied above. Such clusters, however, are not within the scope of this volume.

The majority of the industrial clusters in China are concentrated in the coastal region, especially in Zhejiang, Guangdong, Fujian, and Jiangsu provinces. At the beginning of the 21st century, a quarter of the 404 administrative towns in the Pearl River Delta in Guangdong made up some 100 clusters of specialized activity. The province of Zhejiang, for example, possesses more than 300 clusters, which, in terms of production capacity, might have entered the world's top 10 in their sectors, respectively, with more than 100 others in second position (Ganne and Lecler 2009); these clusters exist in parallel with the hundreds of SEZs. Many reports have commented on China's export-oriented clusters:

> Buyers from New York to Tokyo want to be able to buy 500,000 pairs of socks all at once, or 300,000 neckties, 100,000 children's jackets, or 50,000 size 36B bras. Increasingly, the places that best accommodate orders are China's giant new specialty cities. . . . Each was built to specialize in making

just one thing, including some of the most pedestrian of goods: cigarette lighters, badges, neckties, and fasteners. The clusters are one reason China's shipments of socks to the U.S. have soared from 6 million pairs in 2000 to 670 million pairs last year [2004]. (Wang 2009)

Because of the difficulty in obtaining data, it is hard to quantify the overall contributions of industrial clusters to China's economic development, but some examples could provide us a bird's-eye view. In 2003, more than 20,000 companies in the footwear clusters in China produced some 6 billion pairs of shoes of various kinds, of which more than 3.87 billion pairs with a total value of US$9.47 billion were exported. Sixty percent of the shoes made in China entered the international market, accounting for 25 percent of the total turnover of the shoe industry in the world. Currently, only Wenzhou's footwear products account for one-quarter of China's and one-eighth of the world's total, with more than 300,000 employees.[18] In the Dalang apparel cluster in Guangdong Province, nearly 2,000 woolen firms with more than 100,000 workers produce some 200 million sets of sweaters, which account for 30 percent of the domestic market. In the Datang socks cluster in Zhejiang Province, nearly 5,000 firms plus 1,600 shops employ about 90 percent of the residents of the town. Hangji, a town of 120 square kilometers and a population of 35,000 people in Jiangsu Province, produce 30 percent of the world's toothbrushes and 80 percent of China's (Wang 2009). In 2007, 228 clusters in Guangdong, with a GDP of RMB 765 billion, accounted for 25 percent of the total provincial GDP and about 8 percent of the total employment (see table 1.5); these clusters have become the main economic driver of the provincial economy. In the town of Xiqiao (Guangdong), the textile cluster accounted for 60 percent of Xiqiao's total GDP, 30 percent of the textile fabrics market of Guangdong

**Table 1.5   Cluster Employment as a Share of Total Employment in Guangdong Province, 2001–07**

|  | 2001 | 2002 | 2003 | 2004 | 2005 | 2006 | 2007 |
|---|---|---|---|---|---|---|---|
| Cluster employees | 52.95 | 182.29 | 241.74 | 266.74 | 370.71 | — | 431.48 |
| Total employees | 4,058.63 | 4,134.37 | 4,395.93 | 4,681.89 | 5,022.97 | 5,250.09 | 5,402.65 |
| Cluster employment (%) | 1.30 | 4.41 | 5.50 | 5.70 | 7.38 | — | 7.99 |

Sources: Chapter 6 of this volume and Guangdong Statistical Yearbook 2009.
Note: — = no data available.

Province, 11 percent of the domestic market, and 6 percent of the global market, employing about 43 percent of Xiqiao's population.[19]

Although the total employment in the clusters in China as a whole is hard to gauge, employment is likely to be much higher in clusters than in the SEZs, because most of the clusters are in labor-intensive sectors.

## Cluster Formation

Each cluster has its own development trajectory and was formed in a different way. By examining many of them, however, we may be able to identify some common elements that led, in varying degrees, to their formation:

- *The Open Door policy and reform.* Almost all the clusters were formed after China's opening up. The reforms and Open Door policies provided a macroenvironment that allowed the private sector to flourish and foreign investment to enter China. Before the reforms, all private businesses were officially forbidden.

- *Long history of production or business activities in a particular sector.* Business activity in a given sector preceded many Chinese clusters. For example, the Wenzhou footwear cluster in Zhejiang Province has a long history of shoemaking, dating back to 422 AD, and has built up local production capacity over time;[20] the textile industry in Xiqiao, in Guangdong Province, first prospered during the Tang Dynasty (618–907 AD) and peaked in the Ming Dynasty (1368–1644 AD) and thus had accumulated strong capacity in silk and yarn production before the reform;[21] and the toothbrush industry in Hangji, Jiangsu Province, dates back to the Qing Dynasty (1644–1911 AD) (Wang 2009).

- *Proximity to major local markets and infrastructure.* In general, most of these clusters are located in the coastal region, close to international markets. In addition, they are also generally based in a town or major city and are thus close to main roads, railways, highways, and ports. This location advantage is especially important for export-oriented clusters.

- *Entrepreneurs with tacit knowledge and skills in production and trading.* The long tradition and knowledge passed down from generation to generation through family and kinship ties have played important roles in cluster formation. For example, in the Wenzhou shoemaking cluster, it was those families with specialties in shoemaking that first started the low-end business after the reforms and the economic opening up.[22] In Xiqiao, almost no one from the first generation of entrepreneurs had graduated from any textile university or college, but most of them had had some processing experience in the past and had acquired some professional knowledge and skills.[23]

- *Foreign direct investment and the diaspora.* Clusters benefiting from FDI and the diaspora are concentrated mostly on the eastern side of the Pearl River Delta region, in the Dongguan, Huizhou, and Shenzhen areas. The economies of these clusters are driven mainly by overseas Chinese and foreign firms because of the region's proximity to Hong Kong, China and the preferential development policies in 1980s.[24]

- *Natural and human endowments.* Such factors are especially important for natural resource–based clusters, such as those in seafood process-ing, fruits, stone carving, aquaculture, ceramics, and furniture, among others, in Guangdong Province. The abundant low-cost but relatively educated labor force is also an important resource that the clusters can leverage.

- *Market pull.* When China was first opened up, there was a huge shortage of almost everything as a result of the centrally planned economy. These desperate market needs provided a powerful reason for the existence of the numerous clusters that sprang up in a short period of time.

- *Government facilitation and industrial transfer.* In recent years, because of rising costs, limited land, and tough environmental requirements, many coastal clusters have begun to move inland; some clusters in the middle and western regions were formed through such transfer. In some cases, the moves were highly influenced by deliberate govern-ment policies; however, such transfers are still based largely on market choice, where government plays mainly a facilitating role. An example is the footwear manufacturing cluster in Chengdu, in Sichuan Province, which was a result of cluster diffusion. By the end of 2005, this region had agglomerated more than 1,200 footwear firms and more than 3,000 related firms that produced more than 10 million pairs of leather shoes per year, accounting for more than 50 percent of the leather shoe exports in western China.[25]

Many of these factors can be found in the industrial clusters in other developing countries, including some African countries as well (Zeng

2008), but some factors appear to be unique to China, such as the long history of production in many small towns, industrial transfer, and the like.

## How the Clusters Succeeded and Took Off

Clusters survive and succeed mainly because they are able to increase the diversity and sophistication of their business activities to achieve greater productivity and efficiency. In an export-led growth model, this ability is especially important. Besides the well-known low-cost labor factor, many other elements have contributed to the success of Chinese industrial clusters. These include, among others, efficiency gains and lowered entry barriers through business value chains, production specialization, and division of labor; effective local government support; knowledge, technology, and skill spillovers through interfirm links, including those with state-owned enterprises (SOEs) and foreign firms; entrepreneurial spirit and social networks; innovation and technology support from knowledge and public institutions; and support from industrial associations.

*Efficiency gains and lowered entry barriers.* In most Chinese clusters, many firms operate in different manufacturing segments as well as in related services, thus forming well-functioning value chains and production networks with efficient division of labor. For example, the Datang socks cluster in Zhejiang Province comprises 2,453 socks firms, 550 raw material firms, 400 raw material dealers, 312 hemstitching factories, 5 printing and dyeing plants, 305 packing factories, 208 mechanical fittings suppliers, 635 sock dealers, and 103 shipment service firms. In addition, Datang Light Fabric and Sock City has 1,600 shops (Wang 2009). In the Wenzhou footwear case, more than 4,000 firms operate in supply, production, sales, and service networks. Because the production process is technically divisible, each small and medium enterprise (SME) tends to cover an individual phase of production and is connected by specialized transaction networks to coordinate interfirm cooperation.[26] Such value chains and production specialization reduce operating costs and greatly enhance the productivity and efficiency of all the business activities in the clusters.

In addition, research on the Wenzhou cases also reveals that clustering deepens the division of labor and specialization and helps lower the technological and capital barriers for new entrants, allowing a large number of small entrepreneurial firms to enter the industry by focusing on a narrowly defined stage of production. Such specialization requires much less fixed investment. Meanwhile, small firms in clusters are able to obtain trade credits from upstream enterprises (Huang, Zhang, and Zhu 2008). All these factors greatly enhance the survivability of small firms.

*Effective local government support.* The success of Chinese industrial clusters is inseparable from local governments' strong support and nurturing. These supports often come during the middle or later stages when the clusters have demonstrated their potential. Although the support is multifaceted, it tends to focus primarily on building a good business environment and on the "market failure" or "externality" areas:

- *Infrastructure building.* Besides basic infrastructure such as roads, water, electricity, and telephone lines, to which the Chinese government has given high priority, local governments have tried to build a specialized market or industrial park to facilitate business activities. Such a market brings suppliers, producers, sellers, and buyers together and helps build the forward and backward linkages, thus greatly facilitating the scaling-up of the clusters. In Xiqiao, to regulate the local market and stimulate mass production and sales, the city government set up the South Textile Market in 1985 to replace the original informal market.[27] In Wenzhou, the municipal government invested RMB 557 million to build an industrial zone—the "Chinese Shoe Capital"—in Shuangyu Town Lu Cheng City, a large industrial complex integrating technological training, trading, testing, production, information services, and shoe-related cultural exhibitions.[28] In the Puyuan cashmere sweater cluster in Zhejiang Province, the township government raised RMB 580,000 from different sources and built a "cashmere sweater marketplace" (comprising more than 4,300 square meters of building space and more than 50 rooms). Meanwhile, it formed a shareholding company and invested RMB 40 million in building a logistics business center, loading dock, warehouse, and parking lot. All these greatly enhanced the cluster's business activities (Ruan, Jianqing, and Zhang 2008). Such examples can be found in many Chinese clusters.

- *Regulations, quality assurance, and standards setting.* To facilitate business generation and help clusters operate normally and maintain dynamic growth, local governments often try to improve services and the regulatory environment. In addition, they enact specific regulations, especially those related to investment type, product quality, and standards, to ensure that the products made in the clusters have a market future. This practice is especially common in the Wenzhou shoe cluster. In the 1980s, Wenzhou shoes experienced a rapid expansion of quantity without quality; as a result, they offered low prices but suffered from a bad reputation. To correct this problem, the municipal government issued strict regulations and quality standards for Wenzhou shoes and helped firms develop branded products.[29] Such a measure actually saved the cluster. In Guangdong in recent years, some cities set standards for investment quality to ensure efficiency, including better use of land and less pollution, for example.[30] In the Puyuan textile cluster in Zhejiang Province, when market competition forced firms to use cheap materials at the expense of quality in the late 1990s, the Puyuan township government issued two decrees: the Quality Control and Inspection System in the Cashmere Marketplace in Puyuan, Tongxiang, and the Product Quality Guarantee Stipulation in Cashmere Sweater Marketplaces. These regulations were strictly enforced by the Administrative Committee of Puyuan Marketplace and ensured the quality of the products.

- *Technology, skills, and innovation support.* Given the importance of innovation and technology learning for a cluster's survival, local governments are increasingly emphasizing technology innovation and upgrading. Because imitation within a cluster is easy, firms hesitate to invest in innovation and technology upgrading, and thus government intervention can be justified. In Guangdong since 2000, the provincial government has invested RMB 300,000 in each specialized town, with matching funds from local governments, to build a public technology innovation center (TIC) to support the clusters' innovation and technology activities. In the case of Xiqiao, the township government first set up the Fabrics Sample Manufacturing Corporation in 1998 to develop new fabrics, new dyeing processes, and new printing formulas. After initial success, and with the support of provincial and municipal governments, in 2000 the town of Xiqiao established the Southern Technology Innovation Center to provide technology and innovation services to enterprises at below-market prices. With the support of the Textile Industry Association of China and R&D institutes, the Xiqiao TIC was able to provide new products and innovation services, such as information and technology consulting; intellectual property rights (IPR) protection; and professional training, testing, and certification. It has since become a platform for cooperation among government, industry, and research institutes and a facilitator for enterprise innovation.[31] A comparison of the economic performance of the Xiqiao cluster before and after the establishment of the TIC reveals quite positive results (see table 1.6). In Wenzhou, the local

**Table 1.6   Performance of the Xiqiao Cluster Before and After the Establishment of the Technology Innovation Center, 1998 and 2003**

|  | Comparison of two years | | | | | | | | | |
|---|---|---|---|---|---|---|---|---|---|---|
|  | 1998 | | | | | 2003 | | | | |
| Firm size by number of employees | Number of firms | Number employed | Output (US$ millions) | R&D (US$ thousands) | Number of patents | Number of firms | Number employed | Output (US$ millions) | R&D (US$ thousands) | Number of patents |
| <10 | 795 | 7,055 | 44.6 | 0 | 0 | 465 | 3,715 | 31.9 | 0 | 0 |
| 10–50 | 583 | 26,235 | 130.1 | 0 | 0 | 534 | 25,299 | 94.5 | 0 | 0 |
| 51–100 | 205 | 19,475 | 106.1 | 0 | 0 | 359 | 33,387 | 323.2 | 2,256.7 | 22 |
| >100 | 7 | 1,094 | 61.5 | 230 | 0 | 22 | 6,445 | 339.2 | 3,648.2 | 166 |
| Total | 1,590 | 53,859 | 342.3 | 230 | 0 | 1,380 | 68,846 | 788.8 | 5,904.9 | 188 |
| Firm average | 32.28 | | 0.21 | 0.14 | 0 | 49.86 | | 0.58 | 4.28 | 0.14 |

*Source:* See chapter 6 of this volume.

government encourages entrepreneurs to set up learning institutions; meanwhile, it invited the shoe manufacturing businesses in Italy to set up a footwear design center in Wenzhou to help the cluster gain innovation capacity. In addition, it has set up or introduced professional shoe leather majors in local colleges and schools to foster professional talent for the footwear industry.[32]

- *Preferential policies and financial support.* To attract qualified enterprises to the clusters, local governments often offer certain incentives, including desirable land, tax reduction or exemption, and access to credits and loans. A series of preferential policies from Foshan and Nanhai (Guangdong Province) include tax exemption for the first two years and a lower tax rate of 15 percent in the following three years for high-tech firms. The town of Xiqiao has also set up an award to encourage individuals to bring qualified enterprises into the cluster. Meanwhile, to help SMEs update their equipment, the local government provides a financing guarantee to assist them in gaining bank loans.[33] In the Puyuan sweater cluster, the local government set up an industrial park and granted preferential land, tax, and credit policies to attract enterprises with famous brands to locate in the cluster (Ruan and Zhang 2008).

**Knowledge, technology, and skill spillovers through interfirm linkages.** In clusters, the colocation of numerous firms provides good opportunities for firms to build knowledge networks and forward and backward linkages, which are crucial for technology learning and collective efficiency. Many firms obtained help from their upstream enterprises. In China, many clusters also benefited from state-owned enterprises (SOEs) and FDI, which provided important initial technology and a crucial impetus for the clusters' development. For example, during the 1980s, with the market-oriented economic reforms, many SOEs were privatized or closed down. Many skilled laborers from the original SOEs were laid off, and they either set up their own businesses or provided their know-how to private enterprises. They also helped diffuse technologies and skills to more workers through training or coaching, as was certainly the case in the Xiqiao textile cluster. In the Wenzhou footwear cluster, the original SOE—Dongfanghong Leather Footwear Factory— gave rise to three major enterprises: Jierde Footwear Co., Ltd.; China Aolun Shoes Co., Ltd., and Wenzhou Dashun Footwear Machinery Manufacturing Co., Ltd., as well as many smaller enterprises. Later on, there were many spin-offs from these enterprises as well, such as the famous Aokang and Hongqingting groups (Huang, Zhang, and Zhu 2008).

In addition, many clusters in the coastal region, especially those in the Pearl River Delta, were driven by FDI, especially from the diaspora in Hong Kong, China; Macao, China; and Taiwan, China. Such examples include clusters in Huizhou and in Dongguan, which was regarded as a major base. Among these clusters, many foreign and domestic personal computer–related companies such as Acer, Compaq, Founder, IBM, Legend, and many other diaspora-invested firms have established plants or parts processing.[34] The Kunshan IT cluster in Jiangsu Province was supported mainly by investors from Taiwan, China. The volume of investment from Taiwan, China in Kunshan accounts for nearly one-quarter of its investment in Jiangsu Province and one-tenth of its investment in the whole country (Lai, Chiu, and Leu 2005). These foreign and diaspora investments have become important sources of technology and skills.

***Entrepreneurial spirit and the social network.*** Many of the regions or cities that host clusters had a long history of business and industry predating the formation of the clusters. Although the planned economy interrupted the industrialization process of China, the spirit of entrepreneurship had lived on in the regions. Once the macroenvironment opened up, these hidden entrepreneurial talents were rapidly released. Such a spirit was coupled with a great drive for wealth after decades of deprivation. The Wenzhou people are especially well known for their willingness to take risks and to learn through trial and error, which provided an essential ingredient to their success.

In addition, as in many other countries, the clusters in China depend heavily on information networks and social capital for their operation. Because many transactions involve a number of different parties in a cluster, the use of formal contracts for each transaction could lead to prohibitive transaction costs, especially where a formal judicial system is incomplete or lacking. As a result, most SMEs prefer oral agreements (Ruan and Zhang 2008). Although the agreements are not legally binding, SMEs tend not to break them because of fierce market competition and informal enforcement mechanisms, such as community ties, reputation, opportunity cost of losing business, and so forth. This social trust has significantly reduced transaction costs, and many firms actually operate on funds borrowed from friends and relatives or on trade credits provided by upstream or downstream enterprises. Such a model is quite prevalent in many Chinese clusters, especially in Wenzhou.

*Innovation and technology support from knowledge and public institutions.* In addition to government support, institutions such as universities and research institutes also provide support for innovation and technology upgrading in clusters. In the case of Wenzhou, Wenzhou University has played an important role in supporting technology innovation in the footwear and other clusters. In the shoemaking sector, it has put a great effort into R&D and innovations in leather production and cooperated with several firms in setting up the Leather Production Technology Research Center of Wenzhou in 2004. The center has focused on "green" product development, clean leather production technology, and other high-tech research on leather production. In 2006, the center became the Key Leather Project Laboratory of Zhejiang Province and established the Service Platform for Leather Production Innovation of Zhejiang. In cooperation with Wenzhou University, the laboratory has made significant contributions to producing and testing leather chemicals and to genuine-leather processing technology and performance tests, as well as to environmental management and pollutant treatment.[35] The Dongguan IT cluster has also significantly benefited from its association with Shanghai Jiaotong University, Hong Kong Polytechnic University, and Northeast University, which have established research institutes in Dongguan (Lai, Chiu, and Leu 2005).

*Support from industrial associations and other intermediary organizations.* The industrial associations and other intermediary service organizations are relatively recent phenomena in China; however, many of them, especially those in industrial clusters, have begun to play important roles. In Wenzhou, the shoemaking firms founded the Wenzhou Lucheng Association of the Shoe Industry in 1991—the first shoemakers' association in China. It currently has 1,138 members and 26 branches. It has made important contributions to the cluster through a number of activities: connecting the local authority and the firms, introducing new technologies and helping improve shoe quality, helping firms enter and expand in the domestic and overseas markets through marketing and branding services, providing information services, promoting trade, and providing training in partnership with national footwear institutions and Beijing Leather College. Such activities have provided considerable assistance to the shoe industry in its effort to upgrade.[36] In the Yunhe wood toy cluster in Zhejiang, the Toy Industry Association has played an important role in providing various services, and helped set up the Yunhe Wood Toy Productivity Center, Testing Center, Information

Center, and Research Institute, which have been in operation since 1995 (Zheng and Sheng 2006). These institutions are crucial for the cluster's technology innovation and learning. Such examples can be found in many other clusters as well.

## Reflections on the Experiences of China's SEZs and Industrial Clusters

So far, we have examined the success factors behind China's special economic zones and industrial clusters. Those factors are not necessarily all that have contributed to their success, but they do capture some of the key elements that might be useful to other developing countries that wish to learn from China's industrial experiences. Among the various possibilities, we will highlight several essential points:

- *Strong commitment from the top leadership, and high-level pragmatism, flexibility, and autonomy.* The unswerving determination of the top leaders provided the solid assurance and policy stability needed for the initial SEZs, which then served as the cradle of China's economic reforms and Open Door policy. Such assurance was a key factor for investors, especially for foreign investors, in an otherwise very rigid political, legal, and regulatory environment (Zheng 2009). The unprecedented autonomy and pragmatism enjoyed by the SEZs created a dynamic entrepreneurial and innovative business climate.

- *A gradualist approach toward reform.* Economic liberalization is a means of promoting economic development, not an end in itself. How to proceed effectively with economic liberalization is a question that depends heavily on the situation in a particular economy. The Chinese experience so far seems to suggest, among other things, that a pragmatic, step-by-step approach works better than an attempt to change everything overnight. The key is to minimize avoidable economic, social, and political costs. Using SEZs as laboratories, policy makers have been able to identify problems, sort out issues, develop measures, and test and evaluate results (Ge 1999).

- *Proper role of the government.* As Bhagwati (2004, 54) put it in discussing growth, "Growth was not a passive, trickle-down strategy for helping the poor. It was an active, pull-up strategy instead. It required a government that would energetically take steps to accelerate growth through a variety of policies including building infrastructure such as roads and ports and attracting foreign funds." In the success of the Chinese SEZs and clusters, government at various levels has played a very important role but one limited mostly to addressing market failures and externalities, that is, the public goods and quasi-public goods areas. These range from building better infrastructure—roads, water, electricity, gas, telephone, and so forth—to establishing special marketplaces, technology innovation platforms, R&D centers, and the like. In addition, the government has tried to use the special powers given to the SEZs to create an efficient regulatory system and a conducive business environment, which make the SEZs attractive to investors. Such interventions are quite necessary and also very appropriate. As Justin Lin says, "In addition to an effective market mechanism, the government should play an active, facilitating role in the industrial diversification and upgrading process and in the improvement of infrastructure" (2010, 3). Of course, these SEZs still have more to do in improving the business environment to maintain their competitive edge.

- *FDIs and the diaspora.* Given the severe lack of capital and technologies during the initial stages of China's opening, FDI and assistance from the diaspora were desperately needed. China successfully attracted FDI through its SEZs and clusters, especially those in the coastal region, and they became important sources of capital, skills, technologies, and modern management techniques. FDI also fostered many spin-offs in China. Of course, some have argued that the incentives China gave to foreign investors—such as lower tax rates—were too generous. While that question is still debatable, one thing is certain: FDI policies need to be adjusted according to the stage of development.

- *Public-private partnership approach.* In developing the SEZs and supporting industrial clusters, the government does not necessarily finance everything with its own resources, even in public infrastructure. Instead, government at all levels has adopted many innovative approaches, such as public-private partnerships (PPPs), to address capital constraints. For example, in the early stage of Shenzhen, joint ventures and private developers from Hong Kong, helped develop some basic infrastructure (Yeung, Lee, and Kee 2009). In the Puyuan sweater cluster in Zhejiang, the local government formed a shareholding company with 27 private logistics and transport firms to build the cluster's logistics center (Ruan and Zhang 2008). In the technology innovation center in Guangdong, public institutions and private firms joined forces to conduct R&D.

- *Technology innovation, adaptation, and learning.* Realizing the importance of technology and innovation for the success and competitiveness of the SEZs, the government has increasingly emphasized R&D and innovation by increasing investment, building R&D infrastructure, and offering special incentives to attract high-tech firms. The government has also set up venture financing mechanisms such as the OTC (over-the-counter) in Zhongguncun (Beijing) and ChiNext in Shenzhen—a Nasdaq-style stock exchange for new ventures that opened in 2009. In addition, the government has also designed policies to attract high-quality scientists and engineers. In many clusters, the local government or industrial associations offer all kinds of technical and managerial training to enhance workers' skills. One issue linked with R&D spending is the evaluation and monitoring system, which appears weak in China. Policy makers need to pay close attention to this area; otherwise, huge government-driven efforts might not yield the expected results. To become a truly innovative nation, China needs to build stronger indigenous innovation capacity for the long run.

- *Clear goals and vigorous benchmarking, monitoring, and competition.* Despite the large number of SEZs in China, they all have clear goals and development plans that stipulate the expected targets for GDP growth, employment, exports, and FDI, as well as tax revenues and the like. The central government checks these targets almost every year. In addition, SEZs compete fiercely on performance. Such a competition puts great responsibility and accountability on the government officials in charge of SEZs. Although the clusters do not normally have such clear development plans, the competition over GDP growth is also quite intense, and local governments are pressed to be diligent. Moreover, with the rapid economic growth and increasing environmental challenges of recent years, greater emphasis is now placed on "green" and social development.

The world development community should pay close attention to the lessons provided by China's experience. It offers many useful ideas and approaches for other developing countries, which can learn from them or even replicate them. However, there is "no one size fits all" approach. All the experiences and lessons need to be adapted to local situations. That is how China learned from Western countries and succeeded, and the same should be true for every other country as well.

## Challenges to the Sustainable Development of China's SEZs and Industrial Clusters

Despite the great success of China's special economic zones and industrial clusters, they also face many challenges to sustaining their success, especially given the current global crisis. Although challenges to the various SEZs and clusters might differ in degree, those discussed below pose the major threat to their continued success.

### Moving up the Global Value Chain

Although some high-tech sectors have begun to emerge in SEZs and clusters, in general China still competes mainly on low-cost manufacturing, based on cheap labor and low-tech labor-intensive sectors, that is, at the low end of the global value chain. That position is especially true for the hundreds of clusters. Due to the low technology capacity and the difficulty in protecting intellectual property rights in clusters, thousands of firms compete fiercely on price—a so-called "racing to the bottom" (Wang 2009); such cut-throat competition sometimes pushes firms to resort to illegal means, such as using fake or cheap materials, pirating, and so forth. In the long run, such a situation will adversely affect the future development of these clusters and could even cause them to simply wither away. Although in the special economic zones, the situation in general is better, many SEZs and firms are also seriously constrained by limited innovation capacity and a shortage of skills. Because economic competitiveness increasingly hinges on knowledge, technology, and innovation, how to move China's industries to the high value–added sectors (including services) is a real challenge.

### The Sustainability of Export-Led Growth

China's industrialization is driven mainly by an extraordinary ability to export. In 2009, China replaced the United States as the largest trading nation. The heavy export orientation of China's economy, however, also increases its vulnerability to global market shocks. During the current crisis, the clusters in the Pearl River Delta region, for example, which rely mostly on exports, were particularly hit hard (Yeung, Lee, and Kee 2009). In the first nine months of 2008, some 50,000 out of 1 million industrial enterprises in Guangdong Province had collapsed, and its 30 million migrant workers were inevitably affected (*Straits Times* 2008). Meanwhile, such a growth model often makes China a target of antidumping and trade lawsuits. Global trade frictions will definitely increase in the future, with the increasing global protectionism induced by the economic crisis. All these issues raise questions about the sustainability of the export-led strategy.

### Environmental and Resource Constraints

Related to China's growth model based on low technology and labor- and resource-intensive manufacturing, many SEZs and clusters face serious environmental and resource challenges. With the increasing emphasis on climate change problems, two aspects related to environmental challenges call for particular attention: one is the serious water, air, and land pollution and the huge amount of industrial waste; the other is the increasingly tough eco-standards set by industrial countries for products exported from developing countries. These include RoHS (Restriction of the Use of Certain Hazardous Substances), WEEE (Waste Electrical and Electronic Equipment), and EuP (energy-using products). These challenges are even more severe for clusters, where the technology capacity is much weaker, than for most SEZs.

In addition, with the rapid industrial expansion, land, skilled labor, and energy resources such as oil, water, and electricity have all become more expensive and limited. In some cities, virtually no more land is available for heavily resource-based manufacturing activities, which require a lot of physical space. In many SEZs, the land cost now is several times higher than it was when they were established. These problems have forced some firms to move inland or abroad; however, that is only a short-term solution. In the long run, the SEZs and clusters will need to focus more on growth quality than on quantity.

### Institutional Challenges

China's success began with institutional reforms within the comprehensive SEZs, but now, with the market economy well established across the country, further development will require even better and more efficient institutions demanded by a well-functioning market economy. Such institutions include, among others, a sound regulatory and legal system, including a well-functioning IPR regime; a participatory monitoring and supervisory system; a good evaluation mechanism, especially for public spending; and a sound social safety net. Meanwhile, under the balanced national development strategy, linking the further development of SEZs more closely to the non-SEZ part of a city and the rural area will be an important but difficult task.

### Lagging Social Development

While the special economic zones and clusters have achieved obvious economic success, they are somewhat lagging behind in providing the commensurate social services. Although some SEZs and clusters enjoy a good living environment, many of them do not have sufficient health and education services or public transportation to accommodate their increasing population. Some SEZs are at a distance from their host cities, like an "isolated island" with few cultural and leisure activities,[37] and they worry that once they lose more of their "special" status and preferential treatment, they might not be able to attract more talent and investment.

*Challenges specific to SEZs or clusters.* In addition to the challenges common to special economic zones and industrial clusters, some are specific to one or the other. For SEZs, such challenges include

- *The diminishing of the preferential policies and privileged status.* Whereas the SEZs were "special" by virtue of the exclusive policies and other privileges extended to them in the early years, later on those preferential policies had spread to many other parts of China. After China's WTO accession in 1992, these advantages were further diluted. How they can continue to attract investment, especially FDI, in an environment of enhanced competition could be a challenge for them.

- *The homogeneity problem.* Many of the SEZs or industrial parks now competing in the same or similar sectors lack conspicuous sector or product differentiation. While a reasonable level of competition is good for innovation and growth, too much competition across the country might lead to a waste of public resources, because almost all the zones or parks are government sponsored. It would be more desirable to concentrate the same, similar, or closely related sectors in a few locations where they have the best comparative advantages.

For clusters, some specific challenges include

- *Fragmentation and lack of horizontal linkages.* Many of the Chinese clusters were developed on the model of "one product per village and one sector per town." This approach was very useful in the initial stages for fully mobilizing a village's or town's resources based on their comparative advantages. Once they were successful, however, they found themselves lacking further competitive strength because of small scale, limited human and technology resources, and high-level fragmentation. Towns were actually competing with other towns in the same province or other provinces.[38] How to integrate these similar sectors throughout a city, a province, or a region into a larger value chain so that they can achieve greater economies of scale and have a deeper capacity for innovation is a real question. In addition, research has found that in a cluster, the vertical links are strong, but the horizontal links among similar firms are weak (Shi and Ganne 2009). This weakness will adversely affect their collective efficiency and innovation ability in the long run.

- *Lack of skilled technical and managerial personnel.* In most clusters, the percentage of employees with a college degree or graduate experience is quite low, with the majority having only a senior secondary education or below. Because of the low-end nature of these clusters (many of them are family based), they have difficulty attracting skilled talent and are thus in a disadvantageous position compared to the SEZs (although they too have certain shortages of high-end R&D personnel). This shortcoming constrains their future growth and ability to upgrade.

## Policy Implications

Given these major challenges, China will need to adjust its current development strategy and move toward a more competitive and sustainable development paradigm. How to achieve this goal is a very complex issue, and detailed policy recommendations are not given here, but some general policy directions that might be useful in overcoming the challenges that China's special economic zones and industrial clusters face are provided.

### Gradually Moving toward a More Knowledge- and Technology-Based Development Model

As knowledge and technology are increasingly becoming the drivers for growth and competitiveness and because the cost of resources and labor is rising, along with trade protectionism, China cannot continue the old low-cost labor and factor-based growth model in the long run. Meanwhile, the challenges of climate change and tough eco-standards make such a strategy shift even more necessary. To maintain their competitive edge, China's special economic zones and industrial clusters need to be more innovative and technology intensive. Of course, given the vast pool of labor, such a shift will take time and cannot be completed hastily.

### Putting More Emphasis on Domestic Markets and Consumption as a Source of Growth

While the export-led growth has been very successful for China, the economic crisis and increasing trade friction might make China consider whether it should continue to rely on exports as the main engine for growth. After decades of growth, the domestic market is becoming bigger and more sophisticated, with a middle class rapidly emerging. Under such circumstances, China might be able to gradually increase the share of domestic consumption as a source of growth. This strategy will need a comprehensive approach. Enterprises will need to make more products that cater to domestic consumers, for example, and the government will need to strengthen social security and the social safety net. Meanwhile, opening up and strengthening the service sectors—such as education, health, and rural services—will stimulate consumption significantly. This idea is consistent with China's current balanced national development strategy and will also help move the country toward a more service-based economy.

### Upgrading the SEZs and Industrial Clusters through Technology Innovation and Learning

While China is gradually losing its low-cost labor advantages to other countries such as Bangladesh and Vietnam, it needs to upgrade the current SEZs and clusters through technology innovation, adaptation, and diffusion as well as through skills training. For China to achieve such an ambitious goal, it will have to take a comprehensive approach that will involve but not be limited to the following:

- *Strengthening intellectual property rights protection.* Such protection is important for spurring innovation and attracting high-end FDI, especially in R&D centers. Today, China has good regulations and laws related to IPR protection but suffers from weak enforcement.

- *Providing the right incentives or pressures for enterprise-led innovation.* In addition to fiscal incentives, certain instruments such as government procurement and standards, as well as SOE governance reform and reduction of government ownership through dividend collection and secondary share offerings and the like, could be used (Zhang et al. 2009).

- *Improving SME innovation capacity.* This improvement could be achieved through modernizing human resources management, providing more skills training and vocational education, and establishing certain SME-specific programs such as innovation vouchers[39] and innovation broker-ages.[40] In clusters, because of the frequency of imitation and low entry barriers, the core technologies and skills training have the characteristics of public goods and strong externality. Governments, therefore, need to support such activities, ideally through professional services organizations such as industrial associations. This effort again requires further reform of the intermediary sectors (such as associations and chambers of commerce) to encourage more private and public-private partnership types of providers. In addition, to overcome the fragmentation problem, government-supported technology innovation centers could be designed as *sector-based* in a province to encourage cooperation among firms, instead of *township-based* as is now the case.

- *Strengthening university-industry linkages.* Reinforcing these connections will require policy instruments that encourage joint R&D between universities and industry as well as better staff mobility between these two sectors. Meanwhile, the higher education system should be further reformed to be more responsive to market needs (Dahlman, Zeng, and Wang 2007).

- *Strengthening the financial sector, especially the ecosystem of the venture capital industry.* Building up the financial sector would entail improving the corporate governance of venture capital firms, encouraging institutional investors, and expanding the exit avenues for venture capital investors, among other things (Zhang et al. 2009).

### Implementing Strict Environmental Standards

Enforcing stronger standards will not only improve the environment and increase the focus on quality of growth rather than on quantity, but also force firms to invest more in environmental and energy-related innovations. This measure, however, also needs to be implemented with public assistance. Because many firms in the Chinese clusters or even in the SEZs are operating in the low-tech and environment-polluting sectors, they are unable to comply with certain standards due to lack of innovation capacity, but simply closing them down or moving them away may be not the best solution. Because certain "green" technologies have characteristics of public goods, government and public institutions may need to provide R&D and technological support to enable these firms to upgrade.

We can see, however, that some SEZs and industrial parks have already begun to incorporate green facilities as part of the zone design, such as in the Tianjin Binhai New Area, where a Sino-Singapore Tianjin Eco-City is being developed. The eco-city is envisioned as an "economically sustainable, socially harmonious, environmentally friendly and resource-conserving" city, which will become a "model eco and low carbon city replicable by other cities in China."[41]

### *Further Deepening Institutional Reforms*

Because the SEZs are gradually losing their privileged status, it is important for them to explore new ways of cooperation and integration within a wider territorial and regional context. Meanwhile, they need to deepen institutional reforms and create a better legal environment, a more effective monitoring and supervisory system, a more efficient administrative and regulatory system, and a more conducive business environment overall. In addition, the government will need to withdraw from many functions and let the market and the public-private partnerships play a bigger role. Such a system will be more attractive and more sustainable and will allow the SEZs to stay competitive.

## Conclusion

China has come a long way in a short time, and its rise is the most compelling economic story of the 21st century. Although it still faces many challenges and difficulties in sustaining its rapid growth, it has launched itself on an irreversible growth path and is poised to become a global economic powerhouse and a key economic and financial player. And in today's global crisis, China has become an important engine to drive the world out of the downturn.

While the "China model" offers very useful experiences and lessons for other developing countries, everything has to be put into a local context; there is no panacea for development. I hope this volume on China's two most important growth engines—special economic zones and industrial clusters—will be useful to policy makers, development practitioners, and researchers who are interested in learning from China's experiences.

## Annex A

**Table 1A.1    China's State-Level High-Tech Industrial Development Zones**

| Eastern region[a] | Inland China[b] |
|---|---|
| Province and zone | Province and zone |
| *Beijing* | *Anhui* |
| • Zhongguancun | • Hefei |
| *Fujian* | *Chongqing* |
| • Fuzhou | • Chongqing |
| • Xiamen Torch | *Gansu* |
| *Guangdong* | • Lanzhou |
| • Foshan | *Guangxi* |
| • Guangzhou | • Guilin |
| • Huizhou Zhongkai | • Nanning |
| • Shenzhen | *Guizhou* |
| • Zhongshan Torch | • Guiyang |
| • Zhuhai | *Heilongjiang* |
| *Hainan* | • Daqing |
| • Hainan International (in Haikou) | • Harbin |
| *Hebei* | *Henan* |
| • Baoding | • Luoyang |
| • Shijiazhuang | • Zhengzhou |
| *Jiangsu* | *Hubei* |
| • Changzhou | • Wuhan East Lake |
| • Nanning | • Xiangfan |
| • Wuxi | *Hunan* |
| • Suzhou | • Changsha |
| *Shandong* | • Zhuzhou |
| • Ji'nan | *Inner Mongolia* |
| • Qingdao | • Baotou Rare-earth |
| • Weifang | *Jiangxi* |
| • Weihai | • Nanchang |
| • Zibo | *Jilin* |
| *Shanghai* | • Changchun |
| • Shanghai Zhangjiang | • Jilin |
| *Tianjin* | *Liaoning* |
| • Tianjin | • Anshan |
| *Zhejiang* | • Dalian |
| • Hangzhou | • Shenyang |
| • Ningbo | *Ningxia* |
| | None |

(continued)

**Table 1A.1    China's State-Level High-Tech Industrial Development Zones** *(continued)*

| *Eastern region*[a] | *Inland China*[b] |
|---|---|
| *Province and zone* | *Province and zone* |
| | *Qinghai* |
| | None |
| | *Shaanxi* |
| | • Baoji |
| | • Xi'an |
| | • Yangling Agriculture (in Xi'an) |
| | *Shanxi* |
| | • Taiyuan |
| | *Sichuan* |
| | • Chengdu |
| | • Mianyang |
| | *Tibet* |
| | None |
| | *Xinjiang* |
| | • Urumqi |
| | *Yunnan* |
| | • Kunming |

*Source:* China Knowledge Online 2009.
a. There are 25 high-tech development zones in eastern China.
b. There are 29 high-tech development zones in inland China.

## Annex B

**Table 1B.1    China's 15 Free Trade Zones**

| Province | *Free trade zone* |
|---|---|
| Fujian | Fuzhou |
| | Xiangyu (in Xiamen) |
| Guangdong | Futian (in Shenzhen) |
| | Guangzhou |
| | Shantou |
| | Shatoujiao (in Shenzhen) |
| | Yantian (in Shenzhen) |
| | Zhuhai |
| Hainan | Haikou |
| Jiangsu | Zhangjiagang |
| Liaoning | Dalian |
| Shandong | Qingdao |
| Shanghai | Waigaoqiao |
| Tianjin | Tianjin |
| Zhejiang | Ningbo |

*Sources:* China Knowledge Online 2009; Zhong et al. 2009.

## Notes

1. The historical name *Hong Kong* refers to the period before July 1, 1997, when the former British colony was restored to China; *Hong Kong, China* refers to any time after that date.

2. The historical name *Macao* refers to the period before December 20, 1999, when the former Portuguese colony was restored to China; *Macao, China* refers to any time after that date.

3. The selection of the 14 coastal cities reflected the central government's determination to expose a much greater area to change. From north to south, they include Dalian, Qinhuangdao, Tianjin, Yantai, Qingdao, Lianyungang, Nantong, Shanghai, Ningbo, Wenzhou, Fuzhou, Guangzhou, Zhanjiang, and Beihai.

4. There is a total of 54 HIDZs, but the Ningbo HIDZ was approved only in January 2007.

5. Figures for Xiamen and Hainan are only for the first three quarters (see Yeung, Lee, and Kee 2009).

6. See chapter 3 in this volume for the case of Tianjin.

7. "Hukou" is China's residential registration system.

8. See chapter 3 in this volume for the case of Tianjin.

9. See chapter 2 in this volume for the case of Shenzhen.

10. See chapter 2 in this volume for the case of Shenzhen.

11. See chapter 2 in this volume for the case of Shenzhen.

12. See chapter 3 in this volume for the case of Tianjin.

13. See chapter 4 in this volume for the case of Kunshan.

14. See chapter 2 in this volume for the case of Shenzhen.

15. See chapter 2 in this volume for the case of Shenzhen.

16. See chapter 3 in this volume for the case of Tianjin.

17. In recent years, due to the success of clusters and pressures for cluster transfer, local governments are using cluster policies more and more deliberately.

18. See chapter 5 in this volume for the case of Wenzhou.

19. See chapter 6 in this volume for the case of Xiqiao.

20. See chapter 5 in this volume for the case of Wenzhou.

21. See chapter 6 in this volume for the case of Xiqiao.

22. See chapter 5 in this volume for the case of Wenzhou.

23. See chapter 6 in this volume for the case of Xiqiao.

24. See chapter 6 in this volume for the case of Xiqiao.

25. See chapter 6 in this volume for the case of Xiqiao.

26. See chapter 5 in this volume for the case of Wenzhou.

27. See chapter 6 in this volume for the case of Xiqiao.

28. See chapter 5 in this volume for the case of Wenzhou.

29. See chapter 5 in this volume for the case of Wenzhou.

30. See chapter 6 in this volume for the case of Xiqiao.

31. See chapter 6 in this volume for the case of Xiqiao.

32. See chapter 5 in this volume for the case of Wenzhou.

33. See chapter 6 in this volume for the case of Xiqiao.

34. See chapter 6 in this volume for the case of Xiqiao.

35. See chapter 5 in this volume for the case of Wenzhou.

36. See chapter 5 in this volumefor the case of Wenzhou.

37. See chapter 3 in this volume for the case of Tianjin TEDA.

38. Findings from a field visit to Guangdong by the author in December 2010.

39. The government provides a small number of grants to SMEs that need technology assistance; then SMEs find the relevant universities or research institutes to help solve their technology difficulties. Such a program was implemented in the Netherlands.

40. The government sponsors qualified experts as brokers or agents to help link the SMEs with relevant universities or research institutes to help diffuse technologies from the research community to SMEs, such as the TEFT (Technology Diffusion from Research Institutes to SMEs) program in Norway.

41. It aims to achieve this vision by taking an integrated approach to planning a new urban area in an environmentally sustainable manner. According to the master plan, Sino-Singapore Tianjin Eco-City (SSTEC) promotes integrating land use and urban transport and balancing employment and housing supply. SSTEC promotes the "use of clean/renewable energy and reuse/recycle of resources through innovative technologies and environmentally friendly policies and investments across various sectors," including water, energy, land, and transport, among others. Global climate change and social equity issues are also incorporated into the master plan by explicitly including greenhouse gas reduction and affordable housing targets. The development work of phase one of the project has begun and is expected to be completed between 2011 and 2013 (see Baeumler et al. 2009).

## Bibliography

Andersson, Thomas, Sylvia Schwagg Serger, Jens Sörvik, and Emily Wise Hansson. 2004. *The Cluster Policies Whitebook*. Malmo, Sweden: International Organization for Knowledge Economy and Enterprise Development.

Asian Development Bank. 2007. "Special Economic Zones and Competitiveness: A Case Study of Shenzhen, China." PRM (Pakistan Resident Mission) Policy Note, Islamabad.

Baeumler, Axel, et al. 2009. *Sino-Singapore Tianjin Eco-City: A Case Study of an Emerging Eco-City in China.* Technical Assistance Report, Washington, DC, World Bank.

Bhagwati, Jagdish. 2004. *In Defense of Globalization.* New York: Oxford University Press.

China Knowledge Online. 2009. "China Special Report: Industrial Parks—China's Vehicles for Manufacturing." http//:www.chinaknowledge.com.

Dahlman, Carl, Douglas Zhihua Zeng, and Shuilin Wang. 2007. *Enhancing China's Competitiveness through Lifelong Learning.* Washington, DC: World Bank.

Enright, Michael J., Edith Scott, and Ka-mun Chung. 2005. *Regional Powerhouse: The Greater Pearl River Delta and the Rise of China.* Singapore: John Wiley & Sons (Asia).

FIAS. 2008. *Special Economic Zones: Performance, Lessons Learned, and Implications for Zone Development.* Washington, DC: World Bank.

Fu, Xiaolan, and Yuning Gao. 2007. *Export Processing Zones in China: A Survey.* Geneva: International Labour Organization.

Ganne, Bernard, and Y. Lecler, eds. 2009. *Asian Industrial Clusters, Global Competitiveness and New Policy Initiatives.* Singapore: World Scientific Publishing Co. Pte. Ltd.

Ge, Wei. 1999. "Special Economic Zones and the Opening of the Chinese Economy: Some Lessons for Economic Liberalization." *World Development* 27 (7): 1267–85.

*Guandong Statistical Yearbook.* 2009. Beijing: China Statistics Press.

Hefei ETDZ. 2009. *China State-Level Economic and Technological Development Zone Report (2).* Hefei: Hefei Economic and Technological Development Zone.

Huang, Zuhui, Xiaobo Zhang, and Yunwei Zhu. 2008. "The Role of Clustering in Rural Industrialization: A Case Study of the Footwear Industry in Wenzhou." *China Economic Review* 19: 409–20.

Krugman, Paul, and A. Venables. 1996. "Integration, Specialization, and Adjustment." *European Economic Review* 40: 959–67.

Lai, H. C., Y. C. Chiu, and H. D. Leu. 2005. "Innovation Capacity Comparison of China's Information Technology Industrial Clusters: The Case of Shanghai, Kunshan, Shenzhen and Dongguan." *Technology Analysis & Strategic Management* 17 (3): 293–315.

Lin, Justin Yifu. 2010. "New Structural Economics: A Framework for Rethinking Development." Policy Research Working Paper 5197, World Bank, Washington, DC.

Markusen, Ann R. 1996. "Sticky Places in Slippery Space: A Typology of Industrial Districts." *Economic Geography* 72 (3): 293–313.

Marshall, A. 1920. *Principles of Economics*. London: Macmillan.

McCormick, D., and B. Oyelaran-Oyeyinka, eds. 2007. *Industrial Clusters and Innovation Systems in Africa*. Tokyo: UNU Press.

Meyer-Stamer, Jorg. 1998. "Path Dependence in Regional Development: Persistence and Change in Three Industrial Clusters in Santa Catarina, Brazil." *World Development* 26 (8):1495–511.

Ministry of Commerce (MOFCOM). 2008a. *China Free Trade Zones and Export Processing Zones Yearbook 2008*. Beijing: China Finance and Economics Press.

———. 2008b. *National NTDZ Major Economic Indicators (Chinese)*. http://www.fdi.gov.cn.

MOST (Ministry of Science and Technology). 2009. *China Torch Statistical Yearbook 2009*. Beijing: China Statistics Press.

Mytelka, L. 2004. "From Clusters to Innovation Systems in Traditional Industries." In *Innovation Systems and Innovative Clusters in Africa*, ed. B. L. M. Mwamila et al. Proceedings of a conference in Bagamoyo, Tanzania.

Nadvi, K. 1997. "The Cutting Edge: Collective Efficiency and International Competitiveness in Pakistan." IDS Discussion Paper 360, Institute of Development Studies, Brighton, United Kingdom.

———. 1999. "Collective Efficiency and Collective Failure: The Response of the Sialkot Surgical Instruments Cluster to Global Quality Pressures." *World Development* 27 (9): 1605–26.

National Statistics Bureau. 2006. *China Statistical Yearbook*. Beijing: China Statistics Press.

Porter, Michael. 1990. *The Competitive Advantage of Nations*. New York: Free Press.

———. 1998. "Clusters and the New Economics of Competition." *Harvard Business Review* 76 (6): 77–91.

ProLogis. 2008. "China's Special Economic Zones and National Industrial Parks— Door Openers to Economic Reform." *ProLogis Research Bulletin* (Spring).

Qian, Jinqiu. 2008. "National High-Tech Industry Development Zones." Presentation to the EU Science and Technology Counselors Meeting, Beijing, December.

Ruan, Jianqing, and Xiaobo Zhang. 2008. "Finance and Cluster-based Industrial Development in China." Discussion Paper 768, International Food Policy Research Institute, Washington, DC.

Schmitz, H. 1992. "On the Clustering of Small Firms." *IDS (Institute of Development Studies) Bulletin* 23 (3): 64–69.

Shanghai Pudong Government. 2008. http://www.pudong.gov.cn.

Shanghai Statistics Bureau. 2008. *Shanghai Statistical Yearbook*. Shanghai: Shanghai Statistics Press.

Shenzhen Statistics Bureau. Various years. *Shenzhen Statistical Yearbook*. Beijing: China Statistics Press.

Shi, Lu, and Bernard Ganne. 2009. "Understanding the Zhejiang Industrial Clusters: Questions and Re-evaluations." In *Asian Industrial Clusters, Global Competitiveness and New Policy Initiatives*, ed. Bernard Ganne and Yveline Lecler, 239–66.

Sklair, Leslie. 1991. "Problems of Socialist Development—The Significance of Shenzhen Special Economic Zone for China Open-Door Development Strategy." *International Journal of Urban and Regional Research* 15 (2): 197–215.

Sonobe, Tetushi, and Keijiro Otsuka. 2006. *Cluster-Based Industrial Development: An East Asian Model*. New York: Palgrave Macmillan.

*South China Morning Post*. 2008. November 17, A8.

*Straits Times* (Singapore). 2008. November 15.

Tianjin Statistics Bureau. 2008. *Tianjin Statistical Yearbook*. Tianjin: Tianjin Statistics Press

Wang, Jici. 2009. "New Phenomena and Challenges of Clusters in China in the New Era of Globalization." In *Asian Industrial Clusters, Global Competitiveness and New Policy Initiatives*, ed. Bernard Ganne and Yveline Lecler, 195–212.

Wong, Kwan-yiu. 1987. "China's Special Economic Zone Experiment: An Appraisal." *Geografiska Annaler Serices B, Human Geography* 69 (1): 27–40.

World Bank. 2009. "Clusters for Competitiveness: A Practical Guide and Policy Implications for Developing Cluster Initiatives." International Trade Department, PREM Network, Report, World Bank, Washington, DC.

———. 2010. *Innovation Policy: A Guide for Developing Countries*. Washington, DC: World Bank Institute.

Yeung, Yue-man, J. Lee, and G. Kee. 2009. "China's Special Economic Zones at 30." *Eurasian Geography and Economics* 50 (2): 222–40.

Yeung et al. 2008. "China's Special Economic Zones at 30." *Eurasian Geography and Economics 2009* 50 (2).

Yusuf, Shahid, K. Nabeshima, and S. Yamashita, eds. 2008. *Growing Industrial Clusters in Asia: Serendipity and Science*. Washington, DC: World Bank.

Zeng, Douglas Zhihua. 2001. "Suzhou Technology Park." Research note for WBI Development Series. *China and the Knowledge Economy: Seizing the 21st Century*, Washington, DC: World Bank.

———. 2008. *Knowledge, Technology and Cluster-based Growth in Africa*. Washington, DC: World Bank.

Zhang, Chunlin, Douglas Zhihua Zeng, William Mako, and James Seward. 2009. *Promoting Enterprise-led Innovation in China.* Washington, DC: World Bank.

Zheng, Yu. 2009. "Incentives and Commitment: The Political Economy of Special Zones in China." Unpublished. University of Connecticut, Storrs, CT.

Zheng, Y., and S. Sheng. 2006. "Learning in a Local Cluster in the Context of the Global Value Chain: A Case Study of the Yunhe Wood Toy Cluster in Zhejiang, China." *Innovation: Management, Policy & Practice* 8 (1–2): 120–27.

Zhong, Jian, et al., eds. 2009. *Annual Report on the Development of China's Special Economic Zones.* Beijing: Social Sciences Academy Press.

CHAPTER 2

# China's First Special Economic Zone: The Case of Shenzhen

## Yiming Yuan, Hongyi Guo, Hongfei Xu, Weiqi Li, Shanshan Luo, Haiqing Lin, and Yuan Yuan

Located in the Pearl River Delta, Shenzhen functions as a link and a bridge between Hong Kong, China, and mainland China. The Shenzhen Special Economic Zone (SEZ) was the first such zone created during the early period of modern China's economic reforms. On August 6, 1980, the Standing Committee of the National People's Congress authorized an area of 327.5 square kilometers to be designated as an experimental economic zone. The consequent promulgation of the Economic Zone Ordinance in Guangdong Province marked the formal founding of the Shenzhen SEZ.

Shenzhen's SEZ has been serving as China's "window to the world" and "an experimentation field" ever since the nation's opening up. It is the great passion, creativity, initiative, and diligence of Shenzhen's people that have enabled the city to take the lead in implementing a series of

The authors wish to thank Dr. Douglas Zhihua Zeng, senior economist at the World Bank, for his valuable comments. Thanks also go to Professor David Dodge for his help in improving the English and to Hao Lin for his work in translating the final version. Yiming Yuan, Ph.D., is professor of economics at China's Center for Special Economic Zone Research, Shenzhen University.

important reforms such as the selling out of state-land-use rights, the stock-exchange pilot, the personnel system reform, and the minimizing of administrative approval procedures. In 2007, Shenzhen was ranked first in comprehensive municipal competitiveness among all the cities in mainland China (Chinese Academy of Social Sciences 2008).

Shenzhen's gross domestic product (GDP) reached RMB 780.65 billion[1] in 2008, a 12.1 percent increase over the previous year. The city's total economic output is equivalent to a medium-sized province in China and ranks fourth among major cities nationwide. Shenzhen has become one of China's most productive cities, with the highest per capita income of RMB 89,814 in 2008 (rising from RMB 606 in 1979), and has topped all China's cities for the past 16 years in international trade; its international container port has ranked fourth globally for 11 consecutive years.

Shenzhen has also developed into an important transport hub on China's southern coast and is considered an important economic base for high-tech industries, financial services, exports, and maritime transport services. In the coming years, the city will continue to play an experimental and modeling role in a number of aspects in China's further institutional reforms and its ever-wider opening to the world.

## Background on the Shenzhen SEZ

Shenzhen, a traditional fishing village that has rich land resources and the geographical advantage of bordering the well-developed economy of Hong Kong, China, was chosen as China's window to the outside world and as the field of experimentation for the nation's reform of its economic system. One of the main reasons for the selection was that this formerly remote fishing village had the least resistance to any new institutional change.

In the late 1970s, the Chinese government made the historically significant decision to open up and reform the old system. Within this framework, establishing special economic zones was an important step. These reform initiatives occurred, firstly, because the domestic economy was at a standstill as a consequence of the 10-year long Cultural Revolution and, secondly, because some economies, especially those in regions nearby, were experiencing rapid growth resulting in sharp contrasts to the slow pace of China's growth and its low living standards. To change the situation and catch up with the development of the world, China chose a policy of institutional reform and opening up to the outside world.

## Shenzhen's Unique Geographic Location

On the coast within a 45-minute drive from Hong Kong, China, Shenzhen is the only mainland city bordering this well-developed, modern island city, which had been an international financial center, shipping and regional trading center, and the world's freest market. Shenzhen enjoys a geographic advantage because it has long been the most important channel between the mainland and Hong Kong, China, in commodity circulation and factor imports. More important, Hong Kong, China, has profoundly influenced Shenzhen in its efforts to establish a market-oriented system.

Shenzhen has a total area of 1,985 square kilometers, with a long, narrow coastline of 230 kilometers. It has rich marine resources, an excellent port, and open access to the gulf, all of which contribute to its superior advantages for sea transport. The special economic zone is now an integral part of the city. Except for Hainan Province, Shenzhen is the largest SEZ created in the early stages of reform in China. Its abundant land resources provide potential for further industrial development.

Both the east and the west coastal zones of Shenzhen are also rich in marine resources. Around the city, some 160 streams belong to the East River and Pearl River water system, and 24 reservoirs have a total storage capacity of 5.25 billion cubic meters. The Shenzhen reservoir, on the city's east side, has a storage capacity of more than 4 billion cubic meters and serves as the main water source for the city and for Hong Kong, China.

## Openness and Reform

For various reasons, after 1949, southern coastal provinces such as Fujian and Guangdong (to which Shenzhen belongs) did not receive much attention in development within the planned economic system. In the late 1970s, the region had almost no state-owned industries and its production still heavily depended on agriculture. Most of the area's 31.41 million residents were engaged in fishing and farming before China's reforms, which began in 1978. Shenzhen's GDP was only US$2.87 million in 1978, and per capita GDP was only US$88.86 yearly; the population in the city had low levels of education and living standards. Overall, the society was equal but poor, and its social structure was simple, with no severe conflicts involving different social and economic interests. In this context, given the strong motivation for reform, there was little resistance to the introduction of new economic institutions.

Moreover, people in nearby Hong Kong[2] and Macao,[3] who shared almost the same natural endowments, were enjoying very different living conditions. This sharp contrast created strong incentives among Shenzhen's residents to improve their living standards through changing the prevailing economic institutions and opening up their economy and society to the outside world.

## Development Achievements

After 29 years of development, Shenzhen has become one of China's most important high-tech research and development (R&D) and manufacturing bases. It is now the world's fourth-largest container port, has the fourth-largest airport in China, and draws the fourth-largest number of tourists among Chinese cities.

### Rapid Economic Growth and Industrialization

From 1980 to 2008, Shenzhen's GDP increased from US$4 million to US$114.47 billion, with an average annual growth rate of 26.9 percent. Per capita income increased dramatically from US$122.43 to US$13,196.21.

In 1978, Shenzhen had only 174 factories, with a total industrial output value of less than US$10.25 million. The city's industrialization began in 1980, when the SEZ was announced and implementation began. Shenzhen's industrialization process experienced several stages, with the scale of its industry increasing from small to large, its products from relatively lower value to higher-tech products, and its factor use from labor- and land-intensive to technology intensive. The city has been emerging as a new high-tech industry center.

From 1980 to 2007, the average annual growth rates of the three sectors (agriculture, industry, and services) were 3.3 percent, 37.8 percent, and 24.8 percent, respectively. Starting from a tiny industrial backwater in 1979, Shenzhen's industry has experienced three large leaps in value of industrial output: the RMB 10 billion (US$1.46 billion) increase in just nine years, the RMB 100 billion (US$14.64 billion) increase in the next

**Table 2.1    GDP and Per Capita GDP of Shenzhen, Selected Years, 1980–2008**
US $

| GDP | 1980 | 1985 | 1990 | 1995 | 2000 | 2005 | 2006 | 2007 | 2008 |
|---|---|---|---|---|---|---|---|---|---|
| US$ billions | 0.04 | 0.57 | 2.52 | 12.35 | 32.07 | 72.60 | 85.25 | 99.74 | 114.47 |
| Per capita | 122.43 | 705.13 | 1,279.18 | 2,866.57 | 4,809.38 | 8,915.10 | 10,183.28 | 11,678.15 | 13,169.21 |

*Source:* Shenzhen Statistics Bureau 2008, 2009.

seven years, and the RMB 200-billion (US$29.28 billion) increase in the most recent five years. In 2008, Shenzhen's gross industrial output value grew another 12.4 percent and reached US$521.49 billion.

Since the 1990s, Shenzhen's industrial growth has been the most important driving force in its economic development, contributing half of the growth in GDP. In 1994, industry's contribution was 43.0 percent compared to 11.8 percent in 1979; and since 1994, this number has never been lower than 40 percent (table 2.2).

With rapid industrialization, the proportion of agricultural production has been decreasing steadily. In 1980, tertiary industries were providing mainly basic services. At that time, these basic services and simple assembly industries formed the major part of the economy. Thirty years later, the percentage contribution of the three sectors had changed to 0.1, 48.9, and 51.0 (table 2.3), with secondary and high-tech service industries having become the main sources of economic growth.

Meanwhile, the employment structure has also changed drastically. By the end of 2007, total employment amounted to 7.7 million: some 7,000 in primary industries, about 4 million (roughly 54 percent) in secondary industries, and about 3 million (roughly 46 percent) in tertiary industries.

*Foreign trade.* After 30 years of economic reform and opening up, Shenzhen has developed an export-oriented economy. From 1979 to 2007, total trade volume increased from US$17 billion to US$287.5 billion. Even in the face of the global financial crisis in 2008, total imports and exports of Shenzhen still grew by 4.3 percent and totaled US$299.95 billion, with exports of US$179.7 billion (see figure 2.1). Since 2007,

**Table 2.2  Contribution of Industry to GDP Growth in Shenzhen, 1979–2008**

| | | | Contribution to GDP | |
|---|---|---|---|---|
| Year | Industrial added value (US$ millions) | Industrial growth rate (%) | GDP proportion accounted for (%) | Contribution to GDP growth (%) |
| 1979 | 3.37 | 32.45 | 11.80 | — |
| 1980 | 5.43 | 34.90 | 13.80 | 6.46 |
| 1985 | 149.71 | 41.39 | 26.20 | 61.92 |
| 1990 | 945.60 | 29.28 | 37.60 | 58.90 |
| 1995 | 4,942.08 | 26.08 | 40.01 | 44.61 |
| 2000 | 14,116.57 | 31.34 | 44.01 | 61.06 |
| 2005 | 36,419.21 | 24.41 | 50.16 | 63.35 |
| 2008 | 53,054.55 | 12.40 | 46.40 | — |

*Source:* Shenzhen Statistics Bureau 2008, 2009.
*Note:* — = not available.

**Table 2.3    The Changing Economic Structure of Shenzhen, Selected Years, 1980–2008**

| Year | GDP (US$ billions) | Primary industry (RMB billions) | Secondary industry (RMB billions) | Tertiary industry (RMB billions) | % primary, secondary, and tertiary industry |
|------|------|------|------|------|------|
| 1980 | 0.04 | 0.08 | 0.07 | 0.12 | 29.6, 25.9, 44.4 |
| 1985 | 0.57 | 0.26 | 1.94 | 2.01 | 6.2 , 46.1, 47.7 |
| 1990 | 2.52 | 0.70 | 7.69 | 8.77 | 4.1, 44.8., 51.1 |
| 1995 | 12.35 | 1.24 | 42.21 | 40.79 | 1.5, 50.1, 48.4 |
| 2000 | 32.07 | 1.56 | 108.61 | 108.58 | 0.7, 49.7, 49.6 |
| 2005 | 72.60 | 0.97 | 263.34 | 230.74 | 0.2, 53.2, 46.6 |
| 2006 | 85.25 | 0.70 | 304.95 | 275.71 | 0.1, 52.5, 47.4 |
| 2007 | 99.74 | 0.69 | 340.48 | 338.99 | 0.1, 50.1, 49.8 |
| 2008 | 114.47 | 0.67 | 381.58 | 398.41 | 0.1, 48.9, 51.0 |

*Source:* Shenzhen Statistics Bureau 2008, 2009.

**Figure 2.1    Growth Rate and Total Value of Exports in Shenzhen, 1979–2008**

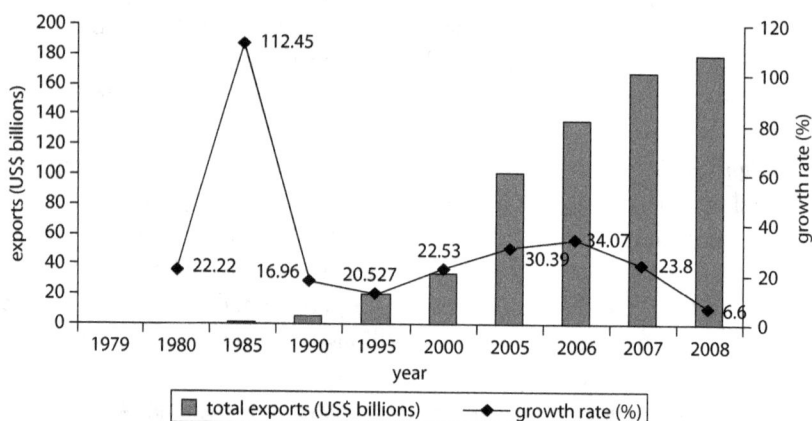

*Source:* Shenzhen Statistics Bureau 2008, 2009.

Shenzhen has ranked first in total trade value among all cities in mainland China for more than 10 years.

*Foreign direct investment.* Foreign direct investment (FDI) has made a tremendous contribution to Shenzhen's industrialization. When the Shenzhen SEZ was established in 1980, FDI amounted to only US$0.73 million. Over the 30 years of China's reform and opening up to the world, together with the implementation of a variety of investment policies, the average growth rate of foreign capital in Shenzhen has been around 28.6 percent per year. In 2008, the inflow of foreign capital was

US\$4.03 billion, a growth of 10.1 percent from 2007 (table 2.4). Manufacturing accounted for 37.5 percent of total FDI; transportation, storage, and postal services for 7.5 percent; tenancy and business services for 9.4 percent; and real estate for 10.6 percent.

In recent years, most foreign capital has gone to service industries, and the actually utilized FDI has been growing rapidly (figure 2.2). In 2008, Shenzhen approved 3,046 new FDI projects, with an actual utilized

**Table 2.4    Growth of Shenzhen's Foreign Direct Investment, Selected Years, 1979–2008**
*US\$ billions*

|  | 1979 | 1980 | 1985 | 1990 | 1995 | 2000 | 2005 | 2007 | 2008 |
|---|---|---|---|---|---|---|---|---|---|
| Amount of foreign capital actually utilized[a] | 0.005 | 0.028 | 0.18 | 0.39 | 1.31 | 1.981 | 2.969 | 3.662 | 4.03 |

*Source:* Shenzhen Statistics Bureau 2008, 2009.
a. The total amount of FDI is the contracted number; actually utilized FDI is part of it.

**Figure 2.2    Actually Utilized Foreign Capital in Shenzhen, 1979–2007**

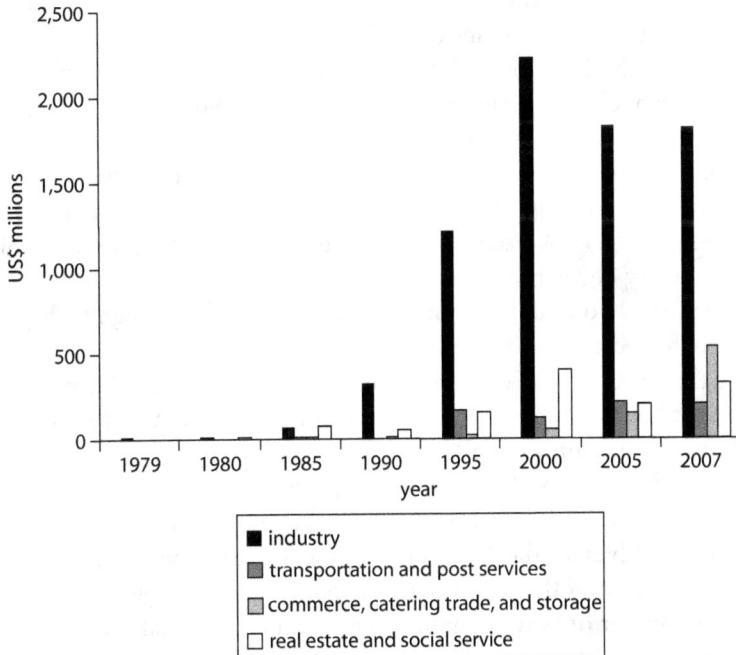

*Source:* Shenzhen Statistics Bureau 2008.

amount of US$7.28 billion. Among these projects, 355 were in the manufacturing sector with US$1.53 billion (actually utilized) and 2,691 in service industries with US$4.94 billion (actually utilized). Of total FDI, secondary industry and tertiary industry accounted for 11.65 percent and 88.35 percent, respectively.

In secondary industry, the foreign capital flowing into textiles and general equipment manufacturing grew by 36.4 percent and 47.0 percent, respectively. In the service sectors, the foreign capital flowing into scientific research, technical services, and geological prospecting grew by 201.7 percent. In wholesale- and retail-sales sectors, the inflow grew by 159.5 percent.

In addition, the world's top 500 multinational companies have invested enthusiastically. By the end of 2008, 164 of them had investments in Shenzhen. Their investment activities brought an inflow of US$4.3 billion in foreign capital. Among the economies of origin of these multinationals, the top three were the United States, Japan, and France, followed by the United Kingdom; Germany; the Republic of Korea; Hong Kong, China; Taiwan, China; Switzerland; Canada; Australia; Singapore; and Finland.

*Development of high-tech industries.* After establishment of its SEZ, Shenzhen began its expansion mainly through processing, trade, and assembly activities. From 1995, Shenzhen's municipal government promoted technological innovations and the development of high-tech industries to encourage the upgrading of the city's production capacity and the transfer of new technologies to associated industries. After 15 years of effort, the high-tech industries of Shenzhen have developed rapidly, and the city has become one of the most important bases for high-tech industry development in China.

From 1991 to 2007, the total output of Shenzhen's high-tech industries increased from US$0.34 billion to US$111.42 billion (table 2.5), more than 300 times. Compared with Beijing, Guangzhou, Shanghai, and Tianjin, Shenzhen's high-tech industry ranks first in both its value added and its contribution to GDP.

Meanwhile, high-tech exports grew continuously. From 2001 to 2008, the value of Shenzhen's high-tech exports increased from US$11.37 billion to US$79.37 billion (the growth rate in 2008 was 9.4 percent), accounting for 44.2 percent of the total value of exports in 2008 (table 2.6).

The number of patent applications in Shenzhen is also growing rapidly. From 1999 to 2008, the proportion of independent innovations in

**Table 2.5    Output Value of High-Tech Industries in Shenzhen, Selected Years, 1991–2008**

| Year | Gross output value (US$10 million) | Growth rate (%) | Gross industrial output value (%) | Share in Guangdong's total (%) |
|---|---|---|---|---|
| 1991 | 33.52 | 50.39 | 7.43 | 27.96 |
| 1995 | 331.11 | 54.46 | 20.33 | 33.54 |
| 2000 | 1,560.78 | 29.84 | 36.08 | 37.39 |
| 2005 | 7,163.12 | 49.51 | 51.06 | 45.74 |
| 2006 | 9,246.89 | 29.09 | 54.02 | 40.56 |
| 2007 | 11,141.88 | 20.50 | 54.90 | — |
| 2008 | 12,772.65 | 14.60 | — | — |
| Annual growth rate(%) | — | 43.98 | — | — |

*Source:* Shenzhen Statistics Bureau 2008, 2009.
*Note:* — = not available.

**Table 2.6    Value of High-Tech Exports from Shenzhen, 2001–08**
*US$ billions*

| | 2001 | 2002 | 2003 | 2004 | 2005 | 2006 | 2007 | 2008 |
|---|---|---|---|---|---|---|---|---|
| High-tech exports | 11.370 | 15.689 | 25.143 | 35.057 | 47.092 | 61.352 | 72.545 | 79.372 |

*Source:* Shenzhen Statistics Bureau 2008, 2009.

high-tech industry increased steadily, with the major high-tech industries changing from importing technologies to independent innovation. By the end of 2008, the output value of high-tech industries with independent intellectual property was as high as US$75.49 billion, growing by 15.6 percent over the previous year and making up 59.1 percent of the total output value of high-tech industries (table 2.7).

### Shenzhen's Contribution to the Nation

In terms of economic size, Shenzhen is the fourth largest city in China. Its contribution to the nation, however, reaches beyond what can be measured by a mere GDP figure. In such areas as economic system reform, social system reform, market competitiveness, and industrial relations, Shenzhen has set an outstanding example for other cities and regions to follow.

*System reform.* The fundamental source of the development of the Shenzhen SEZ is found in the transformation from a planned economy to a market-based system. Adopting market mechanisms has enabled the SEZ to create a new mode of economic development. More generally,

**Table 2.7    Output Value of High-Tech Industries with Independent Intellectual Property, 2000–08**

| Year | 2000 | 2001 | 2002 | 2003 | 2004 | 2005 | 2006 | 2007 | 2008 |
|---|---|---|---|---|---|---|---|---|---|
| Production (RMB billion) | 53.45 | 74.56 | 95.45 | 138.66 | 185.31 | 282.42 | 365.33 | 445.44 | 514.82 |
| Growth rate | 39.37 | 39.49 | 31.00 | 45.25 | 33.35 | 33.35 | 29.40 | 21.90 | 15.60 |
| Percentage of total high-tech industry production | 50.22 | 53.67 | 55.82 | 55.85 | 56.73 | 57.81 | 57.90 | 58.62 | 59.10 |

*Source:* Shenzhen Statistics Bureau 2008, 2009.

Shenzhen has played an important demonstration role in leading China's successive reforms and urban reconstruction, which include land tenure, price system, labor market, financial system, and enterprise reform:

- *Land tenure reform.* Shenzhen was the first city in China to open up the land market and commercialize residential land. Over the period 1980 through 1984, She Kou Industrial Park, one of Shenzhen's industrial areas, introduced commercialized housing for employees, the first attempt of this type of housing reform in China. Subsequently, Shenzhen introduced a "cash transfer" policy to compensate residents while raising rents and house prices to reflect the building costs of the housing provided. Ever since then, Shenzhen has served as a test field for China's housing system reforms and has furnished the original prototype of what has been implemented all over the country in recent decades.

- *Price system reform.* In 1980, Shenzhen began to loosen price controls on capital goods to ease restrictions on the pricing and fees associated with some commodities. The intention was ultimately to set up a market mechanism through which supply and demand decided commodity prices. In 1984, Shenzhen abolished the use of the voucher quota for purchasing food, including edible oil, pork, vegetables, and for purchasing clothing and thus abandoned the administrative allocation system for distributing daily goods. By 1994, food vouchers were no longer in use in China, a national reform that came 10 years later after Shenzhen's initial experiment.

- *Labor market reform.* After the establishment of its SEZ, Shenzhen began carrying out progressive reforms in wage, labor mobility, and labor contracts, among others. Since the 1990s, reforms in labor use, wage determination, and pension insurance have been implemented. In 1984, Shenzhen began to reform the government procedures determining employees' wages that had been integral to the planned economy. In the new system, wages were linked to employees' contributions by dividing the wage into a fixed part (post wage) and a floating part (efficiency wage). By mid-1985, this structural wage reform had been widely accepted and applied in other parts of the nation. To protect low-income people, the municipal government implemented a minimum wage policy in 1992.

- *Financial system reform.* Shenzhen was the first city in China to allow the presence of foreign banks. In 1982, the Nan Yang Commercial Bank, a foreign financial institution, set up its first branch in Shenzhen, which marked a major breakthrough in China's financial reform. In 1987, the Shenzhen Development Bank was set up as the first regional shareholding commercial bank jointly owned by the government, enterprises, and individuals. Such events signaled an end to China's state monopoly over the financial system.

  In 1987, the first securities company in China was registered in Shenzhen, followed in 1990 by the establishment of the nation's first stock exchange, the Shenzhen Stock Exchange. Against the background of tight foreign exchange control in China, Shenzhen went on to establish the first foreign exchange transaction center, a move that greatly encouraged and extended foreign exchange transactions.

- *Reform of state-owned enterprises.* In October 1986, Shenzhen municipal government selected several state-owned enterprises (SOEs) to pilot reform, transforming them into joint-stock enterprises. In the following year, the city's Investment Management Corporation was established and took charge of the management and operation of state-owned assets. July 1988 brought the ratification of the overall planning of state-owned assets management in Shenzhen, and market-oriented state-owned assets management was tested. Finally, in 1990, Shenzhen took the initiative and allowed domestic and foreign investors to invest in former state-owned enterprises. By then, the legal status of joint-stock companies was formally confirmed.

**Creating jobs for rural labor.** As the front-runner in China's reform, Shenzhen has attracted a huge number of immigrants from inland

**Table 2.8    Labor Employed in Shenzhen, Selected Years, 1979–2007**
*10,000 persons*

| Year | State-owned units | Urban collective-owned units | Other ownership units | Urban self-employment | Migrant workers from towns and villages |
|---|---|---|---|---|---|
| 1979 | 3.37 | 0.65 | 1.00 | 0.41 | 9.52 |
| 1984 | 14.14 | 2.15 | 2.04 | 0.50 | 8.43 |
| 1989 | 30.34 | 4.85 | 13.05 | 2.19 | 43.22 |
| 1994 | 38.71 | 8.28 | 35.30 | 54.63 | 135.73 |
| 1999 | 32.94 | 4.17 | 55.41 | 120.86 | 213.22 |
| 2004 | 31.94 | 1.66 | 102.28 | 204.16 | 220.97 |
| 2006 | 39.85 | 1.57 | 142.83 | 267.40 | 193.91 |
| 2007 | 40.03 | 1.50 | 151.51 | 283.74 | 176.76 |

*Source:* Shenzhen Statistics Bureau 2008, 2009.
*Note:* A unit is the business that provides employment.

regions. This large volume of immigrant labor has been not only a major force in the city's ongoing construction and economic growth, but also an important and innovative solution to the employment problems in the less-developed inland areas (table 2.8).

## Development Stages

From the perspective of economic reform, the 30 years of the Shenzhen SEZ can be divided into four stages. The one-by-one measure break-through stage spanned 1980–85, comprehensive reforms occurred over the 1986–91 period, the market framework reform stage took place in the 1992–97 time frame, and the thorough reforms stage began in 1998 and continues into the present.

### Initial Breakthrough Stage

The one-by-one measure breakthrough stage is called the "initial break-through stage." The initial breakthrough stage lasted about five years, from 1980 to 1985, and featured partial reforms and breakthroughs in limited areas. In this stage, the Shenzhen municipal government focused mainly on reforms in the management of infrastructure construction and in pricing, two systems that were heavily influenced by the planned economy and that seriously restricted the development of the special economic zone. The main measures in these reforms included the following:

- *Promoting competition in design and construction.* For infrastructure construction, Shenzhen began piloting project bidding and gradually cemented it as a required procedure. The bidding system changed the old management model, which featured administrative allocation of projects, and formed a market system in the construction industry.

- *Transferring land rights using compensation and land-use fees.* In 1980, the Shenzhen Real Estate Corporation was the first in China to open up a land market, taking the initiative to promote housing commercialization. Later, the Shenzhen government pushed the reform throughout the city. The reform broke the conventional housing system and accelerated the turnover of housing construction capital. Living standards in Shenzhen dramatically improved.

- *Breaking down the planned price management system.* Shenzhen led the way in loosening price controls on capital goods. In 1980, Shenzhen began easing restrictions on the prices of some commodities and promoting market-oriented prices. It abolished voucher quotas and abandoned the administrative allocation system from the planned economy. China discontinued the food voucher quota in 1994 all over the country, ten years after Shenzhen.

- *Implementing a new labor contract system and reforming labor contracts, wages, and pension insurance.* From the pilot labor-contract system, which accompanied experiments in wage reform, to the implementation of the structural wage system, Shenzhen made great efforts to adjust the labor-contract system required by a market economy. At the same time, Shenzhen instituted a major pension reform by establishing a labor insurance company and providing social labor insurance for employees with labor contracts.

- *Adjusting the administrative management system.* Since 1981, Shenzhen has been reforming its administrative management system by simplifying and adjusting economic management departments and establishing industry economic management departments.

- *Reforming the finance and investment system.* Following the establishment of the first foreign bank in Shenzhen in 1982, the Joint Investment Corporation of Bao An County issued the first stock in July 1983. In 1985, Shenzhen set up the Shenzhen Foreign Exchange Center, opening up a new way of allocating foreign exchange in China's highly centralized foreign exchange management system. In addition, Shenzhen unified the rate of income tax.

These "market-oriented" reforms broke the shackles of the planned economy, clearly laid out the direction of reform, changed the way of allocating resources, and successfully completed the preliminary experiments with a market economy.

### Comprehensive Reforms

Between 1986 and 1991, the Shenzhen SEZ adjusted its investment and industrial technology policies. It carried out a series of measures in such fields as enterprise contracting, shareholding, property rights transfer, bankruptcy, financing, banking, taxation, international trade, foreign exchange, state-owned assets management, land use, and housing:

- *Reforming use of state-owned land and commercializing housing.* Shenzhen implemented remarkable reforms in land management, allowing it to become the experiment field for bidding on the use of state-owned land. Shenzhen's first public auction for rights to use state-owned land was known as the "first" revolution in the reform of China's land management system. The municipal government transferred the possession of state-owned land through an auction, bidding, and contracting process, and thus Shenzhen became the first city in China with compensated land use. Shenzhen commercialized the provision of housing and laid the basis for the formation of the city's real estate market.

- *Pursuing additional price reforms.* To break the traditional rigid pricing system, Shenzhen used various measures to limit, adjust, or relax prices and to strengthen price management. Land management and pricing reform were the two areas in which the Shenzhen SEZ broke the old planned economic system and realized market-oriented resource allocation.

- *Establishing a personnel system and pension insurance.* Shenzhen took the lead in reforming the personnel system in China by abandoning government job allocation for graduates of Shenzhen University. Later, China adopted the measures taken by Shenzhen and issued regulations on personnel system reform, replicating the labor-contract system nationally.

- *Instituting a civil service system.* Shenzhen issued the first plan for setting up a civil service system and conducted pilots in such departments as personnel, commerce, taxation, finance, and audit. Detailed regulations on recruitment, evaluation, reward, and discipline were ratified, forming a relatively competitive system.

- *Carrying out comprehensive reforms of the administrative management system.* Shenzhen municipal government put in place substantial reforms by reducing administrative layers and forming the three major systems known as comprehensive management, administrative management, and asset management. Later, the municipal administrative structure and the management system were further reformed, with the aim of completing the administrative management system with comprehensive functions including trade, traffic management, investment attraction, and city management.

- *Encouraging entrepreneurship.* Shenzhen encouraged high-tech professionals to become shareholders of private enterprises by investing in cash, physical goods, individual patents, specially owned technology, brands, and the like and by promoting technologies in production. These measures inspired a number of high-tech professionals to set up private technology ventures.

- *Privatizing state-owned enterprises.* The focus of reform in the second stage was to privatize SOEs. In 1986, Shenzhen became the first city in China to carry out such privatizations. In 1987, Shenzhen set up the Investment Management Corporation to manage and operate state-owned assets. In 1990, Shenzhen became the first city in China to let SOEs go public both at home and abroad.

- *Establishing a securities market.* Shenzhen set up the Securities Corporation of Shenzhen SEZ, which issued stocks to the public and became the pioneer in China's securities market. The first bank set up by enterprises, China Merchants Bank, also was founded in Shenzhen. In 1988, the public debut of the Shenzhen Development Bank marked the birth of the Shenzhen's stock exchange. In July 1990, Shenzhen officially established the Securities Registry Corporation and the Shenzhen Stock Exchange and moved to legalize and standardize the Shenzhen securities market.

- *Creating a foreign exchange transaction center.* After establishing the first foreign exchange transaction center in China in 1985 (which stabilized the foreign exchange market and enhanced international trade), Shenzhen instituted a free trade zone, the Shatoujiao free trade zone, together with the first capital goods market and the future exchange, the Shenzhen Nonferrous Exchange. In addition, the central bank set up a system of credit certificates for enterprises in Shenzhen. These reforms finally established a market economy in Shenzhen.

### A Market System Framework

During the five-year period from 1992 to 1997, the Shenzhen municipal government put forward a series of institutional reforms. Those reforms affected project bidding; labor, wage, and social protection; public utility management; and further SOE privatization:

- *Improving project bidding.* Since 1993, Shenzhen had been implementing changes to the bidding mechanisms in government construction projects. To simplify transactions relating to construction projects and solve the thorny problems of corruption related to project bidding, the city founded the Construction-Project Transaction Service Center.

- *Innovating in the labor, wage, and social protection system.* Shenzhen also initiated innovations in labor, wage, and social protection by breaking the tradition of government job allocation and establishing the so-called two-way selection system, in which employers and employees choose each other in a job market, and adopted a minimum wage and other worker protections. Moreover, the municipal government improved the social security system involving pension, medical insurance, and housing subsidies. All these measures helped promote reform of the allocation of domestic labor.

- *Establishing a modern public utility management system.* The city carried out a series of institutional reforms to strengthen the management of public utilities. These included establishing and improving the structure of corporate governance and experimenting with modern public management methods that met international standards.

**Further reform of state-owned enterprises.** In 1992, the Shenzhen municipal government also expanded the scale of privatization reform of SOEs and created two typical models for privatization. One was to follow the pattern of modern corporations through governance reforms in SOEs. Another was to separate enterprises from the government and then separate the ownership from management. SOE reform was not limited to SOE privatization, but also included reforms of related agencies and systems. For instance, the border management system was improved; the taxation system was modified; the social security system was strengthened; and the scale, structure, and operations of asset-operating corporations were dramatically adjusted to improve the operation and supervision of state-owned assets.

## Thorough Reform

After 1997, the country's reform and opening up entered a new historical period. The remarkable economic growth in China has significantly increased per capita income, and Shenzhen has continued to deepen its ongoing institutional restructuring:

- *Establishing a land trading market.* Shenzhen was the first city in Guangdong Province to sell industrial land. The city government stipulated that the transfer of land-use rights must take place in the open land transactions market. This requirement helped strengthen the regulation of land use and deepened the reform of the land system through building an open, fair, and just market.

- *Providing pensions for workers in the labor-contract system.* In 2001, Shenzhen became the first city to provide pensions for workers in the labor-contract system. Subsequently, this measure was applied all over the country, and the national social security system was established based on the experience of Shenzhen.

- *Establishing a high-tech equity market and a securities market.* To stimulate high-tech industries, in October 2000, Shenzhen established the International High-Tech Equity Transaction Center, which provides a platform for high-tech equity transactions for the whole nation. Later on, the "SME board"[4] was set up in the Shenzhen Stock Exchange.

- *Reforming public service units.* The Shenzhen government carried out a three-step reform of the government-owned public service units (PSUs). First, the government classified these PSUs into three categories: inspection and supervision, business service, and public service. Second, the government deepened reforms of personnel, budget, and materials acquisition for the three different categories of PSUs, respectively. And third, in accordance with the principle of separation of government administration from business operation, PSUs with government administrative power were converted into administrative organizations. These reforms accelerated the corporatization and marketization of PSUs.

- *Increasing efficiency of the government authorization system.* In 1998, Shenzhen began to reform the government authorization system. To increase efficiency and the role of the market in resources allocation, the government streamlined examination and approval procedures and restrained administrative intervention. For better supervision, Shenzhen launched an electronic monitoring system for administrative licensing. In addition, some supervision systems were prepared for important investment projects, and information technology for real-time supervision was applied. Shenzhen also established a unified online platform for government procurement to increase transparency and efficiency and prevent corruption. These measures have all contributed to the improvement of the investment environment in Shenzhen.

- *Evaluating the performance of the audit system.* Shenzhen took the initiative in forming local legislation that required the government to carry out performance audits to improve administrative efficiency. Following this requirement, Shenzhen established an evaluation system for administrative performance and a series of specific auditing regulations on the performance of government-invested projects. For example, the regulations were imposed on the audit of the 12 public hospitals.

Shenzhen has been continuing its efforts to improve the market system. Through these stages of structural reforms and innovations, Shenzhen has preliminarily established an export-oriented market system.

## Roles of the Government

The Shenzhen SEZ came at a critical moment in China's reform and opening up to the outside world. The central government played a leading role in authorizing such SEZs and the associated decentralization of power. The Guangdong provincial government was also prominent in promoting the demand for an SEZ, in taking the initiative in its planning, and in facilitating its establishment. And, finally, the Shenzhen municipal government played a key role in implementing the reform and showed great courage in breaking down the traditional institutions.

### Central Government's Promotion

At the third plenary session of the 11th Chinese Communist Party Central Committee (CCPCC), the central government decided to implement the reform and Open Door policies. It must be credited with taking many unprecedented and groundbreaking steps toward the approval, promotion, and construction of the Shenzhen SEZ.

In mid-1979, the CCPCC and the State Council approved reports written by Guangdong and Fujian provinces asking for special policies and flexible measures relating to foreign economic activities in the provinces and decided to authorize the operation of special zones in Shantou, Shenzhen, Xiamen, and Zhuhai. These were officially named special economic zones.

The SEZs were given more special authority than the rest of the economy. First of all, because the central government considered the development of Guangdong of great importance, it allowed the province to take a first step in implementing special and more flexible policies in the reform and opening up process. Except for the railway, post and telecommunications, banking, civil aviation, and national defense, all other management authority was delegated to the provincial government. Local governments were granted more flexibility in carrying out foreign trade, increasing foreign exchange, and accelerating the development of local economies. In addition, the central government extended the authority of the Guangdong provincial government and the special zone government in such areas as planning, pricing, labor wages, business management, and foreign economic activities. The central government not only encouraged policy innovation but also granted full recognition to well-functioning policies.

In 1992, the central government duly conferred legislative power on the Shenzhen SEZ and provided the Shenzhen Municipal People's Congress as well as its Standing Committee with clear authority to make rules in accordance with specific situations and actual needs, under the provisions of the Constitution, the basic laws, and administrative regulations. At that time, besides the National People's Congress and its Standing Committee, only province-level governments had such power. Even the provincial capital cities were granted only partial legislative authority. All this special treatment by the central government was crucial to maintaining the momentum of policy innovation and ensuring development.

### The Provincial Government's Initiatives

In the process of establishing the SEZs, the Guangdong provincial government has continually reported to the State Council, expressing its strong support. In addition, the provincial government has carried out a series of investigations intended to solve existing problems and to ensure further progress.

During the founding process of the SEZs, the Guangdong provincial government carried out a series of field studies, solicited views of local people, and then submitted the report of the Special Administrative Region to the State Council. The report suggested that Zhuhai and Baoan could be made into high-level bases for industrial and agricultural production and export and had the potential to become resorts for tourists from Hong Kong and Macao. The report also proposed altering the two counties to become medium-sized cities and expressed the hope that the central government would allow Guangdong to implement more special policies and flexible measures and allow it to take the initiative in rezoning Shantou, Shenzhen, and Zhuhai as outward trading areas.

Meanwhile, the Guangdong provincial government asked the central government to further loosen restrictions on opening up wider, to allow more flexibility at home, and to assign more power to local governments. After a series of conferences and discussions, the Guangdong government made the following decisions:

- Given that the provincial government was directly responsible for the political system and economic development in Shenzhen, economic planning was also to be in the hands of the provincial government.

- Powers would be appropriately decentralized to promote international trade: for assembling or processing projects that did not need imported equipment or whose imported equipment was less than US$1 million, the project could be approved by the local government of Shenzhen. If the project were more than US$1 million, the approval power rested with the provincial government.

- According to central government guidelines for establishing special processing zones in Shenzhen and the agreement that Shenzhen could pursue more open approaches than the inland area, the provincial departments were to act promptly on issues related to the establishment of the SEZ. The provincial government was to unify relevant regulations and procedures.

Decentralization of the Guangdong government was successful in increasing the pace of opening up in Shenzhen. And the expansion of local authority helped Shenzhen attract more foreign investment and expand its international trade.

### The Mission of Local Government

The local government expended a great effort to make the SEZ work. Some of the specific measures included:

- *Cultivating a sound investment environment.* The local government of the Shenzhen SEZ spared no effort in development planning and in constantly improving the infrastructure to ensure a favorable investment environment. It also established special fund-raising institutions to guarantee funding for the development of the SEZ.

- *Promoting foreign investment.* In 1979, Shenzhen began introducing three types of foreign-funded enterprises (joint venture, Chinese–foreign equity joint ventures, and solely foreign-owned enterprises) and approved 37 investment projects. In December 1986, Shenzhen ratified the Provisional Regulations on the Approval of Projects Applying to Foreign Investment to reinforce the management of foreign-funded projects. In 1987, Shenzhen set up the Office of Foreign Investment Promotion to take charge of the planning, coordination, approval, management, and provision of services for foreign investment–related projects. In 1996, the Office of Foreign Investment Promotion was replaced by the Shenzhen Investment Promotion Bureau. From 2000 on, Shenzhen has encouraged qualified domestic enterprises to expand to international markets under a "going out" strategy. In 2006, Shenzhen enacted the Scheme for Shenzhen's Strategic Expansion and the 11th Five Year Plan of Shenzhen's Foreign Economic Cooperation. It was regarded as the leading strategy of Shenzhen's development. In the meantime, the Shenzhen Bureau of Trade and Industry held a series of promotional activities for investment both at home and abroad.

  In addition, in 1987 Shenzhen established the Shatoujiao Bonded Industrial Area, the first bonded area in the country, to attract foreign investment. So far, the city has established three such areas, Futian, Shatoujiao, and the Yantian Port Tariff-Free Zone and Bonded Logistics Park. The Futian Tariff-Free Zone with its bridge linking Shenzhen to Hong Kong, China, includes high-tech and modern logistics industries. The Yantian Port Tariff-Free Zone and the Yantian port have facilitated collaboration between the bonded area and the port. They specialize in modern logistics and interact intensively.

- *Creating an orderly market.* Shenzhen also issued a number of policies and regulations concerning intellectual property rights (IPR). Later, the government established the Intellectual Property Office and a specific court dedicated to IPR protection. This move was part of the effort to set up specialized criminal law enforcement agencies with particular jurisdiction over intellectual property rights. In the meantime, a series of policies and measures was enacted to ensure that intellectual property protection was embedded in the laws, regulations, policy formulations, and implementation processes relating to SEZ operations. In 2002, Shenzhen set up the WTO Affairs Center to provide professional services such as consulting, training, forums, and legal counseling related to WTO issues.

- *Continuously improving infrastructure.* Shenzhen has always followed international standards in its urban infrastructure development. The municipal government has invested heavily in developing sea, air, and land transportation networks, including the establishment of a convenient and highly efficient integrated public transportation system consisting of bus and subway services.

- *Encouraging industrialization through industrial parks.* To enhance the potential for economic development and optimize industrial structure, the Shenzhen municipal government gave the Shenzhen Export Processing Zone Management Committee management authority at the municipal level. It is responsible for establishing the Shenzhen Major Industrial Zone, which is located in the northeastern part of Shenzhen and has a planned central area of 39.57 square kilometers. This zone previously had export-processing bases and a national bio-industry park.

  Since the 1990s, the high-tech industries in Shenzhen have experienced rapid development. At the same time, there have been many demands for upgrading infrastructure and for more space to cope with the increasingly fierce external competition. To promote high-tech industries, Shenzhen set up industrial areas that were to specialize in high-tech production. As a result, several high-tech industrial districts were established under the leadership, management, and planning of the municipal government, which was responsible for selecting the industries, making policy, improving the investment environment, and providing services.

- *Strengthening the legal system.* A series of legislative innovations was coupled with the establishment of the Shenzhen SEZ. Since June 30, 2007, the Shenzhen Municipal People's Congress and its Standing Committee have adopted 296 regulations and made decisions relating to all aspects of the city's economy and society. Among these regulations and decisions, about one-third were modeled after those in Hong Kong, China and foreign countries; one-third were ratified with necessary modifications, additions, and refinements of existing laws and regulations based on the economic development needs of the Shenzhen SEZ; and one-third were adapted with the purpose of reinforcing the administrative system, environmental protection, urban management, and cultural development.

## Preferential Policies

The Shenzhen SEZ implemented a series of preferential policies to attract foreign and domestic investments.[5] The main ones involved foreign enterprises, high-tech industries, high-tech venture capital investment, human resources, and land policies.

### *Foreign Enterprises*
Foreign-invested enterprises enjoy a number of preferential policies, including those applying to taxation. For example, the corporate income tax rate is 15 percent, much lower than the 30 percent applied to domestic enterprises. In addition, these enterprises are exempt from the local income tax levied at the rate of 3 percent. Foreign-funded manufacturing enterprises have a two-year exemption from corporate income tax and a half-tax rate for the ensuing two years.

At the expiration of their tax exemption and reduction period, certified export-oriented enterprises have a reduced rate of 10 percent for corporate income tax, provided their export volume accounts for 70 percent or more of their total industrial output. At the expiration of their tax exemption and reduction period, certified manufacturing enterprises using state-of-the-art technologies are entitled to a reduced tax rate of 10 percent during a three-year extension. Foreign-invested enterprises engaged in the services sector with an investment of more than US$5 million and an operational duration of more than 10 years are granted a one-year exemption from corporate income taxes starting from the first profit-making year and a half-tax rate for the ensuing two years.

### High-Tech Industries

For integrated circuits (IC) manufacturing enterprises, from their time of certification until the end of 2010, a refund will be applied to the part of the value-added tax (VAT) exceeding 6 percent for sales of self-produced IC products. General taxpayers will pay VAT at the statutory rate of 17 percent. The refunded tax shall be used by the enterprises for R&D related to IC products and expanded production and shall not be subject to the levy of corporate income tax. IC design enterprises are regarded as software enterprises and enjoy the same tax policies.

As for certified new software enterprises, they may enjoy two years of corporate income tax exemption from the first profit-making year and a half-tax rate reduction for the ensuing three years. Software enterprises recognized by the state, provincial, or municipal governments may enjoy five years of corporate income tax exemption and a half-tax rate for the ensuing five years.

### High-Tech Venture Capital Investment

If venture capital investment agencies invest in the projects listed in the *Guide to Venture Capital Investment in Hi-Tech Industries* (published by the municipal government of Shenzhen) and the total investment exceeds its registered capital or accounts for 70 percent of its total investment and no less than 30 percent is invested in the startup of enterprises, then the venture capital investment agencies can benefit from the preferential policies that apply to high-tech enterprises.

Starting in 2000, the Municipal Finance Bureau has allocated RMB10 million (US$1.46 million) and the Funds for Technologies has allocated RMB 20 million (US$2.93 million) each year to encourage overseas students to start their own businesses in Shenzhen. First, the special-purpose fund is to be used to set up and improve the Overseas Students Venture Park in the high-tech industrial park. And, second, the fund will be used to subsidize loans for high-tech enterprises set up by overseas students.

To support the development of incubators, a maximum of RMB 3 million (US$0.44 million) will go toward subsidizing technological enterprise incubators certified by the technological authority of the municipal government. The intention is to support the construction of public facilities for the technological enterprise incubators, such as public service platforms, network communications, facilities, and instruments for professional laboratories.

## Human Resources

To attract talented people, Shenzhen has undertaken a series of constructive initiatives. These include establishing labor and personnel services companies and setting up a human intelligence market, a senior corporate manager recommendation and evaluation center, and a foreign-related labor market, as well as hosting "talent meetings." The implementation of these initiatives has attracted talented people from China and abroad.

Special policies are in place to attract high-tech talents as well. Software development personnel with university or college educations or above, those with mid- to senior-level professional titles, and those with important inventions, along with their spouses and children (if minors), are allowed to settle in Shenzhen as registered residents and are exempted from the city's infrastructure expansion fee. Furthermore, the municipal government will subsidize postdoctoral scientific research workstations approved by the central government and will subsidize each postdoctoral researcher through a grant of RMB 50,000 (US$7,320.64) for each year after he or she enters the postdoctoral scientific research workstation.

In addition, the Shenzhen government also set up several awards to recognize outstanding talent:

- The Award for Talent in Industrial Development and Innovation of Shenzhen has been set up to acknowledge people who have made outstanding contributions to industrial development and independent innovation in the city's economy.
- The municipal government designates RMB 200 million (US$29.28 million) for these awards as part of its fiscal budget.
- The municipal government has set up specific awards for science and technology, including the Shenzhen Mayor's Award, the Shenzhen Scientific and Technological Progress Award, and the Shenzhen Technological Invention Award. Each year, a sum of RMB 8 million (US$1.17 million) is granted to those technological personnel who make outstanding contributions to the development of the city's high-tech industries.

## Land Policies

To attract investment, certified export-oriented and high-tech enterprises need to pay only half the industrial land-use fees for the first five years. In addition, high-tech enterprises, research projects, and production sites are exempt from transaction fees charged for the transfer of land-use rights, registration fees, trading fees, and charges relating to production and operation facilities and properties. Finally, newly purchased properties for establishing production facilities and operations for high-tech enterprises and projects are exempt from property tax for five years starting from the date of completion of the purchase.

## Key Experiences

Shenzhen has become a model for the reform and opening up process in China, and its experiences have proved to be valuable examples for the rest of the nation. The key experiences include creation of a sound business environment, institutional reform, authority for local decision making, and preferential policies.

### Creating a Sound Business Environment

To ensure orderly economic and urban development and to build investor confidence, the central government and the Shenzhen municipal government have gone to great lengths to produce a sound business environment. That environment includes a good legal system, policy support, and infrastructure provision. Government authorities have also provided effective planning for the SEZ development and have established institutions that protect property rights to ensure a fair market.

### Focusing on Institutional Reforms

As the first city in China to establish an SEZ, Shenzhen has concentrated on the institutional reforms required to build a new market-oriented economic system. Its experiments in reform began at a time when the whole country was still a planned economy, and Shenzhen tried all available means, including learning from foreign experience, to establish a good legal and regulatory environment, an efficient administrative system, a flexible labor market, and the like. Its 30 years of fast development have proved the importance of institution building.

### Granting Sufficient Freedom for Local Decision Making

A special aspect of the Shenzhen SEZ was its authority to trying all kinds of economic experiments. For instance, Shenzhen was the first city to establish a required 24-hour turnaround time for project approval and to shift the personnel system from designated to open hiring. Integral to this special status was the legislative power granted by the central government.

In addition, the SEZ has been granted the privilege of determining its own economic management strategies. All such autonomy is crucial to Shenzhen's success.

### Granting Proper Preferential Policies

The Shenzhen SEZ enjoys great flexibility in the application of foreign funds, the introduction of foreign technologies, and the undertaking of foreign economic collaboration. Preferential policies were granted in such areas as taxation, customs, staffing, land use, and the like. For instance, the profits of foreign firms sent abroad have been exempted from income tax, and such firms are also not liable for property taxes for three years after their establishment.

## Challenges and Recommendations

Despite the tremendous success of the Shenzhen SEZ, it faces many challenges to its future development:

- *Policy changes after WTO accession.* Preferential tax policies for foreign investment led to conflicts of interest relating to foreign investment and domestic investment. First, the overall cost of implementing foreign-investment preferential tax policies is extremely high. According to data released by the National Statistics Bureau, China's FDI accounted for 18 percent of the country's total fixed-assets investment, while the average tax rate of foreign-funded enterprises is at least 4 percent lower than that applying to domestically funded enterprises. Second, because state-owned enterprises, collective companies, and private and personal business have been unable to enjoy the same tax benefits as foreign-financed businesses, they have endeavored to find ways to avoid their tax burden by setting up fake foreign-linked joint ventures. Under such a situation, the FDI policies have to be adjusted based on the WTO requirements.

- *The diminishing effect of institutional reform.* The Shenzhen SEZ is the result of China's pursuit of a change from a planned economy to a market-based economy. It is the product of the necessary system adjustments and an integral part of China's step-by-step reform strategy. In the beginning, the newly established market economy increased people's economic incentives significantly. For a time, Shenzhen enjoyed the positive effects of the institutional reform that brought about the new market system. As the market economy gradually became entrenched, however, this "inspiration effect" decreased.

- *Unsustainable development patterns.* In the early 1980s, China put forward the idea that its economic development mode should be transformed from extensive to intensive. In 2005, the shift from an extensive economy to an intensive economy was again listed as the most severe challenge and the most urgent task in China's 11th Five Year Plan. In Shenzhen, the rapid development of the economy in its early stages depended mainly on small and medium capital investments. Later on, the city's capacity to accumulate funds began decreasing, a trend that posed a direct threat to its capital growth and economic development. After the 1990s, its average capital accumulation growth rate was 36 percent, lower than the 38 percent of Guangdong Province and also significantly lower than the rates in Beijing, Shanghai, and Tianjin that had reached almost 50 percent. The extensive use of resources and the slowing down of the capital growth rate in Shenzhen were alarming calls for a shift to an intensive growth model.

- *Lagging social development.* For a modern nation, economic prosperity and social development comprise two of its most important and mutually reinforcing aspects that should advance in a balanced way. At the early stage of China's reform and opening up to the world, it was necessary to focus more on economic development. In later stages, such economic development needs to be accompanied by an equal emphasis on social development. In the SEZ, for various reasons, economic development has long been the main goal, with social improvement and environmental quality sacrificed to achieve economic growth. As a result, education, science and technology, culture, health care, environmental protection, social security, urban transport, and other important social undertakings have been lagging behind.

- *Increasing resource constraints.* The availability of resources is an important factor in economic growth. With the development of the SEZ and the associated increase in urban populations, the scarcity of resources has become increasingly noticeable. As a consequence, ever more pressure is placed on the natural environment, thus threatening the sustainable development of the economy. Although scientific and technological progress can improve the effectiveness of the use of natural resources, the problem of resource constraints remains largely unsolved. The gaps between supply and demand in relation to land, water, electricity, and other resources have become increasingly apparent.

- *Environmental degradation.* With economic growth as the centerpiece of development, endeavors to raise incomes have received the most prominent attention. At the same time, though, the environment has suffered to a considerable extent, and its quality has been declining rapidly as a result. Moreover, since SEZs have limited natural resources and capacity, their economic growth cannot depend exclusively on such sources. Reliance on external resources therefore becomes an important factor in achieving such growth. Because maintaining environmental quality directly affects the city's ability to attract external resources, the availability of resources has become an important variable for the further development of SEZs. Improving environmental quality has thus become one of its top priorities.

- *Cultural conflicts.* An influx of people from areas with different cultural backgrounds can cause conflicts within society that take time to resolve and can demand considerable coordination efforts. During the development process, building a harmonious society represents a significant challenge for the municipal government.

### The Future of the SEZs

During China's three decades of reform and its opening up to the world, the nation's economy has successfully maintained an astonishing growth rate. Today, the basic framework of the market economy has been established across the entire country. Because of China's special situation as a large developing country, however, problems such as inequality, information asymmetries, and immature institutions still exist. As a result, its market system is far from perfect and signals that the mission of the SEZs as "experiment fields" for economic reform is still important.

The mission of the SEZs has been to resolve emerging problems in the process of China's economic development. The Pudong New Area was established in Shanghai to serve as the stimulus for development in regions such as the Yangtze River Delta and across the country. Similarly, the Tianjin Binhai New Area was launched as China began to integrate into the world economy, which demanded a development strategy with combined planning for land use, effective design of global logistics, and human resources and information flows. China chose the Changsha-Zhuzhou-Xiangtan triangle area, Chongqing, and Wuhan as experimental areas for national urban and rural coordination and associated comprehensive reforms. This is China's major strategy in the development of the central and western parts of the country. Such areas are also regarded as test areas for building a harmonious society by applying a scientific development concept. In the processes of modernization, China may still encounter more problems. Given that the Shenzhen SEZ is the most important experiment field in China's economic development, the larger the role it is able to play, the more development opportunities the city will have.

China's reform began with changes in its economic institutions. A market economy requires a well-functioning legal system, fair competition, and incentives that balance competing interests. This kind of economic system also calls for a suitable political environment, and it is for this reason that reform of the political system plays such a vital role in advancing China's economic development. Nonetheless, reforming the political system clearly involves a wide range of interests, and it is difficult to start such reforms at the national level. Under such circumstances, the SEZs surely become the most appropriate test fields for such reform. This new task for Shenzhen and the other SEZs also grants them new development opportunities at the same time.

## Policy Recommendations

Some broad policy recommendations should be considered, which enable the special economic zones to overcome these challenges and to continue on the path of success. Among them, institutional reform and adjusting the focus of reform from growth to development are particularly important. The SEZs have to focus more on some specific key aspects.

*New reform incentives.* Institutional reform is the key factor behind the success of the Shenzhen SEZ, and local government has been an important player in the required institutional reforms. As a consequence, it is apparent that the incentives provided to the government have served as the original engine of the reform program and have later become the driving force for economic development. For that reason, the Shenzhen SEZ has become the most successful SEZ in China. In the future, this logic of success will continue to hold. During this crucial period of China's modernization, institutional reform is the single most important factor in enabling the Shenzhen SEZ to continue to lead in social and economic development over the next 10 or 15 years. Only if Shenzhen carries on its in-depth reform and opening up further to the world, in the process of building a well-functioning market mechanism, can the city maintain its established front-runner role in China. One precondition for this outcome is to create stronger incentives for government officers to carry on further institutional innovation.

*Adjusting the reform focus.* At this stage, it is also of great importance to deepen the needed administrative reform to ensure the formation of a highly efficient and flexible administrative system that can effectively support economic development and the burgeoning market economy. At present, the administrative bodies of the SEZ are relatively large. The coordination of different departments has become ever more difficult and has resulted in lower efficiency. It is evident, therefore, that the change of government functions has not yet been effectively implemented and much unnecessary administrative intervention in economic activities still occurs. Reforming the government management system by learning from international experiences to ensure that the economy develops sustainably, rapidly, and healthily has become an urgent task.

*From economic growth to broader development.* In the past 30 years, economic growth has been the top priority in China. So far, this goal has been well met through the introduction of foreign capital, advanced management methods, and technologies. In recent years, industries relying on domestic investment have experienced rapid development. As their comparative advantages have slowly faded away and labor and land supplies have decreased, however, the conflicts between social development and economic development, between income generation and environmental degradation, and between economic growth and unequal income distribution are becoming more severe than ever. In the coming years, these aspects need to be taken into account, and the main objective must be shifted from a sole pursuit of economic growth to a wider one that encompasses social development. If this transformation is successfully achieved, then a new development path consistent with given constraints can surely be worked out. Shenzhen can then continue to set an example for China's further development in the new era.

## Notes

1. RMB is the Chinese currency; the yuan is the currency unit.
2. The historical name *Hong Kong* refers to the period before July 1, 1997, when the former British colony was restored to China; *Hong Kong, China* refers to any time after that date.

3. The historical name *Macao* refers to the period before December 20, 1999, when the former Portuguese colony was restored to China; *Macao, China* refers to any time after that date.

4. This is an equity exchange system for small and medium enterprises.

5. This part is largely derived from relevant documents and regulations of the Shenzhen municipal government. Thanks to Dr. Ziling Cai for his valuable help with these materials.

## Bibliography

Chinese Academy of Social Sciences. 2008. *2007 Blue Book of China's City Competitiveness*. Beijing: Social Science Publishing House.

Fan, Gang. 2009. *Research on China's Special Economic Zones: Yesterday and Tomorrow's Theory and Practice*. Beijing: China's Economy Press.

Hongyun, Fan, and Ling Jin. 2008. *Major Legislation Events in Shenzhen*. Shenzhen: Haitian Press.

Jianzhong, Dong. 2008. *Major Economic Changes in Shenzhen*. Shenzhen: Haitian Press.

*Journal of Chai Shui*. 2000. "Notification on Taxation Policies to Encourage the Development of Software Industry and Integrated Circuit Industry." 25.

Shenzhen Reform Office, Integrated Development Institute. 2008. *Shenzhen's Reform of the Past 28 Years*. Study of the Shenzhen Special Economic Zone, the Policy Research Office of the CPC Shenzhen Municipal Committee. Shenzhen: Haitian Press.

Shenzhen Statistics Bureau. 2008. *Shenzhen Statistical Yearbook 2008*. Beijing: China Statistics Press.

———. 2009. *Shenzhen 2008 National Economic and Social Development Statistical Bulletin*. Shenzhen Daily, March 24, Edition A7.

Wei, Meng. 2008. *Major Social Change in Shenzhen*. Shenzhen: Haitian Press.

Yiming, Yuan. 2008. "Endogenous Factors of Industry Development and Its Structural Change in Shenzhen SEZ: An Institutional Economics Analysis." *Management World* 10: 55–60.

Yong-qing, Li. 2008. *Major Administrative Changes in Shenzhen*. Shenzhen: Haitian Press.

# CHAPTER 3

# A Case Study of Tianjin Economic–Technological Development Area

## Xiaoxi Li, Ruijun Duan, and Huanzhao Zhang

The Tianjin Economic-Technological Development Area (TEDA), established officially on December 6, 1984, by the State Council of China, is one of the earliest state-level development areas in China.[1] The past 24 years of growth and experience in TEDA have proved to be a huge success.

This case study starts with a brief summary of the area's development and accomplishments. The second section tells how TEDA was established,

Xiaoxi Li is currently the director of the Institute of Economic and Resources Management, Beijing Normal University; he was formerly the director-general of the Macroeconomic Research Department, Research Office of the State Council. Ruijun Duan and Huanzhao Zhang are research fellows of Nankai University pursuing postdoctoral research. A special acknowledgment should be made to Daihong Xu, minister of the Policy Research Office of TEDA, and to Dr. Bing Sun from Zhou Enlai School of Government, Nankai University. The author's special thanks should also be given to the translation group for this case study, including Ph.D. and master's students in our institute, who have accomplished the translation work with efficiency and great dedication. They are Ran Ren, Huixin Sun, Yimeng Liu, Yi Zhang, Miao Chen, Yamin Du, with Huixin Sun being the chief organizer.

and the third section analyzes the role of government. The fourth section outlines the favorable fiscal policies implemented for the development area, and the sixth section summarizes the successful experience of TEDA's development and opening-up process. The major challenges faced by the development area are summarized in the sixth section. The paper then concludes with lessons learned.

## TEDA's Accomplishments

TEDA is the largest, the fast-growing, and the most profitable among the 57 state-level economic and technology development areas. Covering 40 square kilometers with a residential population of 143,000, TEDA had a 2007 gross regional product of RMB 93.87 billion, a gross industrial output of RMB 335.067 billion, tax income of RMB 19.816 billion, a total import and export value of US$335.01 billion, and a total social investment of RMB 25.577 billion in fixed assets. With per capita disposable income of RMB 41,700 and per capita consumption of RMB 26,100, TEDA has become the flagship of the Binhai New Area and has contributed significantly to the economic growth of the city of Tianjin (http://gaige.chinareform.net/index.html).

Since its inception in 1984, TEDA has seen rapid growth in its economy, trade, investment, and high-tech industries, thanks to favorable local endowments as well as preferential economic policies. It has experienced three development stages. The first stage, from 1984 to 1994, was characterized by investment predominantly in primary goods with little value added or technological content. During the second stage, from 1994 to 2004, with continuous upgrading and restructuring, the high-tech industries became the leading force in TEDA. Since 2004, TEDA, as part of the Binhai New Area, has been focusing on specialization and cooperation across regions. In particular, the reform experiment zone established in the Binhai New Area in 2006 has provided new development opportunities for TEDA.

### Economic Growth and Efficiency

TEDA has maintained outstanding economic performance since its establishment 24 years ago. In 1986, TEDA's gross domestic product (GDP) was only RMB 9.35 million. About 20 years later, in 2007, TEDA's GDP had reached RMB 93.87 billion and in 2008 RMB 106.5 billion, maintaining an annual growth rate of 20 percent. Its gross industrial output grew rapidly as well: that number for 1986 was RMB 38.72 billion compared to RMB 335.067 billion in 2007 and RMB 373 billion at the end of 2008 (see figures 3.1 and 3.2).

Output per capita was RMB 13,700 in 1987 compared to RMB 285,100 in 2007. Labor productivity has kept growing, increasing from RMB 59,500 per capita in 1987 to RMB 564,700 per capita in 2000 (see table 3.1). Although productivity has declined slightly since 2000, partly because of

**Figure 3.1    Gross Regional Output and Gross Industrial Output of TEDA, 1986–2008**

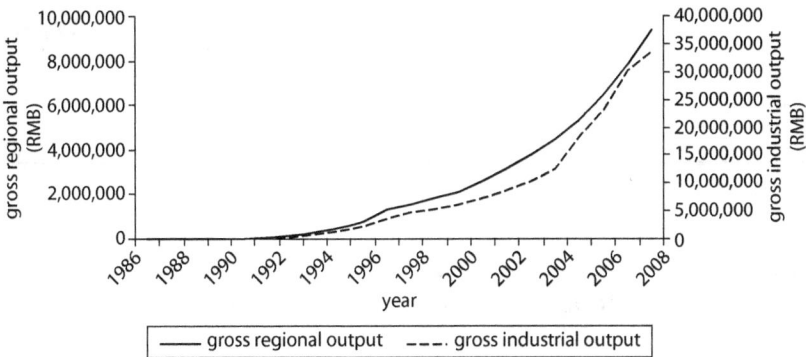

*Sources:* Li Yong 2004; Economic Bureau of TEDA 2001–07; 2008 data from the statistics of www.bh.gov.cn.

**Figure 3.2    Growth of Gross Domestic Product and Gross Industrial Output of TEDA, 1996–2008**

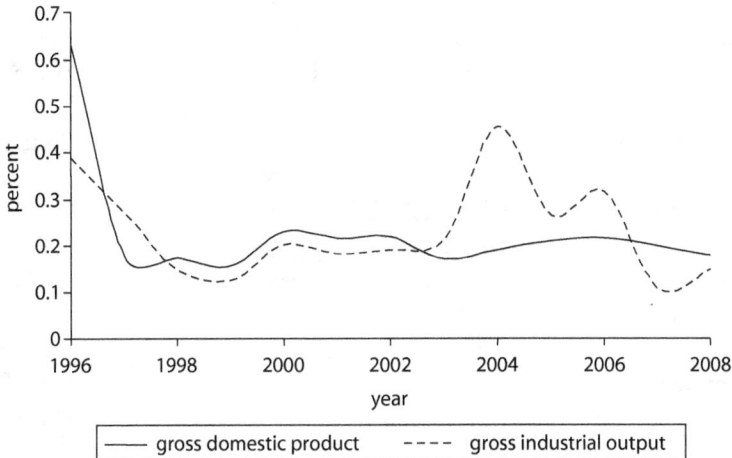

*Sources:* Li 2004; Economic Development Bureau of TEDA 2001–07; 2008 data from the statistics of www.bh.gov.cn.

**Table 3.1    Performance of Employees of TEDA, 1987–2007**

| Year | GDP per capita (RMB 10,000) | Productivity (10,000 per person) | Year | GDP per capita (RMB 10,000) | Productivity (10,000 per person) |
|---|---|---|---|---|---|
| | 1987–97 | | | 1998–2007 | |
| 1987 | 1.37 | 5.95 | 1998 | 10.75 | 46.09 |
| 1988 | 2.23 | 7.58 | 1999 | 11.58 | 49.52 |
| 1989 | 2.30 | 7.01 | 2000 | 13.46 | 56.47 |
| 1990 | 1.73 | 8.81 | 2001 | 15.64 | 35.04 |
| 1991 | 3.13 | 14.73 | 2002 | 18.10 | 21.08 |
| 1992 | 3.38 | 15.09 | 2003 | 19.23 | 22.10 |
| 1993 | 4.61 | 19.14 | 2004 | 20.08 | 25.62 |
| 1994 | 5.79 | 24.36 | 2005 | 22.28 | 24.11 |
| 1995 | 7.10 | 31.19 | 2006 | 24.72 | 26.45 |
| 1996 | 10.08 | 39.40 | 2007 | 28.51 | 29.92 |
| 1997 | 10.17 | 43.54 | | | |

*Sources:* Li 2004; Economic Development Bureau of TEDA 2001–07.

higher labor costs and industrial restructuring, TEDA's productivity has remained relatively high, at RMB 299,200 per capita in 2007.

## Trade Growth

Since its establishment, TEDA has emphasized foreign trade. The volume of export has grown continuously, through higher value-added and more high-tech products.

*Fast-growing exports.* The export trade of TEDA, initiated in 1986, began with just six export enterprises, but by 2007 that number had grown to 783, with the value of exports increasing from US$2.02 million in 1986 to US$18.5 billion in 2007 (see table 3.2). The leading enterprises of TEDA have played a significant role: in 2007, 98 individual enterprises achieved an export value of more than US$10 million. Their total exports were valued at US$17.556 billion, accounting for 94.9 percent of regional exports. Twenty-three enterprises had exports exceeding US$100 million, and their total export value was US$15.199 billion, accounting for 82.2 percent of regional exports.

Export products have been continuously upgraded. In the early years of foreign trade, the exported products of TEDA consisted mainly of primary goods, such as special local products, plastic, garments, hardware, and daily supplies, with a low technology level and added value. Since 1992, more technology-intensive products have been exported, and the

**Table 3.2    TEDA's Number of Exporters and Value of Products Exported, 1986–2007**
*US$ millions*

| Year | Exporter (company) | Export value (US$ millions) | Year | Exporter (company) | Export value (US$ millions) |
|---|---|---|---|---|---|
| | *1986–96* | | | *1997–2007* | |
| 1986 | 6 | 2.02 | 1997 | 263 | 2,004.15 |
| 1987 | 23 | 16.16 | 1998 | 285 | 2,081.35 |
| 1988 | 38 | 37.80 | 1999 | 385 | 2,553.80 |
| 1989 | 56 | 46.04 | 2000 | 397 | 3,266.91 |
| 1990 | 75 | 63.70 | 2001 | 446 | 4,035.00 |
| 1991 | 99 | 113.48 | 2002 | 396 | 5,706.00 |
| 1992 | 137 | 160.22 | 2003 | 466 | 6,886.00 |
| 1993 | 151 | 292.35 | 2004 | 481 | 11,175.00 |
| 1994 | 184 | 544.26 | 2005 | 575 | 13,971.00 |
| 1995 | 221 | 901.03 | 2006 | 604 | 17,145.00 |
| 1996 | 253 | 1,450.20 | 2007 | 783 | 18,500.00 |

*Sources:* Li 2004; Economic Development Bureau of TEDA 2001–07.

percentage of fine finishing products was 72.7 in that year. In 1994, export products were concentrated in 24 categories, primarily in electronics, electrical industry, machinery, chemical industry, pharmaceutical industry, clothing, and food, shifting from labor-intensive to technology-intensive products. With further structural upgrading in 1996, electronic and electric products took the lead, accounting for 64.62 percent of the total export value in that year. Since 2000, more technology-intensive products have been added, such as mobile phones, integrated circuits, semiconductors, li-ion batteries, color televisions, digital cameras, and the like. In 2007, the value of high-tech exports was US$13.21 billion, accounting for 80.4 percent of TEDA's total, and the export value of mechanical and electrical products was US$17.09 billion, accounting for 92.4 percent of regional exports (see table 3.3).

***Foreign trade and growth.***  In its start–up period, TEDA exported mainly to Hong Kong,[2] Japan, the Republic of Korea, and the United States. It expanded its market to Europe in 1988. In 1994, export trade to Hong Kong, Japan, the United States, Korea, the United Kingdom, and Taiwan, China accounted for 90.3 percent of the total. By 2007, TEDA had established trading relations with 188 countries and regions, among which the United States ranked as the leading partner with an export value of US$5.24 billion, accounting for 28.3 percent of total foreign trade in the area (see table 3.4).

**Table 3.3    Value of TEDA's High-Tech Exports and Their Share of Total Export Value, 2001–07**

|  | 2001 | 2002 | 2003 | 2004 | 2005 | 2006 | 2007 |
|---|---|---|---|---|---|---|---|
| Export value of high-tech products (US$ millions) | 2,344 | 3,335 | 3,405 | 9,011 | 11,281 | 13,777 | 13,213 |
| % of high-tech products in total exports | 58.1 | 58.4 | 49.5 | 80.6 | 80.7 | 94.1 | 80.4 |

*Source:* Economic Development Bureau of TEDA 2001–07.

**Table 3.4    Value of Exports to Six Countries, Economies, or Regions and Their Share of Total Export Value, 2007**

| Country, economy, or region | Export value (US$ millions) | Percentage of total export value |
|---|---|---|
| United States | 5,243 | 28.3 |
| European Union | 3,151 | 17.0 |
| ASEAN | 2,707 | 14.6 |
| Republic of Korea | 1,556 | 8.4 |
| Japan | 1,112 | 6.0 |
| Hong Kong, China | 1,019 | 5.5 |

*Source:* Economic Development Bureau of TEDA 2007.

### Growth of Foreign Direct Investment

Foreign direct investment (FDI) has played a crucial role in the development and construction of TEDA. Today, the volume of FDI in TEDA continues to grow and to produce better-quality investment projects.

TEDA was challenged by slow investment growth in its start-up period. From 1985 to 1990, 217 projects were approved, valued at only about US$400 million. Since 1992, FDI has grown significantly, and at the peak in 1993, 909 projects were approved. After 1993, the number of investment projects has declined, but the total value is rising, as well as the average investment size (see table 3.5). At the end of 2007, there were 4,485 foreign enterprises from 74 countries and regions with an investment value of US$40.33 billion,[3] contracted foreign capital of US$30.04 billion, actually utilized foreign investment of US$16.93 billion, and an average project size of US$8.99 million. Some 657 enterprises had an investment value of more than US$10 million, and 31 enterprises had an investment value of more than US$100 million.

***Changing trends in foreign investments in TEDA.*** Before 1987, none of the foreign-funded enterprises in TEDA had increased their investment,

**Table 3.5    Foreign Investment in TEDA, by Number of Approved Projects and Total Investment Value, 1985–2007**

*US$ millions*

| Year | Number of approved projects (company) | Total investment (US$ millions) | Average size (US$ millions) | Year | Number of approved projects (company) | Total investment (US$ millions) | Average size (US$ millions) |
|------|------|------|------|------|------|------|------|
|  | | 1985–96 | |  | | 1997–2007 | |
| 1985 | 14 | 31.92 | 2.28 | 1997 | 172 | 1,495.76 | 8.70 |
| 1986 | 27 | 43.42 | 1.61 | 1998 | 194 | 1,482.07 | 7.64 |
| 1987 | 34 | 22.80 | 6.70 | 1999 | 106 | 1,428.84 | 13.48 |
| 1988 | 48 | 84.82 | 1.77 | 2000 | 99 | 2,779.02 | 28.07 |
| 1989 | 40 | 105.69 | 2.64 | 2001 | 94 | 1,204.00 | 12.81 |
| 1990 | 54 | 122.37 | 2.27 | 2002 | 109 | 1,537.00 | 14.10 |
| 1991 | 121 | 185.65 | 1.53 | 2003 | 161 | 1,122.00 | 6.97 |
| 1992 | 462 | 702.61 | 1.52 | 2004 | 165 | 2,551.00 | 15.46 |
| 1993 | 909 | 1,235.36 | 1.36 | 2005 | 223 | 2,553.00 | 11.45 |
| 1994 | 487 | 1,522.78 | 3.13 | 2006 | 232 | 3,186.00 | 13.74 |
| 1995 | 361 | 1,811.29 | 5.02 | 2007 | 186 | 3,725.00 | 20.03 |
| 1996 | 187 | 1,916.04 | 10.25 | | | | |

*Sources:* Li 2004; Economic Development Bureau of TEDA 2001–07.

but the situation changed in 1988. Before 1993, enterprises increased investment at a smaller scale, with the maximum only around US$50 million. After 1994, enterprises took a more active approach, and the investment increased both in total value and in average value. The increased investment on average reached a high of US$41.96 million in 2000 (see table 3.6). As of 2007, altogether there were 1,666 foreign-funded enterprises that had increased their investment in TEDA, for a total investment of US$16.67 billion.

*Improving quality of foreign-invested projects.* Initially, the investment projects in TEDA were mainly low technology, with a maximum individual investment of US$5 million. Since 1992, as foreign funding has significantly increased, foreign investment from multinational companies began to move out of the initial medium or small investment. The level of technology rose remarkably, and some even filled the technology gaps in China. Many products manufactured in TEDA became brand names and market leaders. As of 2007, 137 companies from 10 foreign countries and regions were investing in TEDA, 62 of which were multinational companies in the Fortune 500. TEDA has attracted a great number of

**Table 3.6    Foreign Investment in TEDA, 1988–2007**

| | Enterprises with increased investment | Value of increase (US$ millions) | Average increase (US$ millions) | Year | Enterprises with increased investment | Value of increase (US$ millions) | Average increase (US$ millions) |
|---|---|---|---|---|---|---|---|
| | | 1988–97 | | | | 1998–2007 | |
| 1988 | 6 | 4.82 | 0.80 | 1998 | 78 | 520.00 | 6.54 |
| 1989 | 1 | 0.19 | 0.19 | 1999 | 50 | 746.00 | 14.92 |
| 1990 | 5 | 13.71 | 2.74 | 2000 | 55 | 2,308.00 | 41.96 |
| 1991 | 15 | 15.26 | 1.02 | 2001 | 56 | 1,284.00 | 22.93 |
| 1992 | 26 | 51.09 | 1.97 | 2002 | 79 | 1,070.00 | 13.54 |
| 1993 | 48 | 50.90 | 1.06 | 2003 | 82 | 1,169.00 | 14.26 |
| 1994 | 59 | 314.22 | 5.33 | 2004 | 144 | 850.00 | 5.90 |
| 1995 | 62 | 979.00 | 15.79 | 2005 | 244 | 1,710.00 | 7.01 |
| 1996 | 97 | 867.00 | 8.94 | 2006 | 252 | 1,934.00 | 7.67 |
| 1997 | 52 | 340.00 | 6.54 | 2007 | 255 | 2,439.00 | 9.56 |

*Sources:* Li 2004; Economic Development Bureau of TEDA 2001–07.

multinational companies that represent the most advanced technology worldwide, such as Coca-Cola, Halliburton, Honeywell, IBM, Kodak Polychrome, Pepsi, and Motorola.

## Rapid Growth of High-Tech Industries

TEDA has been focusing on the development of high-tech industries and has made significant progress. At the beginning stage, TEDA paid special attention to the development of high-tech industries and strengthened the supporting facilities, including policy, human capital, and financial services, to create a favorable environment. In 2004, the output of high-tech products exceeded RMB 100 billion and went as high as RMB 197.35 billion in 2007, accounting for 58.9 percent of the total (see table 3.7). Information and communications technology is the leading force of TEDA's high-tech industry, while biomedicine, aviation technology, new energy, new materials, and environmental protection are playing an increasingly significant role.

TEDA's objective is to attract foreign funds and develop its high-tech industries, which have grown rapidly; as of the end of 2007, TEDA included 218 high-tech enterprises and 46 certified software enterprises. At present, with major funding from multinational companies, TEDA has six high-tech industry clusters: the electronic information cluster, with General Semiconductor, Mitsui, Motorola, Panasonic, and Samsung; the

**Table 3.7    Value of High-Tech Products in TEDA and Percentage of Gross Industrial Output, 2001–07**

|  | 2001 | 2002 | 2003 | 2004 | 2005 | 2006 | 2007 |
|---|---|---|---|---|---|---|---|
| Output of high-tech products (in millions of RMB) | 50,042 | 61,664 | 71,987 | 109,693 | 143,152 | 186,658 | 197,354 |
| High-tech products as % of gross industrial output | 57.8 | 59.8 | 57.5 | 60.2 | 62.1 | 61.6 | 58.9 |

*Source:* Economic Development Bureau of TEDA 2001–07.

optical, mechanical, and electronic integration cluster, with Honeywell and Merlin Gerin; the biomedicine cluster, with Novo Nordisk and Smithkline Beecham; the new material cluster, with BBA and PPG; the new energy cluster, with Energizer and Tong Yee; the machinery cluster with leading companies such as SEW, SMG, and Toyota; and the environmental protection cluster, with Veolia Water and Vestas (http://www .teda.gov.cn).

TEDA has created a favorable environment for technology innovation. As of 2007, there were 11 incubators, with a total incubation area of 296,800 square meters, 245 incubated enterprises, 27 engineering technology research centers, 35 enterprise technology centers, 45 research and development (R&D) centers established by multinational companies, and 7 venture capital companies in TEDA. Companies in TEDA have made great progress in researching, developing, and transforming bio-chips, membrane technology, the electric automobile, stem cells, and nanometer technology. As of 2007, TEDA enterprises have obtained 2,520 patents, 1,029 of which are invention patents and 1,790 of which are owned by domestic enterprises.

### The Driving Economic Force of Tianjin

TEDA has become an increasingly significant force driving Tianjin's economic development. From 1986 to 2007, TEDA's GDP increased from RMB 9.35 million to RMB 93.87 billion, and gross industrial output from RMB 38.72 million to RMB 335.07 billion. In the same period, the GDP of Tianjin City increased from RMB 19.47 billion to RMB 501.83 billion, and gross industrial output from RMB 34.473 billion to RMB 1,050.291 billion. The economic growth rate for TEDA was much higher than that for Tianjin City (see table 3.8). The percentage of GDP, gross industrial output, export value, and number of employees of TEDA increased from

**Table 3.8   Major Economic Indicators in TEDA, 1986–2007**

| Year | % of GDP | % of gross industrial output | % of exports | % of employment | Number of employees (in 10,000) |
|------|----------|------------------------------|--------------|-----------------|----------------------------------|
| 1986 | 0.05 | 0.11 | 0.16 | 0.02 | 0.11 |
| 1987 | 0.40 | 0.47 | 1.07 | 0.14 | 0.64 |
| 1988 | 0.74 | 0.70 | 2.25 | 0.19 | 0.86 |
| 1989 | 0.65 | 0.73 | 2.73 | 0.17 | 0.80 |
| 1990 | 0.80 | 1.15 | 3.57 | 0.31 | 1.45 |
| 1991 | 1.96 | 2.38 | 7.06 | 0.45 | 2.14 |
| 1992 | 3.12 | 3.21 | 9.14 | 0.78 | 3.79 |
| 1993 | 4.72 | 5.01 | 15.05 | 1.10 | 5.52 |
| 1994 | 6.65 | 8.50 | 22.68 | 1.64 | 8.42 |
| 1995 | 8.60 | 14.18 | 30.05 | 2.19 | 11.29 |
| 1996 | 11.68 | 17.00 | 35.82 | 2.74 | 14.02 |
| 1997 | 12.15 | 19.19 | 39.94 | 3.08 | 15.79 |
| 1998 | 13.10 | 21.08 | 37.85 | 3.38 | 17.16 |
| 1999 | 13.89 | 22.12 | 40.33 | 3.55 | 18.05 |
| 2000 | 15.07 | 23.75 | 37.86 | 3.92 | 19.11 |
| 2001 | 16.26 | 25.70 | 42.47 | 3.99 | 19.50 |
| 2002 | 17.67 | 27.74 | 49.21 | 4.18 | 20.59 |
| 2003 | 17.27 | 28.63 | 47.91 | 4.54 | 23.20 |
| 2004 | 17.04 | 29.46 | 53.56 | 4.89 | 25.81 |
| 2005 | 17.37 | 32.15 | 50.96 | 5.31 | 28.83 |
| 2006 | 17.91 | 34.02 | 51.12 | 5.61 | 31.57 |
| 2007 | 18.71 | 31.90 | 48.50 | 5.36 | 32.93 |

*Sources:* Li 2004, Economic Development Bureau of TEDA 2001–07.

0.05 percent, 0.11 percent, 0.16 percent, and 0.02 percent, respectively, in 1986 to 18.71 percent, 31.90 percent, 48.50 percent, and 5.36 percent respectively, in 2007—an increase of 18.66 percent, 31.79 percent, 48.34 percent, and 5.34 percent, respectively.

## Background on TEDA

Establishing special economic zones (SEZs) and economic and technological development areas, which is a vital decision in the face of domestic and international circumstances, is considered an important experiment in China's development policy. As forerunners of China's export-oriented economic development, the southeastern cities have competitive advantages and abundant resource endowments, favorable geographic locations, solid capital foundations, and good management skills and technology bases. TEDA was established in 1984 after thorough research on location options, preferential policies, industry categories, capital funding, and management systems.

## The Drive toward Opening up and Reform

Before China adopted the opening up-policy, its economy suffered from slow growth or economic stagnation and faced challenges of capital shortages, out-of-date technology skills, foreign exchange restrictions, and employment pressures. With the new science and technological revolution driving the world economy at a faster pace, China was lagging farther behind in economic as well as in scientific and technological strength. In the Third Plenary Session of the 11th Central Committee held in December 1978, the Communist Party shifted its focus to Socialist modernization and adopted the opening-up policy. In July 1979, China began experimenting with special zones in Shenzhen, Zhuhai, Shantou, and Xiamen.[4] Those SEZs have achieved miraculous results, attracting attention throughout the world. The success of the four special economic zones provided valuable experience for China at that time.

In February 1984, Deng Xiaoping said, "In addition to existing special economic zones, we may consider opening more port cities. We would not call them special economic zones, but similar policies could be applied" (Deng 1983, 3: 51–51). The objective of opening up more cities and establishing more economic-technological development areas in coastal areas was to take advantage of their geographic locations, to build up a favorable business environment to attract foreign investment to these small regions as soon as possible, to promote the development of an export-oriented economy, and to increase the degree of opening up. Tianjin, as a vital port and traffic hinge in northern China—with an advanced domestic and international trade system as well as a solid industrial base—was considered a good location for establishing an economic and technological development area. After thorough research and with the approval of the State Council, the Tianjin Economic-Technological Development Area was officially established in December 1984.

## TEDA's Abundant Endowments

In addition to the necessary conditions for an economic-technological development area, TEDA has unique endowments that have played an important role in promoting its rapid economic growth. These endowments include abundant land, rich natural resources, transportation infrastructure, and solid technology and human capital.

*Abundant land.* TEDA is west of Bohai Bay on a saline fluvial plain, land that used to be a beach. It has an average elevation of 2.5 meters, but after it was filled with earth for development, its elevation increased to 3.5 meters. It is part of the neo-cathaysian structural system. Its soil is soft, and there is no seismic fault running through it. Currently, TEDA covers 40 square kilometers. Its southern part, known as the southern living zone, is for residential apartments, government units, and financial services, while the northern part, known as the industrial zone, is for manufacturing. The living zone covers about 11.3 square kilometers, the industrial zone about 26.4 square kilometers, and the college zone and the forest park about 3.1 square kilometers (http://www.teda .gov.cn). The planning area of TEDA is 2,270 square kilometers, of which 1,100 square kilometers are saline-alkali wasteland, including tidal flats, and some are low-yield farmland. The 1,100 square kilometers of wasteland provide the land source for future development.

*Rich natural resources.* Tianjin is rich in fuel, metallic ore, nonmetallic minerals, and terrestrial heat resources. Dagang Oilfield and Bohai Oilfield have plenty of natural gas reserves as well as wide distribution, thick oil formations, good penetrability, low sulfur content, and high economic value. TEDA could develop its petrol-chemical industry and marine chemical industry, taking advantage of Tianjin's solid foundation in the chemical industry. Tianjin possesses a wide variety of metallic ores and nonmetallic minerals, many of which are rare. Tianjin also has plenty of coal reserves, and the largest medium- and low-temperature terrestrial heat field among China's cities. Tianjin's terrestrial heat resources are characterized by shallow embedment and good water quality. The regions around Tianjin are also known for their rich natural resources. For instance, Kailuan's coal, Renqiu's petroleum, Luanxian's iron ore, and Jidong's architectural and refractory material are all within 200 kilometers of Tianjin. In addition, the coal base in Shanxi Province and the fur production area in Neimenggu are not far from Tianjin, about 500 kilometers away (Gu 1984).

*Convenient transportation.* Within a 500-kilometer radius of TEDA are 17 percent of the nation's population and 11 big cities, each of which has a population of more than 1 million.[5] Beijing and Tianjin have a combined population of more than 20 million. Tianjin is also the transportation hub (with both land and sea routes) for northern China. Tianjin port was the first to use containers in China and takes a leading role in port throughput capacity, storehouse area, port facilities, and automation. In the 1980s, Tianjin port ranked third in scale and fifth in port throughput capacity in China, accommodating about a thousand foreign ships annually with more than 20 ocean shipping routes and trading with 168 countries and regions (Gu 1984). Tianjin is the economic center and the industrial base of northern China, with an advanced railway and highway network. The well-developed transportation infrastructure has contributed much to the region's economy, politics, science, and technology as well as to its social development, making TEDA the center of commerce, trade, and goods in the northern and northwestern regions.

*Technology and human capital.* Tianjin has provided significant support to technology and human resources for TEDA. Tianjin, an old industrial city, serves as an important industrial base, with a full range of industrial sectors, strong manufacturing capacity, high-quality industrial products, and advanced production technology and therefore provides strong economic returns. Tianjin's leading enterprises and brand names are of great importance in China. Furthermore, Tianjin has a competitive advantage in research and development. A large number of engineers work here, and scientific research institutions play a central role in this region of northern China.

Science and technology in some industries and disciplines take the leading role in the country. Tianjin's colleges and universities have also made outstanding scientific and technological discoveries in both fundamental theory and applied science, which have helped the city strengthen its technology base and improve its economic productivity. In this context, the labor force in Tianjin is well educated (see table 3.9), but compared to Beijing, Guangzhou, and Shanghai, labor costs in Tanjin are relatively low.

**Table 3.9    Highest Educational Attainment of TEDA's Labor Force, 2008**

|  | College and university degree | Senior high school (including technical secondary) | Junior high school | Primary school |
|---|---|---|---|---|
| Number of people | 5,121 | 8,218 | 9,263 | 2,239 |
| % of population | 19.7 | 31.7 | 35.7 | 8.6 |

*Source:* Li 2008. Based on the statistics of the fifth population census of Tianjin.

## *Importance of TEDA to Tianjin's Economic Development*

The establishment of TEDA was of vital importance to Tianjin's economic development because it helped promote the export-oriented economy, introduce advanced technology from abroad, and explore new patterns of economic development. TEDA relies on Tianjin for a supportive environment and in return fosters the economic development of the whole city.

***Promotion of an export-oriented economy.*** TEDA places a high priority on using foreign investment and developing export-oriented industries. A series of preferential policies has been implemented in TEDA to attract foreign investment, such as a lower income tax rate of 15 percent for foreign-funded enterprises, and special policies for high-tech and exporting companies. For foreign-funded enterprises, the foreign share of the enterprises' profit can be remitted abroad without paying income tax. All these preferential policies have made TEDA a priority for foreign investors. More important, TEDA sets a good example of how to improve the climate for foreign investment. TEDA has gradually become the base for Tianjin's export-oriented economy and has promoted the awareness of foreign trade in developing the regional economy.

***Introduction of advanced technology from abroad.*** The objectives behind the establishment of TEDA are stated as follows:

> TEDA shall introduce advanced technology in urgent need from abroad; TEDA shall establish Sino-Foreign joint ventures and cooperative ventures as well as foreign owned scientific research institutions in order to develop cooperative production, collaborate research, discover new techniques, and manufacture high end products; in this way, TEDA could boost export, and share new technology and management experience with the inland areas (Notice of State Council 1984).

Therefore, TEDA has focused primarily on high-tech and high value-added programs to promote technology upgrading and industrial restructuring. The leading enterprises in TEDA—mostly high-tech companies, some of which have world-class production technology—have fueled rapid technology development in Tianjin as well as in its neighboring regions. Meanwhile, some multinational companies have invested in TEDA, which also benefits TEDA's technology upgrading.

*Reliance on and service to the city.* TEDA relies on the city of Tianjin, which provides the nurturing environment for TEDA's development, including infrastructure, manufacturing industries, and human capital. In return, TEDA provides crucial services for the city's development. Generally speaking, the advanced technology introduced in TEDA promotes technological progress and industrial restructuring in the entire city. TEDA has accumulated valuable experience in location choice, construction planning, land utilization and management, and municipal construction, which set a good example for the city and fuel new development in Tianjin. TEDA is dedicated to developing high-tech industry through top-of-the-line projects and to serving as the engine driving the technological progress of the city. TEDA helps the city attract a large volume of foreign investment, with many foreign-funded enterprises, mainly exporting companies, in an effort to expand the city's foreign trade.

## The Role of Government in the Construction of TEDA

The Tianjin municipal government and its authorized organization—the TEDA Administrative Commission—have played an important role in the construction of TEDA. Together, they have conducted land exploitation and administration, created an excellent investment environment, and attracted outside investments by various means.

### Land Exploitation and Administration
The government of TEDA implements its land exploitation policy primarily through four patterns. The first pattern is called "indebted exploitation." In TEDA's early years, a national development loan of RMB 370 million was offered for indebted land exploitation, enabling the building of infrastructure for a 3-square-kilometer industrial zone and a 1.99-square-kilometer living zone, which laid a sound foundation for TEDA's further development. The second pattern is "roll exploitation," which entails first aggregating the land, then exploiting it, and finally reclaiming it. A combination of income from land-use charges and financial support from the Administrative Commission was reinvested in land exploitation, with priority on the construction and improvement of infrastructure, thereby creating a positive cycle of exploiting and reclaiming land while investing. Given the insufficient funding, TEDA's roll exploitation approach ensured rapid land exploitation and provided a good environment for large-scale foreign investment.

The third pattern is called "segmented land exploitation" and operates mainly in three ways (Pi and Wang 2004):

- First, the TEDA Administrative Commission, as owner of the land, designates a certain piece of land and takes the exempted charge for the use of land as the capital stock of the government. Then investment is introduced to make joint development, and then the developed land is sold, with profits for both sides.
- Second, a potential foreign investor buys a piece of land from TEDA's Administrative Commission at a low price and creates a commercial development, which is then sold to another investor at a profit.
- Third, the TEDA Administrative Commission uses the land as its share of investment and establishes a real estate company jointly with other foreign investors, developing land and obtaining profits through the transfer of land.

This segmented land exploitation pattern accelerated TEDA's infrastructure construction and met the needs of TEDA's rapid development; it also relieved TEDA's burden of land exploitation by itself and significantly enhanced the scale and speed of land exploitation.

The fourth land exploitation pattern is the direct transfer of land-use rights to foreigners. As the first development area in China to make compensated land-use rights available to foreign investors, the Land Administration Bureau of TEDA signed a contract for "assignment of the right to the use of land" with the U.S. MGM Commercial Co. in August 1989, offering the right to use 5.37 square kilometers of land for a maximum term of 70 years. The fourth pattern has greatly propelled reform of the land-use system in China and has expanded foreign investment as well. These four types of land exploitation have generated large profits for TEDA, with the total exploited land increased by 20.6 percent annually within 18 years, from 4.99 square kilometers in 1988 to 42 square kilometers in 2006 (http://www.teda.gov.cn).

To ensure effective land administration, the government of TEDA has set up special organizations and issued a series of provisions and regulations on land administration. As the official land administration authority, the Construction Development Bureau Office of TEDA specializes in the following administrative functions: implementing the city planning law of China, managing the cadastre of state-owned land in TEDA, administering the assignments and transfers of land, registering land transfers, managing land mortgages and donations, issuing certificates for the use of state-owned land, collecting taxes and charges on the use of state-owned land, supervising the land market, and evaluating land values. The regulations on land administration released by the government of TEDA include mainly the following: Provisions on Land Administration in TEDA in July 1985, Regulations on Compensated Assignment and Transfer of the Right to the Use of the Land in TEDA in December 1988, Measures on Applying to Use Land in TEDA, Measures on Charges for Compensated Transfer of the Right to the Use of the Land in TEDA, Implementation Measures on Compensated Assignment and Transfer of the Right to the Use of Land in TEDA, Provisional Regulations on the Right to the Use of Land in TEDA in December 1988, Provisional Measures on the Auction of the Right to the Use of Land in TEDA in July 1999, and so forth. The government of TEDA has implemented effective land administration through the Construction Development Bureau Office and through the administrative provisions and regulations mentioned above.

## TEDA's Government and the Investment Environment

To promote the development of TEDA, the government formulated an integrated development plan. In addition, it has constructed infrastructure and a good physical environment, established specialized institutions to promote investment, and provided sufficient financing.

*Integrated development plan and implementation.* An integrated development plan provided the guidelines for the overall construction of TEDA, including regional function orientation, industrial development planning, strategies for attracting foreign investment, social and cultural environment, environmental protection, regional image marketing, and the like. The planning was rather simple at the beginning. The government did not create the preliminary development plan until 1985. The TEDA Administrative Commission constituted the Comprehensive Master Plan of TEDA in 1996, which was further developed and adjusted according to the construction and development practices of TEDA in 2001. In January 2008, the comprehensive plan was further revised and extended in accordance with the overall development requirements of Tianjin and the Binhai New Area. For planning administration, the TEDA Administrative Commission issued the provisions on planning and design administration of TEDA in March 1997, including the compilation and approval of the comprehensive plan as well as detailed plans, administration of land planning for construction, administration of construction projects, legal liabilities, and so on. All of these were intended to reinforce the planning administration, to ensure the implementation of the plan, and to promote balanced economic and social development.

***Infrastructure and the environment.*** With regard to infrastructure, TEDA had set a goal of "creating a favorable international investment environment" early on. The slogan had a number of implications. On the one hand, the exacting environment suitable for the operation of modern industrial enterprises was to be built according to international standards. On the other hand, foreign enterprises were treated much as they were in other countries. The infrastructure of TEDA consisted not only of residential buildings, schools, hospitals, banks, post offices, custom bureaus, and so on, but also a convenient transportation network. Currently, among the national economic-technological development zones, TEDA is considered to have the best comprehensive infrastructure and facilities.

For planting and ecological construction, TEDA administrative authorities have issued Administrative Regulations on the Maintenance of Green Lands, Administrative Regulations on the Transplant and Chopping of Trees, Green Lands Management and Specification, and so on. The authority has also promulgated the "green guaranty," which mandates that enterprises in TEDA operate according to its environmental standards. The administrative leadership is responsible for the major greening and planting projects. In addition, obligatory tree-planting activities are held every year.

The above measures have proved effective, with a continuously enlarging green area in TEDA and a green coverage rate exceeding 30 percent. The Environmental Protection Office of TEDA, founded in 1985, was restructured as the Environmental Protection Bureau in 1990, responsible for environmental protection and supervision. At the end of 2000, TEDA took the lead in passing the ISO14000 urban environmental certification. By 2003, the planning of an eco-industrial park in TEDA was completed, and in 2004 the plan was approved by the State Bureau of Environmental Protection. In September 2007, the supervisory committee of the National Eco-Industrial Demonstration Area came to TEDA for field research, confirming that TEDA satisfies 19 of the 21 standards issued by the State Bureau of Environmental Protection's Criteria of Integrated Eco-industrial Areas (trial edition) (http://www.teda.gov.cn).

### Promotion of Foreign Investment

Because attracting investment is TEDA's key task, the investment promotion authority serves an important role. Among its activities, it establishes specialized organizations to attract investment, continually adjusts TEDA's focus and approach, and administers industrial parks.

***Specialized organizations for attracting investment.*** The Investment Promotion Bureau and the Economic Development Bureau are mainly in charge of investment promotion in TEDA. The former is responsible for preparation, negotiation, and approval of investment projects; organizing activities; marketing and maintaining investment clients; and facilitating TEDA's overall operation. The Economic Development Bureau assists the Investment Promotion Bureau in attracting investment, with a special focus on domestic investment projects. The offices of TEDA have been set up in many domestic cities including Beijing, Shenzhen, Shanghai, and Hong Kong, China, and as well as overseas, including the United States, Japan, Singapore, and Europe. These offices are responsible for communication with governments, enterprises, and other organizations, for marketing TEDA, and for Tianjin's favorable investment environment. Furthermore, many well-known native and foreign experts are employed as consultants for TEDA, which serves as an additional means for expanding the network to attract investment.

***TEDA's focus and approach.*** When TEDA was established in the late 1980s, the focus on attracting investment meant upgrading technology and promoting foreign trade. By 1993, that adjustment had been made, and priority shifted to larger projects and bigger financial syndicates to strengthen cooperation with multinational companies. In 1996, the focus changed again, expanding beyond industry to include infrastructure, commerce, and finance, among others.

Since 2000, TEDA has put more emphasis on technology innovation and has transformed itself from an export-oriented manufacturing district into a high-tech industrial center. Along with the shifting emphasis, TEDA's approach to attracting investment has been adjusted accordingly. At the beginning, the project contract system was adopted to make administration uniform, with a focus on marketing and networking. In 1993, as more aggressive guidelines for attracting investment were put in place, TEDA undertook large-scale marketing with an emphasis on large multinational companies. Since 2000, TEDA has strengthened its comprehensive approach to attracting investment by promoting technology investment, industry investment, international investment, brand investment, and domestic investment, among others.

*Industrial parks.* To promote investment, TEDA offers good services to industrial parks. It administers three major industrial parks: TEDA Microelectronics Industrial Park, TEDA Yat-Sen Scientific-Industrial Park, and TEDA Chemical Industrial Park. TEDA Microelectronics Industrial Park was built in 1996 with the objective of becoming China's Silicon Valley. The industrial park accommodates the specific needs of individual companies by making regular visits to the enterprise. By 2006, the total accumulated investment amounted to US$1.12 billion in TEDA Microelectronics Industrial Park, with 92 registered enterprises located in the park, 61 of which were foreign-funded enterprises and 31 domestic. TEDA Yat-Sen Scientific-Industrial Park was built in 1993 and offers high-quality services to the enterprises in the park. By 2006, the total project investment amounted to US$826 million. The industrial structure was initially intended to focus on electronics, automobile components, and machinery manufacturing. TEDA Chemical Industrial Park was established in 1995, with an emphasis on the development of marine chemical industries, fine chemical industries, and downstream petrochemical products. In 2005, the Chemical Industrial Park was named most valuable petrochemical park for investment in China. By the end of 2006, there were 40 registered enterprises in the park, and the total investment was US$585 million (http://www.teda.gov.cn).

## TEDA's Preferential Tax and Fiscal Policies

TEDA's outstanding economic development relies heavily on a series of favorable tax and fiscal policies. These policies have been constantly adjusted to sustain fast economic growth in the region.

### Taxes and Tariffs

The favorable tax policies implemented during TEDA's initial period affected mainly enterprise income tax, sales tax, and tariffs. The enterprise income tax rate for foreign-funded manufacturing enterprises was 15 percent. Those established more than 10 years could enjoy two years of income tax exemption from the year they started making profits and could pay half the tax in the following three years ("two-free three-halves," for short). Those whose annual export value exceeded 70 percent of their total annual production could enjoy a 10 percent enterprise income tax rate. High-tech enterprises could enjoy three more years of half-tax. Foreign enterprises that introduced advanced technology to China for free or on favorable terms were exempted from business tax and enterprise income tax, and the income from technology transfer was exempted from sales tax.

During TEDA's rapid development, the favorable tax policies gradually became more specific. Complementing the existing policies, new tax policies came into being. Accordingly, foreign-funded enterprises investing in infrastructure were to pay an enterprise income tax rate of 15 percent and, from their first profitable year, enjoyed a tax exemption for the first five years, followed by a half-tax rate for the next five years. Advanced technology and high-tech enterprises, from their first year of production, were to enjoy "two-free three-halves" as well as a favorable enterprise income tax rate of 10 percent for three more years. And foreign financial institutions, from their first profitable year, were to pay an income tax rate of 15 percent and to enjoy a one-year tax exemption and half-tax for the next two years.

Preferential tariff policies in TEDA have remained stable except in 1996. For TEDA enterprises, export is exempted from export tariffs. Construction materials, manufacturing equipment, raw materials, parts and accessories, vehicles, office supplies, and management equipment imported by enterprises for self-use, as well as goods and vehicles that foreign entrepreneurs imported for home use, are exempted from import tariffs. The exemption policy for import tariffs was abolished in 1996 but restored in 1998. Foreign enterprises' share of profits is exempted from export tax when remitted abroad. Products processed in TEDA with materials or semifinished products from the mainland, and with value added of more than 20 percent, could be regarded as products of the development zone and be exempted from export tariffs. Foreign-funded enterprises are exempted from import tariffs and import-related taxes when they import self-use equipment that could not be manufactured in mainland China.

### Favorable Fiscal Policies

TEDA is allowed to issue favorable policies and regulations in support of enterprises using discretionary government revenues. At the beginning, these favorable policies were mainly for the manufacturing sector. As TEDA developed, fiscal policies tended to favor high-tech industries and the service sector. Specifically, TEDA's favorable fiscal policies aim to encourage high-tech industries, promote a modern service sector, and expand the outsourcing of services.

***Encouraging high-tech industries.*** The administrative council of TEDA allocates 5 percent of its disposable annual revenue to a scientific and technology development fund to support the development of high-tech industries. High-tech enterprises and R&D institutions that purchase land for production or R&D in the zone receive corresponding construction support according to the scale and density of the investment and quality of the project. High-tech enterprises that enjoy a favorable income tax rate of 15 percent receive 100 percent financial support in the first two years and 50 percent in the following three years. High-tech enterprises in the start-up stage can receive rent subsidies for up to three years when they rent buildings for research, administration, or production. High-tech manufacturing enterprises can receive subsidies for up to 50 percent of the interest on their loans when investing in fixed assets.

*Promoting a modern service sector.* TEDA has established the TEDA Modern Service Sector Development Fund with RMB 100 million from its annual budget to support modern service enterprises. Headquarters of domestic-funded enterprises and regional headquarters of multinationals can receive operational support ranging from RMB 10 million to RMB 20 million, according to their registered capital, and their business and enterprise income tax can be exempted for two years from the approved year and halved for the following three years. Financial enterprises set up in the zone can receive operational support ranging from RMB 2 million to RMB 10 million in accordance with their registered capital, and their business tax can be exempted within the first two years after approval of the application and halved for the following three years. Professional services, logistics, trade, culture, and the conference and exhibition industry can also receive financial support to offset the value-added tax, business tax, enterprise income tax, loan interest, and so on.

*Expanding service outsourcing.* Enterprises that meet the requirements of the Regulations on Promoting the Development of Service Outsourcing of TEDA can receive subsidies when they purchase or rent office buildings in the zone. Service outsourcing enterprises engaging in software R&D and technology R&D and design can take advantage of national and municipal tax supports. For other types of service outsourcing enterprises, from the year of establishment, part of the business tax and income tax collected by the municipal government can be exempted for the first two years and halved for the following three years. Service outsourcing training institutions that meet the requirements of the regulations can receive fiscal support amounting to 50 percent of municipally collected business tax and enterprise income tax for five years starting from the year of establishment.

### Other Favorable Policies

Besides preferential fiscal and tax policies, TEDA has also implemented special treatment for enterprise operations:

- TEDA's examination and approval power for foreign investment is similar to the practice in the four special economic zones and has even a higher quota for using and borrowing foreign exchange.
- TEDA attracts a talented labor force for R&D in enterprises or scientific research institutions in the zone through favorable housing policies, research funding, and subsidies for children's education as well as assistance in Hukou[6] transfer and the evaluation of positional titles.
- Administrative fees have been abandoned, except those required by law and regulations.
- The establishment of nonprofit organizations for education, culture, science and technology, and health, among other aspects of public welfare, can benefit from discounts or exemptions from venue fees after approval from the administrative council of TEDA. Enterprises investing in the construction and operation of the water supply, gas, electricity, heating, sewerage, roads, and other infrastructure projects pay reduced venue fees or are exempted from them. Land used for production, infrastructure projects, standard factory buildings, high-tech industries, venture capital, manufacturing, and service sectors can enjoy favorable land rents according to the needs of different projects and in some instances can be exempted from them.

## TEDA's Success

After 24 years of reform and development, TEDA is the development area with the strongest overall strength in China and has also become the new driving force for Tianjin's social and economic development. Binhai New Area, with TEDA at the center, has become one of the three major sources of China's economic growth and the economic center of northern China, along with Shenzhen City in Guangdong Province and the Pudong economic zone in Shanghai. During the development and opening up process, TEDA gained important experience and learned valuable lessons, which are elaborated in this section to provide guidance for other economic and technology development areas.

### TEDA's Low-Cost Advantage in Land, Labor, and Infrastructure

TEDA's land costs were fairly low in its early stage of development. TEDA is located on a saline-alkali wasteland, 45 kilometers east of its home city, Tianjin. The preliminary planning area was 33 square kilometers. Because the saline-alkali wasteland is state-owned land, TEDA obtained the land-use rights free. Consequently, the land expropriation cost was largely reduced. Furthermore, because the wasteland was unpopulated, no relocation costs were involved. Therefore, TEDA's initial advantage of low-cost land provided a solid foundation for its future development.

The high-quality but low-cost labor force has also attracted enterprises to TEDA. The home city of Tianjin has always been an important manufacturing center of China. The number of workers in various sectors in Tianjin has been growing steadily and their labor skills continuously improving, satisfying the different demands for labor resources. Therefore, enterprises in TEDA have easy access to skilled employees. At the same time, the wages in Tianjin have been far below the average in other coastal cities in eastern China, which strengthens the competitiveness of the enterprises that settle in TEDA.

The industrial environment and infrastructure in TEDA also facilitate lower-cost production. Tianjin provides a solid industrial base with comprehensive industry sectors easily coordinating with one another. Therefore, enterprises here can find compatible supporting vendors without much difficulty. As a result, enterprises in TEDA can not only guarantee quality of production, but also cut the transportation costs of importing parts and accessories from overseas. The sound supporting environment is able to reduce overall manufacturing costs and facilitate TEDA's sustainable and balanced development.

### TEDA's International Transportation and Communications

TEDA has an obvious geographical advantage: its proximity to Tianjin port. Tianjin port, which is adjacent to TEDA, is the largest port in northern China and also ranks among the top 10 artificial deepwater ports in the world. It is an important foreign trade port in northern China, having trade relations with more than 400 ports in more than 180 countries and regions. Tianjin port possesses large throughput capacity and has become an important port in international trade. With convenient access to Tianjin port, TEDA has a gateway to the world in northern China and the front runner in trade cooperation.

TEDA also has an obvious advantage in transportation, with more than a dozen roads and highways connecting it with other big cities and industrial centers and its railway systems linked to the national railway network. Commodities can be transported to any part of the country and can be reexported to Europe through Mongolia, which is the shortest and most convenient route to Europe. Tianjin International Airport, right next to TEDA, with 39 international and domestic airlines, is the largest air cargo center in northern China and is considered a substitute international airport for Beijing.

In addition, TEDA has a historical and cultural heritage of international communication and exchange. Tianjin is an old commercial port city, first opened as a trading port in the 19th century. The city has a long history of foreign trade and close commercial interaction with countries around the world. The residents in Tianjin have a good understanding of foreign customs, lifestyles, values, and beliefs after years of experience in international communications and exchange. Meanwhile, Tianjin is a popular residential location for foreigners who have become familiar with local customs. It offers a good example of how cultural exchange promotes commercial interaction.

### Committed Government and Efficient Public Services

TEDA has gained the attention and commitment of the central government. In the early stages of planning, the central leadership considered many locations and conducted field investigations before choosing TEDA. During the construction of the development area, the central leadership often gave guidance, solved problems on the spot, and issued preferential policies for TEDA's development. In 1986, when Deng Xiaoping visited TEDA, he was pleased to make the inscription, "TEDA is a promising development area," which greatly inspired the people involved in TEDA's construction and development. In the meantime, as a state-level development area, TEDA can often communicate directly with and make recommendations to central ministries and commissions. Ministries and commissions can also directly respond to TEDA. This interaction has effectively promoted its development.

The government of TEDA is pragmatic and innovative. It pays a lot of attention to the training of a talented labor force, invites Nankai University and other well-known institutions to build their campuses in the development area, experiments in vocational education, cooperates with partners in Germany and Spain to facilitate multilevel support for talent, and has transformed TEDA into an educational base. The government of TEDA emphasizes innovation in science and technology as well as construction of major scientific and technology innovation platforms, such as innovation parks, R&D centers, and industrialization bases. The government operates according to law, makes regulations conforming to international conventions, and forms internal management systems of laws and regulations. In the process of streamlining economic laws related to foreign trade after China joined the World Trade Organization (WTO), the legal system in TEDA rose to the challenge.

In addition, TEDA boasts efficient public services. The government strives to create a "compatible international investment environment" according to international standards, to build up infrastructure in line with the requirements of international investors, to place the rights of enterprises first, and to restrain from intervening in legitimate business activities. The government of TEDA aims to create a "service-oriented government" with simple and efficient approval processes and to avoid administrative fees. As a separate office of the Tianjin government, the TEDA management committee is structured efficiently, combining relevant functional departments and establishing fiscal administration that ensures independent taxation and budget processes. This management system is highly delegated and specialized with sole concentration on economic development; it strives to achieve lower costs and enhanced efficiency.

### Policy Advantages of the Special Economic Zone
Shortly after TEDA was established, the central government provided some preferential tax and finance policies that allowed TEDA to speed up its development. At the same time, TEDA also established some specific policies, such as giving preferable land terms to well-known enterprises and offering financial support to investing enterprises. TEDA's initial purpose was to attract foreign investment, which requires reforming policies for taxation, foreign exchange, finance, and customs. For example, allowing foreign companies to recruit and fire Chinese workers was an unprecedented approach at that time. These policy reforms made breakthroughs in TEDA's practices and distinguished TEDA from other development areas, contributing to the concentration of high-quality resources in the area and to the formation of an optimal operational environment for the enterprises. All the high-quality resources are used efficiently in TEDA and have greatly affected the area's development. Thanks to these favorable policies, TEDA has realized remarkable economic development and has become the area with the most vibrant economic activity and the fastest rate of economic growth.

### Environment for Sustainable Development in TEDA

TEDA's administrative committee is in a separate office from the Tianjin government. It performs general administrative functions and is authorized to enact reforms in the role of government, organizational structure, planning, and construction. To ensure a smooth transition from traditional administration, the Tianjin TEDA Administrative Regulation granted legal status to TEDA at its inception. The legislation regulates land transfer, registration of foreign companies, and employment policy by foreign companies. TEDA is legally authorized to experiment with various pioneering reforms. Given the incomplete legal system in China at that time, the legislative guarantee for the development of the export-oriented economy represents one of the innovative approaches in TEDA. In addition, innovation pushes forward the internal reform of TEDA, as it implements institutional autonomy and efficiency.

At present, institutional reform relies heavily on the knowledge of relationships among different institutions. The comprehensive reform now being instituted is aimed at resolving unbalanced institutional relationships. The central government has approved Binhai New Area as a pilot area to put in place these broad reforms. As one of the core functional regions in the pilot program, TEDA can now provide important support for such reforms. Therefore, these reforms have become a new institutional advantage for TEDA. In accordance with the general rules of socioeconomic development, TEDA can make full use of the first-mover advantages of the reform and seek specific policies and regulations suitable for its development. In other words, compared with the neighboring area, the most important institutional advantage of TEDA is the authority to carry out reforms and experiments. TEDA has continually expanded the spectrum of reform and promoted sustainable development through a combination of major breakthroughs and general innovation, of economic system reform and reform in other aspects, and of practical problem solving in local areas and theoretical problem solving.

## Challenges Faced by TEDA

TEDA has already made extraordinary achievements, moving Tianjin's social and economic development forward. Many lessons have been drawn from this process. As an innovative experiment, however, TEDA has accumulated valuable experience that can be shared with development areas in other countries and regions.

### Balancing Favorable Policies and Market Competition

The central government has granted certain preferential policies to support the development of TEDA. And TEDA itself has also created favorable policies critical to the fast development of the area. With its entry into the WTO and the deepening of its opening-up reforms, China has witnessed profound changes in its economy and society. But development zones, along with the local special economic zones, now suffer from the diminishing advantages of favorable government policies. According to the principles of fair trade, transparency, and fair competition, those favorable policies were weakened or even abolished after China's entry into the WTO. In effect, enterprises from home and abroad now enjoy the same policy environment, enterprises from inside or outside are to be treated equally, and nondevelopment zones will also benefit from similar favorable policies, such as taxation, land, and investment. For instance, the enterprise income tax on enterprises in development zones used to be 15 percent, compared to the average tax rate of 24 percent. The Enterprise Income Tax Law of China (2007) indicates that the enterprise income tax in all areas should be levied equally eventually. Moreover, favorable policies should be made and executed in line with standards and regulations on transparency, and afterward those policies implemented in the development zones can be applied to areas outside the zones.

TEDA's policy advantages are gradually diminishing. Because regional policy disparities will be eliminated and information can be shared between development zones, TEDA must deal with competition from other zones and the conflicts arising from attracting investment among development zones. TEDA, however, has already achieved an excellent reputation, making it an attractive option for investors:

- TEDA is a national development zone with standard management and high reliability, which makes a difference when it comes to negotiating with foreign investors interested in TEDA, because they trust national-level development zones.
- Owing to close contact with foreigners, TEDA has trained a team of talented people with advanced knowledge and high productivity.
- TEDA provides an exceptional investment environment and excellent public services. As a national development zone, TEDA can directly communicate with central ministries and commissions and lobby on behalf of the enterprises in the zone.

### Dealing with Land Use

To some extent, TEDA's fast development and expansion came at the price of rapid land exploitation. Land was not considered a scarce resource at the beginning stage of TEDA's development. To attract investment, the zone adopted several land-use measures, such as indebted exploitation, roll exploitation, financing exploitation, and the like to accelerate land exploitation, which solved the land-use problem and boosted the real estate industry and service sectors. The low cost of transferring land-use rights, however, was used to attract foreign investment. For example, when TEDA was first established, the lowest market price for land was only 14 yuan per square meter, which was just 10 percent of its cost (Pi and Wang 2004). Therefore, the price of land did not reflect its real value and cannot be treated as an independent commodity.

At present, TEDA's restriction on land resources has already become a challenge to its future development for several reasons. First, demand for land is rising continuously as the scale of manufacturing grows larger and larger. TEDA is faced with diminished land resources because neighboring administrations are unwilling to transfer land to TEDA. Second, the price of neighboring land has been rising rapidly as a result of TEDA's prosperity. Land exploitation cost per acre is several times higher than it was when TEDA was launched, making land expansion a daunting task. TEDA cannot expand without substantial expenditures on more land. Thus, the most urgent issue for TEDA now is to figure out how to control its scale, how to restructure its industrial composition, and how to use land efficiently.

### Dealing with the Relationship between TEDA and Tianjin

TEDA relies on the home city of Tianjin and in turn serves the city as well. On the one hand, TEDA's smooth development relies on the indispensable benefits of the sound infrastructure, industrial environment, and labor force of the home city. On the other hand, the development zone provides a stimulus for the city's further economic development with its intensive industrial capacity and modern technology, making itself a new pillar for the home city's growth. However, frictions between the two arise for several reasons.

The first reason is distance. TEDA is in a remote area of the city, like a "lonely geographic island," which has led to the high cost of infrastructure construction, diseconomy of scale, and high operational costs of the enterprises in the zone. Moreover, other elements of the zone are incomplete as a result of its focus on industry. Business facilities, tourism, leisure, culture, and recreation are not provided for, and as a result the zone is almost empty after working hours. Being distant from the home city reduces the environmental advantage of the zone.

The second reason is attracting investment. As the policy advantages lessen, foreign investors will prefer to invest in the home city, which has more comprehensive city amenities, for the sake of lower cost. Currently, enterprises want to register in the zone in the hope of favorable policies and services but physically locate in the city for better facilities. This phenomenon has become common, creating frictions between the zone and the city.

The third reason is administrative conflict. In its initial years, TEDA's gross production and scale of economy were relatively small, contributing little to the city's GDP. After 24 years of rapid development, today the development zone has become the fastest-growing area in Tianjin and has close contact with the outside world and therefore more interaction with the city. The power delegated to TEDA's administrative committee has been gradually diluted through various administrative regulations by different government departments, and in some circumstances its authority has been revoked by the municipality, resulting in longer government procedures and lower government efficiency.

### Dealing with Industrial Development in the Zone

TEDA takes modern manufacturing as its leading sector, aiming to become a modern high-tech manufacturing base featuring multinational corporations. These corporations, however, set up only their manufacturing facilities in TEDA, which is the least-profitable link in the business chain. The more-profitable parts, those with higher value added, are not based in TEDA. Take Motorola as an example. Motorola's materials procurement and sales are in Beijing, while its R&D is performed abroad, leaving only manufacturing in TEDA. Of the three production centers for multinational corporations—manufacturing, production services, and R&D—the manufacturing center is not the focal point of competitiveness anymore, R&D having taken its place. Because TEDA specializes mostly in manufacturing rather than R&D, technology innovation and high-tech industry are relatively weak. Few corporations have obtained their own intellectual property rights in TEDA. Therefore, the serious challenges for TEDA are how to induce R&D departments of multinational corporations to come into the zone and how to accelerate the development of technology innovation.

The modern service sector has developed as the result of industrial restructuring and upgrading, which have affected the city's development direction and economic performance. Industry-oriented development in TEDA has resulted in a relatively backward service sector. As shown in table 3.10, the proportion of tertiary industry production in 1999 was only 22.4 percent and fell to only 17.5 percent in 2007. Because of the backward service industry and the long distance from the urban district, the cost of living and commuting in the zone is comparatively high. This situation is not only inconvenient for people working in TEDA, but also detrimental to the industrial development of the area. How to accelerate the modern service sector is an urgent issue for TEDA. At present, TEDA is emphasizing the "headquarters' economy," which means promoting a full spectrum of services by introducing company headquarters into the zone, leading to more opportunities for employment and economic expansion.

## Lessons Learned from TEDA

TEDA's experiences offer broadly applicable lessons. Based on TEDA's successful experience, we have arrived at the following policy recommendations for economic and development areas in other countries and regions.

### Give Priority to Advanced Open Port Areas

Coastal areas—with more advanced transportation systems, industrial bases, technology, managerial capacity, and education—are experienced in foreign trade and in economic and technology cooperation with inland areas (Notice of State Council 1984). These advantages are important

**Table 3.10    Proportion of Secondary and Tertiary Industry Production in TEDA, 1991–2007**

*percent*

|  | 1991–99 | | | | | | | | |
|---|---|---|---|---|---|---|---|---|---|
|  | *1991* | *1992* | *1993* | *1994* | *1995* | *1996* | *1997* | *1998* | *1999* |
| Secondary | 93.5 | 92.8 | 70.6 | 80.2 | 84.2 | 84.5 | 82.3 | 77.7 | 77.6 |
| Tertiary | 6.5 | 7.2 | 29.4 | 19.8 | 15.1 | 15.5 | 17.7 | 22.3 | 22.4 |
|  | 2000–07 | | | | | | | | |
|  | *2000* | *2001* | *2002* | *2003* | *2004* | *2005* | *2006* | *2007* | |
| Secondary | 79.1 | 78.6 | 78.9 | 79.7 | 83.1 | 84.3 | 83.9 | 82.5 | |
| Tertiary | 20.9 | 21.4 | 21.1 | 20.3 | 16.9 | 15.7 | 16.1 | 17.5 | |

**Sources:** Adapted from *Journal of Tianjin Economics and Technology Development Zone; Tianjin Economics and Technology Development Zone 2001–07.*
**Note:** No primary industry exists in TEDA currently.

factors for attracting foreign investment. In addition, with a long history of international exchange and communication, coastal areas are less constrained by tradition and more open to new ideas. Therefore, the reforms required for investment, employment, market, and government regulations can be more easily implemented with fewer struggles to break free from the old system. Given favorable policies, the coastal areas can promote science and technology, share management experience, boost domestic markets, expand foreign trade, and train the workforce to support and facilitate economic development in their adjacent regions as well as across the country.

### Adjust Favorable Policies according to Contract Commitment and Development Stage

Favorable policies were crucial to TEDA's development in the early period. The special policies helped attract foreign funds and allocate domestic resources to TEDA to accelerate its development. We should be cautious about adjusting these policies, however, because policies, if adjusted frequently, directly affect investors' confidence in the government and negatively affect prospective development in the region. For example, the tax exemption for the equipment imported by foreign-funded enterprises was abolished in 1996. Because of this policy change, many multinational companies suspended their investment plans, and many prospective investors backed away. As a result, the follow-up projects in TEDA slowed down and as did economic growth. Although the policy was reinstated in 1998, the initial change led to huge losses for the development area in just a short time. Of course, though, with economic development and a changing market environment, some policy adjustments are inevitable. Since the accession of China into the WTO, the favorable policies in general have declined in number, and the policies for equal competition have been strengthened. Contract commitment and appropriate policy adjustment should be given more attention.

### Grant Administrative Autonomy for Provision of Public Services

The role of government is key to the future of TEDA. It is very important for the local government to give the administrative committee of TEDA appropriate autonomy so that TEDA can form an innovative managerial system that meets market needs and permits dealing with foreign investors more flexibly and efficiently. Certainly, it is critical to define the role of the government of TEDA, with a clear relationship between government and market. The main responsibilities of the government are to establish sound regulations for foreign-funded enterprises, to work efficiency, and to provide the good facilities and convenient living conditions necessary for foreign investors. The government of TEDA should be involved only in regulating markets and should not be involved with or interfere in business operation. Nor should the enterprises depend on the government. The government pursues service-oriented management for enterprises, creates a sound market economy in TEDA, and empowers enterprises with full autonomy in operation without interference in legal business activities. The new pattern of government-business relationships helps the government provide better public services and helps enterprises maximize their profits, creating a win-win situation.

### Allocate Resources in a Local Context with a National Perspective

TEDA's development should make full use of its comparative advantages, relying on its rich local resources. For example, if the local area has abundant skilled workers, it should take advantage of lower labor costs. On the one hand, optimizing resource allocation can lower cost, improve profitability, and turn the resource advantage into incentives for faster industrial development. On the other hand, through favorable institutions and policies, the development area can compensate for its own resource disadvantages by introducing the basic elements for economic development that are missing in the area.

Pioneering institutions and policies help the area attract resources throughout the country for more effective allocation. For example, capital, technology, and talented labor from other parts of the country relocate in TEDA because of its favorable institutions and policies.

### Government Plan, Market Control

TEDA's great success relies on the government's commitment and promotion. At each development stage of TEDA, the government prepares development plans, ensuring the right direction for industry. The framework defined by the government, however, should be complemented by market forces instead of being regulated only by the government, an approach that might be called "government plan, market control." It is one of the principles that TEDA adheres to for its development and land planning. Government should support the enterprises that comply with the industrial development plan through favorable tax and fiscal policy instead of intervening through administrative measures. Industrial restructuring and upgrading in the development area are related to the quantity and quality of foreign investment, particularly from large multinational companies. Therefore, industrial upgrading should take into account the development strategy of multinational companies. In this way, the development area is able to make full use of market regulation and improve the investment climate to attract more foreign multinational companies.

## Notes

1. If not otherwise stated, all the data are from the Web site of the Tianjin Economic–Technological Development Area.
2. The historical name *Hong Kong* refers to the period before July 1, 1997, when the former British colony was restored to China; *Hong Kong, China* refers to any time after that date.
3. The foreign enterprises include investment in Hong Kong, China; Macao, China; and Taiwan, China.
4. The term *special economic zone* was officially adopted in 1980.
5. In China, 32 cities have a population of more than 1 million people.
6. Hukou is China's residential registration system.

## Bibliography

Administration Commission of Changsha National Economic and Technical Development Zone. 2004. *Kaifaqu Yuanyou Zhengce Youshi Ruohuahou Ruhe Zaichuang Zhaoshang Yinzi Xin Youshi, China Development Area Yearbook 2003*. http://china.org.cn/english/SPORT-c/75823.htm.

Administration Commission of TEDA. 1996. *Tianjin Kaifaqu Shinian Jianshe Zongjie*, Office for Economic Restructuring of State Council. *China Development Area Yearbook 1995*. Beijing: China Financial and Economic Publishing House.

Deng, Xiaoping. *Selected Works*. Vol. 3, *A Summary of the Symposium on Some Coastal Cities*. Beijing: People's Literature Publishing House.

Department of National Economic Statistics. 2005. *1949–2000 China Statistical Data Compilation*. Beijing: China Statistics Press.

Economic Development Bureau of TEDA. 2001–07. *Annual Report on the National Economy and Social Development of Tianjin Economic-Technological Development Area (2001–2007)*. http://en.investteda.org/.

Fan, Gang. 2009. *Zhongguo JIngji Tequ Yanjiu*. Beijing: China Financial and Economic Publishing House.

Gong, Wen. 2006. *Cheng Gong De Shijian, Baogui De Jing Yan, Association of China Development Zone: China Development Zone Yearbook 2005*. Beijing: China Financial and Economic Publishing House.

Gu, Shutang. 1984. *Tianjin Jingji Gaikuang.* Tianjin: Renmin Chu Ban She.

Li, Xiaoxi. 2006. *Xinshiji Zhongguo JIngji Baogao.* Beijing: People's Press.

Li, Yong. 2004, 2008. *Chorography of Tianjin Economic Technological Development Area.* Beijing: Zhonghua Book Company.

Notice of State Council. 1984. *A Summary of the Symposium on Some Coastal Cities.* May 4.

Pi, Qiansheng. 2006. "On Strategic Thinking of Overall Reform in Tianjin's Binhai New District." *Gangkou Jingji* 2.

Pi, Qiansheng, and Wang Kai. 2004. *Zou Chu Gu Dao.* Beijing: Sanlian Bookstore.

Special Zone Office of the State Council, *Dayou Xiwang De Shiye,* Office for Economic Restructuring of State Council. 1996. *China Development Area Yearbook 1995.* Beijing: China Financial and Economic Publishing House.

Tianjin Economics and Technology Development Zone. 2001–07. *National Economics and Social Development Bulletin of Tianjin Economics and Technology Development Zone (2001–2007).* Beijing: National Statistics Bureau.

Tianjin Statistics Bureau. 2008. *Tianjin Statistics Yearbook 2008.* Beijing: China Statistics Press.

Wu, Jinglian. 2006. *Zhongguo Zengzhang Moshi Jueze* Shanghai: Shanghai Yuandong Publishing House.

Xiao, Jincheng. 2006. *Disan Zengzhang Ji De Jueqi.* Beijing: Economic Science Press.

Zhao, Yundong. 1996. *Pengbo Fazhan De Jingji Jishu Kaifaqu.* Office for Economic Restructuring of the State Council. *China Development Area Yearbook 1995.* Beijing: China Financial and Economic Publishing House.

# CHAPTER 4

# From County-Level to State-Level Special Economic Zone: The Case of the Kunshan Economic and Technological Development Zone

## Jianming Wang and Ming Hu

The Kunshan Economic-Technological Development Zone (KETD) was established in 1985 and was recognized as a provincial-level development zone in 1991. Then in 1992, because of its success, the State Council elevated it to the national level. With 20 years of development experience, KETD has expanded from 3.75 square kilometers to 115 square kilometers

Jianming Wang is professor and deputy dean of the College of Education and Public Administration, Suzhou University of Science and Technology; Ming Hu is deputy secretary general of the Kunshan People's Political Consultative and the guest researcher of Kunshan Research Center of Taiwan, China Institute at Tsinghua University. Appreciation is extended to Jian Shen, assistant to the director of the Administrative Committee of KETD, and to Cheng Guixiang, chief secretary of KETD of the General Affairs Office for their generous help.

Relevant research support and statistics were provided by the Research Department of the Municipal Party Committee and municipal government, Economic and Trade Commission, Foreign Trade and Economic Cooperation Bureau, KETD, and other related departments.

and has become the leading force in Kunshan's economic development and scientific and technological progress. From 2001 to 2008, KETD was ranked among the top four national development zones for eight consecutive years by a comprehensive nationwide assessment of state-level development zones conducted by the Ministry of Commerce (MOFCOM) (Administrative Committee of KETD 2009, 5). Some comparisons between Kunshan and other major state-level development zones can be seen in table 4.1.

This case study will analyze KETD's background and history and the roles that the local government has played during the process of its development. The chapter will start with KETD's development performance and then summarize its successful experiences and lessons. It will conclude by putting forward some suggestions and policy measures for future development.

**Table 4.1    Key Indicators for Kunshan and Other Major State-Level Development Zones in China, 2008**

| Indicator | Tianjin | Suzhou | Guangzhou | Kunshan | Qingdao | Yantai | Beijing |
|---|---|---|---|---|---|---|---|
| GDP (RMB 100 million) | 1,066 | 1,002 | 1,140 | 843 | 725 | 650 | 566 |
| GIP (RMB 100 million) | 3,730 | 3,000 | 2,945 | 3,317 | 2,016 | 1,950 | 2,020 |
| Tax revenue (RMB 100 million) | 238 | 197 | 235 | 86 | 93 | 77 | 158 |
| Local general budget revenue (RMB 100 million) | 76 | 95 | 109 | 36 | 74 | 32 | 70 |
| Total imports and exports (US$100 million) | 333 | 620 | 218 | 506 | 130 | 235 | 244 |
| Actually utilized FDI (US$100 million) | 25.1 | 18.0 | 10.3 | 9.2 | 12.5 | 5.5 | 5.4 |
| High-tech enterprises (number) | 225 | 384 | 212 | 54 | 134 | 135 | 597 |
| High-tech enterprise output (RMB 100 million) | 1,999 | 1,482 | 945 | 704 | 1,387 | 1,429 | 1,630 |

*Source:* Administrative Committee of KETD 2009.

## The Major Achievements of KETD

Since its inception in 1984, KETD has made remarkable achievements. These achievements include those in the investment environment, in foreign investment, in the regional economy, in the contribution of large-scale industries, in park construction, and in industrial spillover.

First, the investment environment has been significantly improved. Kunshan, situated to the west of Shanghai and to the east of Suzhou, has a unique geographical location. Over more than 20 years, KETD has spent nearly RMB 20 billion on the infrastructure, including transportation, telecommunications, water, energy, and environmental protection, among others. Kunshan has more than 100 kilometers of local major and minor roads, and on average, each of them has four to six lanes covered with asphalt. They are connected to the Shanghai-Nanjing Expressway, State Highway 312, the Shanghai Hongqiao International Airport Road, and the Shanghai-Nanjing railway, offering very convenient transportation. Furthermore, it has set up international schools, foreign-funded hospitals, foreign enterprise service centers, and an inland customs office. KETD has also established an ISO14000 national demonstration zone, which has created a good environment for investors.

Second, it has attracted a high volume of foreign investment. As of 2009, KETD had introduced some 1,600 foreign investment projects from 43 countries, economies, and regions such as Europe; the United States; Japan; Republic of Korea; Hong Kong, China; and Taiwan, China, with contracted foreign direct investment (FDI) of US$14.6 billion and actually utilized foreign capital of more than US$8 billion. Among these investments, those from Taiwan, China accounted for 55 percent. The newly introduced FDI is more likely to finance larger-scale projects, wholly foreign ownership, and a higher level of new technologies. Up until 2009, 41 projects had an investment value of more than US$100 million, and 511 projects had more than US$10 million. Worldwide, 45 of the world's top 500 firms have invested in Kunshan or set up factories (Administrative Committee of KETD 2010, 1–2). A number of high-tech enterprises such as InfoVision and Nan Ya have their roots in the Kunshan Development Zone.

Third, the regional economy is developing rapidly. In 2009, the regional gross domestic product (GDP) saw a year-on-year rise of 14.4 percent, reaching RMB 96.4 billion. The industrial output value realized was RMB 375.34 billion, up by 13.1 percent on a year-on-year basis.

More than 40 enterprises have a total output and sales value exceeding RMB 1 billion. The total value of exports and imports reached US$53.3 billion, increasing by 5.5 percent, with the value of exports reaching US$36.5 billion. Nearly 30 companies had more than $0.1 billion worth of exports. The tax revenue has grown steadily year after year, and in 2009, it exceeded RMB 10 billion for the first time in history, reaching RMB 11.98 billion, up by 28.81 percent (Administrative Committee of KETD 2010, 1–2). The tax revenue of Kunshan has continuously ranked number one among the counties of Suzhou. The open development of KETD has driven the industrialization, urbanization, and urban-rural integration of Kunshan and has also laid a solid foundation and provided strong momentum for Kunshan to become a modern industrial and commercial city.

Fourth, certain large-scale industries have formed. Three major industries—electronic information, precision machinery, and living supplies—have arisen in KETD, and the degree of their contribution to the economic development of the region continues to increase. The electronic information industry especially has taken advantage of clustering and has developed rapidly over these years. Owing to the effects of scale, this industry has made an outstanding contribution. In 2009, output of the regional information and communications technology (ICT) industry reached RMB 210 billion, with a sharp increase of 30 percent. The regional production of personal computer notebooks reached RMB 60.67 million, which is more than 40 percent of the global total. The digital camera output was 18 million pieces, accounting for about 15 percent of global production. Clearly, Kunshan has become an important production base for the ICT industry both nationally and globally (Administrative Committee of KETD 2010, 1–2).

Fifth, the park construction is quite satisfactory. KETD has always focused on the specialized parks to promote economic development, and it has established different functional parks such as export-processing zones (EPZ), an overseas student pioneer park, an electronics industrial park, a science and technology industrial park, a precision machinery industrial park, and the Small and Medium Enterprises Garden. All these parks are located in one area and can easily interact with each other. Table 4.2 shows that the Kunshan Export-Processing Zone compares favorably with other major EPZs in the region. In 2009, the optoelectronics industry in KETD made a great breakthrough: after successfully creating its own brand, it was awarded as the National Opto-electronics Production Base by the Ministry of Industry and Information Technology. The State

**Table 4.2 Key Indicators for the Jiangsu Kunshan Export-Processing Zone and Other Export-Processing Zones in Its Surrounding Area, 2008**

| | Shanghai, Songjiang | | | Jiangsu Kunshan | | | Jiangsu Suzhou | | | Jiangsu Wuxi | | |
|---|---|---|---|---|---|---|---|---|---|---|---|---|
| | Volume or number | Growth rate | Accumulation | Volume or number | Growth rate | Accumulation | Volume or number | Growth rate | Accumulation | Volume or number | Growth rate | Accumulation |
| Volume of imports & exports (US$100 million) | 390.7 | 1.2 | n.a. | 352.4 | 11.6 | n.a. | 123.6 | 1,448.6 | n.a. | 86.1 | −18.3 | n.a. |
| Volume of exports (RMB 100 million) | 284.7 | 10.8 | n.a. | 243.6 | 16.8 | n.a. | 89.3 | 1,659.2 | n.a. | 48.4 | 4.4 | n.a. |
| Industrial output (RMB 100 million) | 2082.2 | −2.2 | n.a. | 1589.4 | 26.5 | n.a. | 85.6 | 206.2 | n.a. | 258.1 | −48.1 | n.a. |
| Electronics and information industry (RMB 100 million) | 1937.4 | −6.0 | n.a. | 1405.1 | 26.7 | n.a. | 81.0 | 252.0 | n.a. | 235.1 | −37.4 | n.a. |
| Sales of industrial products (RMB 100 million) | 2030.6 | −5.4 | n.a. | 1582.7 | 26.7 | n.a. | 84.9 | 202.6 | n.a. | 252.9 | −43.8 | n.a. |
| Profit of industrial enterprises (RMB 100 million) | 20.9 | −14.7 | n.a. | 19.8 | −19.4 | n.a. | 3.8 | 3321.5 | n.a. | 15.7 | −52.4 | n.a. |
| Approved projects (number) | 10 | 25.0 | 94 | 10 | −37.5 | 113 | 5 | 0 | 60 | 1 | −80.0 | 33 |
| Utilized contracted FDI (US$100 million) | 1.2 | −4.3 | 8.7 | 1.1 | 15.6 | 9.4 | 3 | 40.3 | 9.7 | 0.3 | −96.1 | 23.9 |
| Employees (hundred) | 9.0 | n.a. | n.a. | 10.0 | n.a. | n.a. | 6.0 | n.a. | n.a. | 3.0 | n.a. | n.a. |
| Inspected square meters (number) | 4.28 | n.a. | n.a. | 2.86 | n.a. | n.a. | 2.70 | n.a. | n.a. | 1.70 | n.a. | n.a. |

*Source:* Lu 2009.
*Note:* n.a. = not applicable.

Council then approved a comprehensive bonded zone planning area of 5.86 square kilometers, which became the eighth state comprehensive bonded zone. The provincial government has recognized many enterprises as high-tech firms. Fifteen provincial-level high-tech enterprises, 90 high-tech products (including software) and 2,600 patent applications were added to the list in 2009. The Microsoft Technology Center, an opto-electronics industrial patent information platform, and a number of public technical service platforms have been established. Some important enterprises like Sany and Nano have built a research and development (R&D) and engineering center. Currently, 13 foreign-funded R&D institutions are located in Kunshan (Administrative Committee of KETD 2010, 1–2).

Sixth, the effect of industrial spillover is significant. Since 1992 when the first supplier district was set up, KETD has helped introduce more than 300 foreign-funded projects to a dozen rural industrial support districts, and the value of contracted foreign investment has surpassed US$2 billion. To help domestic firms plug into supply chains through FDI is one effective way for KETD to generate spillover effects. Currently, more than 1,600 domestic suppliers provide 2,300 supporting projects. The annual sales income has now exceeded RMB 40 billion, and the number of enterprises whose contracting service revenues are more than RMB 10 million reached 640 (Administrative Committee of KETD 2010, 3; data calculated from 1992 to 2009). The establishment of local supply chains has not only helped domestic private enterprises but has also helped foreign enterprises take root in Kunshan. Table 4.3 shows the growth of Kunshan's supply services since 1997.

## Background and History of KETD's Development

Before the mid-1980s, agriculture dominated Kunshan's economic structure, and the industrial base was relatively weak. After 30 years of reform and opening up, however, Kunshan has become a successful example of open economic development among counties in China. Kunshan's export-oriented economic development falls into three phases, and each phase has presented different challenges and opportunities.

### Start-up and Opening Phase: From the Early 1980s to the 1990s

In 1978, the industrial output value of Kunshan County (upgraded to a city in 1989) was only RMB 0.28 billion, and the percentage contribution

**Table 4.3    Kunshan's Export-Oriented Supply Services, 1997–2008**

| Year | Number of supply enterprises | Number of supply projects | Supply services revenues (RMB 100 million) | Tax revenues from supply services (RMB 100 million) |
|------|------|------|------|------|
| 1997 | 199 | 374 | 11 | 1.6 |
| 1998 | 237 | 408 | 20.2 | 2.2 |
| 1999 | 200 | 605 | 33 | 4.1 |
| 2000 | 349 | 619 | 45.2 | 5.3 |
| 2001 | 376 | 668 | 58.2 | 6.8 |
| 2002 | 479 | 816 | 73.9 | 8.5 |
| 2003 | 584 | 1,002 | 102.6 | 10.9 |
| 2004 | 685 | 1,156 | 132.8 | 14.8 |
| 2005 | 958 | 1,292 | 193.7 | 18.9 |
| 2006 | 1,058 | 1,560 | 232 | 19 |
| 2007 | 1,503 | 1,878 | 316.2 | 33.3 |
| 2008 | 1,585 | 2,378 | 419.3 | 41 |

*Source:* China Executive Leadership Academy 2009.

of the three industry sectors (agriculture, industry, and service) to Kunshan's GDP was 51.4 percent, 28.9, percent, and 19.7 percent, respectively. Agriculture dominated the economy, and urban and rural residents had saved on average only RMB 22. With the development of township enterprises in southern Jiangsu Province—an important national commodity grain base—Kunshan faced an important choice for its future development path. The grim realities required Kunshan to change its production methods. Under such a circumstance, Kunshan County government made a crucial decision to shift its economic development from predominantly agrarian to industrial.

Benefiting from its location advantage adjacent to Shanghai, Kunshan seized the opportunities of Shanghai's industrial upgrading and relocation of some labor-intensive industries, as well as the transfer of certain military enterprises from inland to coastal areas. Using the overall strategy of "relying on Shanghai to the east, depending on the military enterprises to the west, associating the villages and towns with the relevant enterprises," it successfully attracted some military enterprises from Guizhou, Shanxi, and other provinces, and soon they were converted from military to civil production. Kunshan also established more than 500 joint-venture enterprises with Shanghai. All these efforts laid a preliminary foundation for industrialization. In 1985, the proportional contribution of the three sectors to Kunshan's GDP had changed to 30.7 percent (agriculture), 50.2 percent (industry), and 19.1 percent (services), marking the transformation of its economic development model from an agriculture basis to an industry basis. This change not only prepared the manufacturing base for its future export-oriented economic development, but also helped the people of Kunshan County learn more about the market economy and eventually connect with the global economy.

In early 1983, a general manager of the Japanese enterprise SWANY came to China to look for places to invest. After visiting six places in the Yangtze River Delta region, he finally chose Kunshan, which is 40 kilometers from the Shanghai Hongqiao airport, because of its advantageous geographic location. He immediately decided to set up the first joint-venture corporation producing and exporting medium-high-level gloves in the eastern part of Kunshan County in Jiangsu Province. This program was approved in June 1984 and officially began in February 1985. It marked the first step in the transformation of Kunshan's economy from domestic production to export-driven production.

In April 1984, the central authorities decided to open 14 coastal port cities and establish economic and technological development zones (ETDZ). Given the economic and jurisdictional status of Kunshan at that time, it was not included and so was unable to enjoy the benefits conferred upon ETDZs. To further attract FDI and promote export-oriented development, Kunshan, imitating other open cities, decided to establish its own self-funded development zone in 1984. Following this decision, the county government opened a new industrial area of 3.75 square kilometers in the southeast part of town, forming the embryonic state of the Kunshan Economic and Technological Development Zone. After January 1985, the self-funded development zone officially entered a substantial development phase: the area was expanded from 3.75 square kilometers to 6.18 square kilometers, and in 1998 it officially received the name Kunshan Economic and Technological Development Zone. In 1991, it was designated a key development zone in Jiangsu Province.

In the beginning stages of the zone's development, the government adopted a policy of "planning richly, developing economically." *Planning richly* means focusing on the long-term perspective and building the zone with full modern features to high standards. *Developing economically* means self-reliance, hard work, and accomplishing more with less money. With this spirit, Kunshan's average per kilometer construction cost was only one-eighth that of the other 14 coastal port cities at that time, and its realized profits and taxes were 2.37 times as much as the cost of its infrastructure construction.

After its foundation, by virtue of its superior location and policy advantages, KETD attracted many foreign-funded enterprises. From 1985 to 1991, Kunshan's contracted foreign investment increased from US$1.51 million to US$59.34 million, up 38 times. The early start on the constructing of the development zone helped Kunshan win opportunities in the export-oriented economic race of the late 1990s. According to statistics, from 1985 to 1991 the actually utilized foreign capital in Kunshan accounted for half the total foreign investment in Suzhou and one-fifth the total foreign investment in Jiangsu Province. The change in focus of Kunshan's economic development from internal to external helped accelerate its industrialization process. In 1990, the proportional contribution of the three sectors to Kunshan's GDP was now 22.6 percent, 56.5 percent, and 20.9 percent, respectively, and the proportion of the industrial sector increased further.

### Rapid Expansion Phase: 1992–2001

During this period, changes in the domestic and international economic environment brought rare opportunities for KETD and its export-oriented economic development. With globalization, international competition became increasingly fierce. Many multinationals of developed countries began to shift their traditional capital-intensive industries and labor-intensive sectors to emerging economies and regions. These moves provided a great opportunity for developing countries and regions to participate in the global division of labor led by the multinationals.

In 1990, pushing for further reform and opening up, the central government opened the Shanghai Pudong New Area as a special economic zone, and in 1992, the State Council also approved KETD as a state-level economic and technological development zone. Taking advantage of this rare opportunity, Kunshan actively integrated with Pudong's development and caught the wave of industrial transfer from multinationals. From 1991 to 1992, Kunshan's actually utilized foreign capital rose from US$15.48 million to US$126.43 million, up by 717 percent, and in 1995, the actually utilized foreign capital increased by 300 percent compared with 1992. Meanwhile, the quality of FDI was also improved, with larger size and higher-level technologies. From 1992 to 1995, the number of foreign-funded programs greater than US$10 million reached 73.

During the 1997 Southeast Asian financial crisis, the industries of Taiwan, China were hit hard, and many of them, especially in the information technology (IT) sector, were seeking industrial transfer opportunities. The Kunshan government and KETD decisively adjusted their FDI policy to "focus on introducing capital from Taiwan, China," and following this policy, they went to Taiwan, China eight times to attract investment. Such a strategy worked well and made KETD a superstar in attracting foreign capital. From 1996 to 2001, average actually utilized foreign capital increased by 6.8 percent, and the amount of annual actually utilized foreign capital was more than US$500 million.

Meanwhile, KETD sped up building various industrial parks to attract foreign investments and also gradually changed its industry structure from traditional to high-tech. Based on the experience of the Hsinchu Industrial Park of Taiwan, China, Kunshan set up the Kunshan Export-Processing Zone in April 2000. In October of the same year, it began operation. The establishment of the Kunshan Export-Processing Zone sped up the customs processing of imported and exported products, further increasing KETD's attractiveness to foreign-funded enterprises, especially for the high-tech ones that had higher demand for fast delivery. At the same time, among all the counties in the country, Kunshan was the first to set up a national overseas student pioneer park. As a high-tech incubator, it attracted many overseas returnees and domestic students who wanted to set up high-tech ventures. In addition, Kunshan also set up the Zhouzhuang Sensor Industrial Base, Yushan Module Park, Bacheng Software Park, and other high-tech industrial parks to promote the agglomeration of special industries. These parks have gradually become the growth pole of regional economic development. More than 90 percent of the utilized foreign investment and total trade and more than 80 percent of Kunshan's GDP were generated in these functional parks. By the end of the 20th century, the IT, precision machinery, fine chemicals, and consumer goods industries had become the leading industries in KETD. From 1996 to 2001, the IT industry grew by 20 percent annually. In 2001, the output value of the industry stood at RMB 9.347 billion, accounting for 21.5 percent of the city's major industrial output value, and IT has become the leading industry in Kunshan. The output value of precision machinery and fine chemical industries accounted for 10.2 percent and 7 percent, respectively.

### Enhanced Development Stage: After 2000

Since 2002, after the amount of FDI had reached a certain level (tables 4.4 and 4.5 show the FDI amount and its sources) and the leading industries had been formed, KETD's FDI policy became more selective; that is, it paid more attention to the quality of foreign investment, focusing on technology and industry. Meanwhile it made great efforts to improve

**Table 4.4** Export-Oriented Economic Development of Kunshan Development Zone, 1984–2008

| Year | Number of new, approved foreign-funded projects | Total investment of new, approved foreign-funded projects (US$10,000) | Amount of contracted FDI (US$10,000) | Actually utilized FDI (US$10,000) | Number of foreign-funded enterprises in operation | Number of projects spending below US$10 million |
|---|---|---|---|---|---|---|
| 1984 | 1 | 150 | 74 | 30 | — | — |
| 1985 | 1 | 340 | 174 | 40 | 1 | — |
| 1986 | — | — | — | — | 2 | — |
| 1987 | 2 | 289 | 94 | 30 | 2 | — |
| 1988 | 1 | 336 | 174 | 13 | 4 | — |
| 1989 | 4 | 724 | 299 | 173 | 5 | — |
| 1990 | 4 | 2,165 | 853 | 97 | 8 | — |
| 1991 | 18 | 4,937 | 4,047 | 733 | 12 | — |
| 1992 | 66 | 39,240 | 28,709 | 4,374 | 24 | 16 |
| 1993 | 99 | 47,213 | 43,877 | 12,915 | 68 | 33 |
| 1994 | 46 | 59,668 | 55,534 | 25,111 | 124 | 52 |
| 1995 | 53 | 61,196 | 59,978 | 32,863 | 153 | 66 |
| 1996 | 73 | 60,700 | 58,998 | 37,916 | 206 | 77 |
| 1997 | 58 | 39,503 | 37,055 | 35,160 | 243 | 89 |
| 1998 | 52 | 69,894 | 66,358 | 37,400 | 273 | 109 |
| 1999 | 73 | 60,596 | 58,249 | 33,408 | 296 | 127 |
| 2000 | 107 | 125,856 | 139,951 | 38,477 | 328 | 160 |
| 2001 | 136 | 135,760 | 133,766 | 37,543 | 361 | 192 |
| 2002 | 134 | 218,708 | 217,432 | 56,491 | 413 | 226 |
| 2003 | 131 | 22,800 | 95,423 | 47,468 | 514 | 270 |
| 2004 | 104 | 182,984 | 88,824 | 52,253 | 582 | 358 |
| 2005 | 93 | 244,453 | 92,936 | 63,103 | 641 | 391 |
| 2006 | 98 | 183,617 | 92,071 | 73,710 | 593 | 431 |
| 2007 | 137 | 236,838 | 133,797 | 87,892 | 677 | 462 |
| 2008 | 113 | 272,657 | 142,877 | 92,442 | 831 | 485 |

*Source:* Zhong and Zhang 2009, 221.
*Note:* — = not available.

**Table 4.5    Countries, Economies, and Regions Invested in KETD, 2008**

| Country, economy, or region | Number of approved projects | Amount of contracted foreign investment (US$10,000) | Total of approved projects (number) | Total of contracted foreign investment (US$10,000) |
|---|---|---|---|---|
| Austria | 1 | 197 | 3 | 443 |
| Britain | 2 | 254 | 10 | 4,025 |
| Brunei | 3 | 232 | 26 | 4,111 |
| Cambodia | 0 | 0 | 1 | 500 |
| China, Macao | 0 | 0 | 4 | 87 |
| China, Hong Kong | 18 | 35,925 | 228 | 286,958 |
| China, Taiwan | 17 | 1,473 | 357 | 105,510 |
| Denmark | 0 | 0 | 5 | 3,448 |
| France | 0 | 69 | 12 | 4,347 |
| Germany | 1 | 1,121 | 24 | 5,523 |
| India | 1 | 19 | 2 | 422 |
| Indonesia | 0 | 0 | 5 | 9,039 |
| Italy | 1 | 214 | 6 | 1,373 |
| Japan | 6 | 2,016 | 132 | 100,473 |
| Korea, Rep. | 3 | 1,668 | 48 | 12,086 |
| Luxembourg | 0 | 640 | 2 | 4,308 |
| Malaysia | 0 | 0 | 9 | 3,710 |
| Mauritius | 0 | 3,642 | 31 | 28,272 |
| Myanmar | 0 | 0 | 2 | 80 |
| Netherlands | 1 | 5 | 7 | 10,335 |
| Seychelles | 1 | 70 | 1 | 70 |
| Singapore | 2 | 1,866 | 72 | 49,015 |
| Spain | 0 | 35 | 7 | 188 |
| Thailand | 0 | 0 | 2 | 2,039 |
| Total | 113 | 142,877 | 1,564 | 1,344,795 |

*Source:* Zhong and Zhang 2009, 222.

domestic production and service systems. It placed strong emphasis on promoting technology innovation, aiming to transform its products from "made in Kunshan" to "created in Kunshan." To build upstream and downstream of the industrial clusters, the whole region focused mainly on electronic information, precision machinery, fine chemicals, and consumer goods as its four pillar industries.

At the same time, Kunshan actively supported the development of domestic private enterprises so that they could participate in the international industrial division of labor and become part of the supply chains for the FDI operating locally. By 2008, KETD had more than 20,000 private enterprises, and the total registered capital was more than RMB 50 billion. These figures put Kunshan at the top of Jiangsu Province's county-level cities. By 2008, the number of private service enterprises inside and outside the zone had reached 1,600, and the electronic information industry had become Kunshan's leading sector. Nearly 300 foreign-funded electronic information enterprises are in the zone, one-third of the city's total number, and their total investment is US$6.37 billion, or one-half the city's total investment. Now the output value, sales, and imports and exports of the electronic information industry account for a large proportion of the city's and province's total, making it a uniquely endowed leading industry. Particularly worth mentioning is that in this period, high-tech industries of KETD had achieved a significant breakthrough. Key technology projects were set up and went into production stages in optoelectronics, semiconductors, and new energy industries. One example was the formation of a new optoelectronics industry chain through the InfoVision core program, which exemplified KETD's important breakthrough in industrial transformation and upgrading.

With the continuous expansion of the manufacturing sector, KETD also realized the importance of developing modern service industries, especially the "producer services," which are between the secondary industry and tertiary industry industries. In contrast to the development of Shanghai, KETD focused on developing logistics, exhibitions, marketing, business services, and other productive service industries and also built an industrial park to promote the service industry. In 2006, KETD set up the province's only economic development zone—Huaqiao Economic Development Zone—with the service industry as the dominant focus. Applying its previous experiences to developing its service industry, KETD followed the same ideas of openness, good planning with high standards, and actively introducing foreign capital. The amount of service-oriented foreign capital constantly increased, and the proportion of registered foreign-funded services in 2008 reached 38 percent of total foreign capital. According to statistics, KEDT had introduced more than 700 service projects with a total investment of US$5 billion. Table 4.6 shows KETD's main economic indicators.

## Preferential Policies for Foreign-Funded Enterprises

After KETD was approved as a state-level development zone, all FDI (foreign enterprises and enterprises with foreign investment) in the development zone began to enjoy the same preferential policies that applied

**Table 4.6    KETD's Economic Indicators, 1984–2008**

| Year | GDP (RMB 100 million) | Total industrial value (RMB 100 million) | Total exports (US$ 10,000) | Total industrial profits and taxes (RMB 10,000) | Fiscal revenue (RMB 10,000) | Infrastructure investment (RMB 10,000) |
|------|------|------|------|------|------|------|
| 1984 | — | — | — | — | — | 50 |
| 1985 | 0.1 | 0.6 | 218 | 518 | — | 106 |
| 1986 | 0.4 | 1.7 | 448 | 994 | — | 250 |
| 1987 | 0.8 | 3.1 | 834 | 1,528 | 350 | 621 |
| 1988 | 1.1 | 4.6 | 2,000 | 2,423 | 480 | 801 |
| 1989 | 1.2 | 5.1 | 1,152 | 2,255 | 680 | 882 |
| 1990 | 1.4 | 5.6 | 2,348 | 3,557 | 770 | 1,185 |
| 1991 | 3.1 | 11.7 | 6,500 | 7,568 | 661 | 1,496 |
| 1992 | 3.5 | 21.1 | 10,040 | 10,168 | 5,970 | 8,000 |
| 1993 | 7.7 | 30.1 | 15,050 | 16,761 | 6,118 | 20,000 |
| 1994 | 14.2 | 45.0 | 20,030 | 23,068 | 12,100 | 20,000 |
| 1995 | 18.6 | 65.0 | 30,338 | 23,083 | 11,843 | 21,000 |
| 1996 | 30.4 | 100.0 | 12,743 | 34,706 | 22,670 | 10,100 |
| 1997 | 41.5 | 130.0 | 70,136 | 43,653 | 29,259 | 11,147 |
| 1998 | 56.0 | 157.0 | 86,913 | 68,099 | 37,733 | 11,148 |
| 1999 | 65.0 | 185.0 | 119,600 | 72,849 | 59,434 | 13,000 |
| 2000 | 84.6 | 253.0 | 158,233 | 229,704 | 89,003 | 21,515 |
| 2001 | 113.3 | 347.5 | 198,649 | 282,013 | 177,216 | 60,298 |
| 2002 | 180.4 | 535.0 | 365,234 | 347,016 | 225,283 | 10,100 |
| 2003 | 272.3 | 852.1 | 631,002 | 456,872 | 346,154 | 311,000 |
| 2004 | 411.4 | 1,261.2 | 1,139,149 | 667,330 | 528,351 | 240,000 |
| 2005 | 535.9 | 1,760.7 | 1,610,985 | 777,723 | 541,732 | 154,454 |
| 2006 | 539.3 | 2,028.1 | 2079,856 | 984,805 | 540,431 | 187,003 |
| 2007 | 673.2 | 2,587.6 | 2,762,792 | 1,426,664 | 717,596 | 210,736 |
| 2008 | 843.5 | 3,317.5 | 3,310,261 | 2,251,349 | 9,29,864 | 229,369 |

*Source:* Zhong and Zhang 2009, 220.
*Note:* — = not available

to all other state-level development zones. These policies included those applying to taxes and dividends:

- The income tax is levied at a reduced rate of 15 percent on manufacturing enterprises with foreign investment. Those scheduled to operate for a period of more than 10 years (inclusive of 10 years) are exempted from income tax in the first two profitable years and granted a 50 percent reduction in the next three years. The income taxes levied on enterprises with foreign investment in the fields of energy, transportation, and large-scale integrated circuits are to be exempted for the first five profitable years and granted a 50 percent reduction in the next five years.

- Export-oriented enterprises with foreign investment are to pay their income tax at a reduced rate of 10 percent upon expiration of the tax exemption and reduction period. Enterprises involving state-of-the-art technology are granted a 50 percent reduction for another three years before enjoying the 10 percent income tax rate after the period of tax exemption and reduction.

- Enterprises with foreign investment that reinvest in China to set up another export-oriented enterprise, or one applying state-of-the-art technology with a business term of no less than five years, are refunded all the collected income tax on the reinvested portions, after examination and approval from the relevant tax authorities.

- The remittance of dividends to foreign countries obtained from enterprises with Chinese and foreign investments will be exempted from the income tax on the remitted amount.

Besides the preferential policies already described, companies within the KETD Export-Processing Zone (KEPZ) can also enjoy the "within territory but out of customs" policy, namely, the "four noes," the "four exemptions," the "one bonded," and the "one return" policies. Specifically, the "four noes" refer to no bank deposit system, no customs registration system, no (value-added tax) VAT or consumption tax on processed products, and no import-export quota or export license. The "four exemptions" refer to the duty exemption on machines, equipment, and modules to be used in production and the spare parts to be used in repairs; the duty exemption on machines and equipment to be used in the construction of infrastructure or the building materials to be used for factory and warehouse construction; the duty exemption applied to a reasonable amount of office supplies imported for self-use by enterprises and administrative institutions; and the duty exemption on final products, leftover pieces, or defective or waste pieces that are processed in the zone and are to be sold abroad. "One bonded" refers to raw materials, spare parts, components, packaging materials, and expendables imported for processing export products that are bonded for the total value. "One return" refers to goods that are sold to companies within KEPZ; these are considered exports and are eligible for a tax return.

KEPZ is the first among all EPZs in China to allow the final or semifinal products turned out by companies within the zone to be moved freely to companies outside the EPZ for further processing.

In addition, preferential policies are available in the Kunshan Business Incubator for Overseas Chinese Scholars. The Chinese diaspora can enjoy several benefits that were once located in the Kunshan Business Incubator:

- The management provides the business with offices and standard factory buildings at discounted rates for three years.
- The income obtained from technology transfer, technical innovation, and technical consultation is exempted from the sales tax.
- The equipment imported for the purpose of technical innovation and technology transfer is exempted from duty and import-related VAT.
- The state's favorable policies regarding enterprises with foreign investment, software, and integrated-circuits design companies are also applicable in the incubator.
- An apartment will be offered to overseas Chinese scholars, rent-free, for a period of three years.
- Overseas Chinese scholars, their spouses, and their children under 18 can transfer their permanent residence to Kunshan free of charge.
- The relevant authorities will give priority to making adequate arrangements for those young or middle-aged experts with outstanding achievements in their field.

Apart from the items mentioned above, KETD also grants additional preferences to those with needed talents, such as experts younger than 50 with advanced professional titles and suitable specialties or those less than 45 years old with intermediate professional titles and suitable specialties; they will be exempted from the three kinds of expenses mentioned above, and their spouses and children can also enjoy the same benefits according to the related regulations. Talented candidates younger than 30 with assistant-level professional titles and a suitable specialty will be granted a reduction of 50 percent on the expenses noted above, and their spouses and children can also enjoy such reductions. Graduates with less than five years of work experience and a suitable specialty can enjoy a 50 percent reduction on the three types of expenses.

In addition, the Kunshan municipal government provides foreign staff with high-quality apartments or villas, such as Lijing Garden, Baodao Villa, Jinshan Mansion, Big Shanghai Golf Resort, and the like, which have sound property management and are well equipped (Nankai University's Multinational Study Center Research Group 2006, 141).

## The Essential Experiences of KETD's Development

The success of KETD's development can be attributed to applying the right strategy to local practice and bringing local advantages into full play while continuously aligning its development practices with the latest trends in the international division of labor. In addition to choosing the right strategy and building on comparative advantages, KETD has also benefited from having strong government support, applying flexible strategies, making best use of industrial parks, setting up industrial chains, taking a "people-first" approach, and promoting indigenous innovation.

### Choosing the Right Strategy and Building on Comparative Advantages

In the mid- and late 1980s, Kunshan wisely chose an open development strategy. After the reform and opening up in 1978, Kunshan relied mainly on agricultural industries. In the manufacturing sector, the rural and township enterprises started fairly late and suffered shortages of capital and technology; in addition, they faced conflicts over property rights as well. With respect to state policy, Kunshan had difficulty getting fiscal inputs and policy incentives from the state like those in special economic zones. Under such circumstances, Kunshan could rely only on overseas capital and technologies as the road to development.

An open-economy strategy fit with Kunshan's comparative advantages and location. Kunshan had a strong human capital base and a relatively high-level labor force. In addition, with Shanghai to the east, Kunshan is located in a key area of the Yangtze River Delta, making it easy to get people, logistics, information, and capital for its processing trade.

### Strong Government Support

A forward-thinking government, with clear ideas, was essential to KETD's fast development. Since the establishment of the national industrial zone in 1984, Kunshan's leaders have changed quite frequently, but the development strategy of an open economy that relies on FDI for exports has never changed. Every leader has been determined to work wholeheartedly for the planning and construction of KETD and has carried forward its development vision.

An executive system with innovation and a reasonable structure was another essential ingredient for the fast development of KETD. After the formulation of the development strategy and goals, the leadership became the decisive factor. KETD carefully selects high-quality cadres to form the management of KETD and strongly encourages management innovation. In such an atmosphere, Kunshan has many "firsts" to its credit in Jiangsu Province: it established the first self-financed development zone, the first Chinese-foreign joint venture, and the first wholly foreign-owned enterprise; it was the first to carry out the land payments on compensatory transfers; and it set up the nation's first county-level export-processing zone.

A service system with credibility, diligence, and high efficiency was a third critical ingredient of government support. Such a system was achieved through the following approaches:

- *Constantly innovating service ideas.* Every year the Kunshan municipal government and the KETD Administrative Commission put forward distinctive goals for services to foreign investors. For instance, in 1999 the objectives of sincere service, good administration, decreasing cost, and increasing effect were set. In 2000, probusiness ideas like securing business and serving business were put forward to build a good investment environment. In 2001, after China joined the World Trade Organization (WTO), the goals of international practices, teamwork, and efficiency and effectiveness were established. To build an even more open, transparent, service-oriented, and highly efficient government, in 2002 Kunshan adopted the policy of proficiently serving the foreign companies and implemented regular, transparent, and highly efficient cooperation along with an emphasis on win-win outcomes. Further, in 2004, professionalism and high effectiveness in building a harmonious social environment while developing the export-oriented market economy became the goals.

- *A continuously innovating service system.* From 1998 on, the government of Kunshan has constantly issued decrees and regulations to improve the service environment. Many of them were related to business inspection and approval, registration, licensing, and administrative efficiency. As a result, an efficient Kunshan has been established, and certain systems such as the notification-promise system, deadline-binding system, first-acceptance responsibility system, department consultancy system, and so on are fully functioning.

- *Constantly innovating service platforms.* In recent years, KETD successively built the administrative examination and approval service center, foreign investment promotion and service center, domestic private investment promotion and service center, and enterprise complaint and solution center. In 2005, in response to a need, *Mashangban*, a center specifically serving enterprises in Taiwan, China, was set up. With the increase in investment diversity, service centers for European and American enterprises and domestic private enterprises were also established. At the same time, the contract system between KETD leaders and foreign- and private-invested enterprises was implemented, providing 24-hour immediate services. Every September, KETD brings together governmental department leaders to perform credit services for foreign-invested enterprises and to solve practical problems.

- *Continuously evaluating services.* The Kunshan municipal government and KETD Administrative Commission took the lead in Jiangsu Province in implementing an effectiveness evaluation mechanism for government services, including voting for effectiveness, accountability systems, Internet supervision, service innovation award, and so on. In 2009, the Electrical and Electronic Association of Taiwan, China ranked Kunshan number one on the investment environment of mainland cities.

### Flexible, Realistic Investment Promotion Strategies
The goal of flexible, realistic strategies was first evident in KETD's change in foreign investment promotion targets. In the early and mid-1980s, KETD attracted mainly military industries and industrial transfer projects from Shanghai, such as the Shanghai Jinxing TV Factory, Guizhou Fenghua Fridge Factory, Hongshan Bearing Factory, and so on, which were all big factories for Kunshan at that time and laid a foundation for its industrial development. In the early 1990s, seizing the opportunity of the opening of the Shanghai Pudong New Area, KETD successfully attracted many small and medium labor-intensive enterprises to enlarge its industrial base quickly. In 1997, KETD implemented the important strategy of targeting investments from Taiwan, China and dispatched eight groups there to attract investment. From then on, Kunshan gradually became one of the three major areas for investment from Taiwan, China, especially in the IT sector.

To diversify its FDI investments, starting in 2005, the Kunshan municipal government and the Administrative Commission of KETD began to target Japanese and Korean as well as European and American investments, the proportion of European, American, Japanese, and Korean investments noticeably increasing. The newly approved European and American investments increased by 128 percent, and the Japanese and Korean investments by 78 percent. Besides attracting FDI, from 2006 on, Kunshan also began to emphasize developing domestic private enterprises and the service industries that are related to its manufacturing sectors. This approach greatly helped build the industrial value chains.

While its manufacturing sector was maturing, Kunshan again began to focus on the technology intensity of its industrial sectors and tried to increase the percentage of R&D projects. In 2008, the Kunshan municipal government and the Administrative Commission of KETD put forward the new strategy of shifting Kunshan's industrial structure from common manufacturing industries to high-level manufacturing and modern service industries.

Kunshan also has effective ways of attracting FDI. One is to build industrial value chains or clusters. Inviting leading firms and then helping them extend their vertical and horizontal links is Kunshan's secret to building its industrial sectors in a relatively short time. Kunshan's IT and optoelectronics are all good examples in this regard. In addition to attracting firms, Kunshan also tries to attract R&D institutes to serve its industries. Currently, KETD has more than 90 foreign-invested R&D centers, technology centers, engineering centers, and laboratories, which are building strong technological and innovative foundations for industrial restructuring and upgrading.

In addition, Kunshan has also built logistics centers to attract investors. Through the electronic purchasing center, the stowage center, and the Jiangsu Huaqiao business center, among others, Kunshan quickly formed an integrated commercial service area. It includes the functions of electronic commerce, modern logistics, delivery, industrial training, and information services and energetically promotes the commercial and trade service industries. Many service projects have successively settled in KETD, such as the East China Businessmen's Children's School of Taiwan, China; the Zong-Ren Yu Qing Memorial Hospital of Taiwan, China; the Chang Hwa Bank of Taiwan, China; American International Assurance; Federal Express; Singapore YCH Logistics; and so on, which have significantly improved the city's functions and enhanced the business environment for industrial development.

And finally, Kunshan also tries to explore new fields. Besides developing manufacturing and service trade, Kunshan has also put much effort into attracting agriculture and some newly emerging industries. Seventy-two agricultural projects have been approved, with registered foreign capital of $200 million. Some new industries such as special vehicles, biomedical, and new materials manufacturing are also moving into Kunshan.

### Effective Use of Industrial Parks

Since the 1990s, based on successful past experiences, KETD has built industrial parks according to the modern concept of separating industrial, residential, and living and entertainment activities into different functional areas, a practice that greatly enhances the efficiency of land use. Meanwhile, KETD set up an export processing-zone, a pioneering park for overseas scholars, a Japanese industrial park, and so forth to target different groups of investors. In 2010, Kunshan will pay more attention to coordinating the relationships among different investment parks to avoid duplication of similar projects and vicious competition in attracting investment. It will try to enhance support and complementarities in the various parks.

### Attracting Investment through Industrial Chains

To tap into the global division of labor more effectively, KETD has set up industrial chains to attract FDI, helping build the up- and downstreams for the industries it intends to attract. Examples of its efforts include the following:

- After successfully attracting a foreign enterprise, especially a leading enterprise, KETD will try to track down its domestic and overseas up- and downstream enterprises and attract them to Kunshan. For example, after bringing in Infovision Optoelectronics to the zone, KETD investigated InfoVision's value chains and subsequently persuaded Dexing Electronics to settle beside InfoVision. KETD preserved the surrounding land for its up- and downstream enterprises, such as American liquid crystal glass producers and domestic producers of liquid crystal display (LCD) televisions, which laid the foundation for the LCD industry in KETD.

- Targeting the missing links in local industrial value chains, KETD has focused on filling the gaps to enhance its ability to attract FDI, especially multinationals. One official of KETD used to disassemble his laptop to show which components had not been produced in Kunshan to persuade relevant foreign enterprises to settle in the development zone. Through such efforts, a complete IT industrial chain formed in Kunshan rather quickly.

- Kunshan has also vigorously developed the local supplier market for FDI. In 1997, the Kunshan municipal government set up a special office and designated highly competent officials to work on the supporting industries for FDI. The main measures included

- o *Building platforms.* Every year the special office involving all the major functioning departments of the municipal government jointly holds discussions for domestic private enterprises and enterprises from Taiwan, China to promote cooperation and investment opportunities for the two parties. In addition, the office holds forums for the domestic suppliers every year to promote interfirm cooperation and reward the key performers for the previous year. A virtual platform has also been set up to provide information on product supply and demand for both domestic and foreign enterprises.

- o *Policy support.* To encourage innovation and technology-based sectors, the Kunshan government has implemented many programs to support R&D and encourage large firms to obtain brand products with their own intellectual property rights and core technologies. Meanwhile, it has issued laws and regulations to enhance product standards and quality and to protect intellectual property rights (IPRs).

### A "People-First" Strategy

The effectiveness of investment attraction relies mostly on the quality of the investment promotion team. Investment promotion personnel should have four strong qualities: passion, integrity, service consciousness, and professionalism. To build such a team, the Kunshan municipal government and the KETD Administrative Commission set up special foreign investment promotion and service institutes to provide professional training and even send qualified candidates to domestic and overseas colleges and universities for study and training. Meanwhile, they provide incentives to reward high-performing investment attraction and service personnel.

### Promoting Indigenous Innovation

Indigenous innovation is the essential ingredient for the sustainable development of an open economy. The Kunshan municipal government and KETD actively participate in supporting indigenous innovation and the building of an enterprise-led innovation system. Concrete steps include

- *Continuously increasing investment in technology innovation, especially in the form of risk investment for high-tech projects.* For this purpose, KETD set up a venture investment fund. In 2006, the municipal government appropriated RMB 30 million in specific funds to promote indigenous innovation and invested RMB 50 million in high-tech projects through the venture investment fund. Meanwhile, the government-run assets operation company of KETD directly helped high-tech firms secure finance; for example, in 2006, it helped Infovision Optoelectronics obtain a joint loan of US$350 million from seven banks.

- *Assisting high-tech firms or firms with brand products with land application, planning, and construction.*

- *Attracting highly talented people in the fields of technology and management through strong incentives, such as housing, health care, provision of children's education, and the like.*

## Challenges and Some Policy Suggestions

Given increased globalization, wide fluctuations in international markets, and the intensified competition among the regional economies, KETD, with its open economy, faces new challenges and increasing limitations on its current and future development. Some of these challenges include attracting international capital, technology, and industrial transfers.

First, as a traditional state-level development zone, Kunshan cannot rely solely on industry, foreign capital, and foreign trade for continuous development. It needs to redefine the concept of "open economy" and establish a development mode for improving its competitiveness by responding to the demands of both domestic and international markets and optimizing industrial and economic structures.

Second, KETD, which is in the process of industrialization and urbanization, is increasingly constrained by shortages of land, capital, and human resources and by the need to preserve the environment. KETD has been transformed from an entity with a single economic function—that is, growth—to one that has multiple functions, including comprehensive construction, development, and management.

Third, the improvement of regional competitiveness and the transformation and upgrading of industries in KETD face two big hurdles. The first is the huge task of transforming and upgrading "initial industries," and the second is how to optimize the "newly emerging industries" such as those associated with environmental protection and cartoon production.

And fourth, regional investment promotion and industrial configuration in KETD face more intensified and increasingly homogeneous competition from the rest of the country. Competition among different provinces, cities, and regions over land prices, taxes, rebates, and cash bonuses, as well as competition in the same region, is rather fierce. The homogenization or overlaps of industrial layout and construction and repetitive investments are becoming a key problem for many industrial parks across China.

To overcome these challenges, state-level development zones need to consider their industrial structures in the overall framework of national planning and regional integration and take fully into consideration their own comparative advantages and development needs. For Kunshan to overcome the above-mentioned challenges, it needs to expand its service sector substantially—the sector accounted for only 16 percent of KETD's GDP in 2008–and to further enhance indigenous innovation to move up the global industrial value chain.

During the 12th Five Year Plan, KETD should put a strong emphasis on "second ventures." The second venture of KETD should bridge the past and future and accelerate the transformation from reliance on resources to reliance on talent, science, and technology; the transformation from extensive development to intensive development; and the transformation from a focus on expansion to an emphasis on quality. KETD should also pursue excellence in industry, innovation, and talent and improve its independent innovation capability, its international competitiveness, and its capacity for sustainable development capacity. It should carry on its role as the *engine* for future economic growth, as *pioneer* in transformation and upgrading, as *pilot* for modern city development, as *ice-breaking ship* for systematic innovation, and as *manifestation* of social harmony (Wang 2009, 1).

### Continue to Be the "Engine" for Future Development

The primary task of the second venture for KETD is to use the status quo as a base for future planning and to build the "engine" for the future economic growth of Kunshan. During the next three to five years, KETD should ensure the achievement of several targets of economic growth: that is, increasing industrial output value by RMB 300 billion, increasing fiscal revenue by RMB 200 billion, and increasing trading volume by RMB 100 billion. KETD, in its role as engine, is moving forward in the following four ways.

***The TFT-LCD High-Gen project.*** With the TFT-LCD High-Gen project as a breakthrough, KETD is about to reach a critical point in the acquisition of high-end industry. The construction of the TFT-LCD High-Gen project has laid a solid foundation for the rapid development of KETD's future economy. With the start of the High-Gen project and the successive settlement of projects in the Kunshan Optoelectronic Village—such as glass substrate, color filter, polarizer module, and machinery, among others—the Kunshan Optoelectronic Village will become a top-level producer in the international flat panel industry both at home and abroad after three to five years of development. The park should grow into an industrial cluster with US$10 billion of total investment and RMB 200 billion of output value.

*"Three old machines."* KETD should consolidate and expand its traditional advantage of the "three old machines" to stabilize the growth of its industrial clusters. It is a major global laptop manufacturing base, and the three old machines—the laptop, the digital camera, and the cell phone—have together become one of the pillars of the industrial economy of Kunshan. The output value of the Kunshan IT industry, dominated by KETD, accounts for 31 percent of the value of Jiangsu Province's total output. With Compal and other three leading enterprises increasing their investment in KETD to build regional headquarters, an R&D center, and a second manufacturing base, a new output volume of 30 million laptops or LCD TV sets will undoubtedly be achieved.

*Integrated innovation as a source of growth.* In one example of how integrated innovation might work, as the IT industry, the precision machinery industry, and technologies like bionics become more integrated, they could serve as an incubator for the digital medical industry, an emerging industry expected to achieve breakthroughs in the development of the Chinese digital medical equipment industry. In another example, the technological integration of IT and the special machinery industry could lead to breakthroughs in the automation equipment manufacturing industry. KETD will also build on the huge automobile electronics, spare parts, and components industry to support the development of special vehicles and energy-efficient automobiles, which will bring new engines of growth to KETD's economy.

*Opportunities in domestic trade.* KETD should take advantage of the growth opportunities in domestic trade for traditional service industries and the state-level comprehensive bonded area. In the next five years, traditional service industries in KETD, serving industry and the domestic trade in the state-level comprehensive bonded area, will bring in more than RMB 100 billion of trading volume for KETD. Currently, the import and export volume of the Kunshan Export-Processing Zone ranks at the top of export-processing zones in China, and the key is to exploit further its potential for promoting trade.

### Continue to Be a "Pioneer" in Transformation and Upgrading

One of KETD's major tasks is to promote industrial development and the transformation and upgrading of regional economic growth by relying on technology innovation. KETD's development has entered a new historic period in which it confronts new challenges brought on by the global economic crisis and the new international economic order. It needs to comply with the new requirements of development stages, accelerate structural readjustment, promote transformation and upgrading, and strive for excellence in industry, innovation, and talent to cope with crisis and to strengthen its capability in indigenous innovation, international competition, and sustainable development.

It is also important to constantly improve the investment environment and perfect the service functions of KETD. This effort includes fully utilizing the advantages of the various industrial parks to attract technological resources and to speed up the construction of service platforms—such as the outsourcing and distribution center, the supply and allocation center, and the exhibition and transaction center—and to strengthen critical functions like commercial, financial, information, public technology, and policy services.

### Continue to Be the "Pilot" for Modern City Development

The critical task for KETD in its second venture is to promote its transformation from an industrial park–oriented development zone to a comprehensive urban development zone, constantly improving the level of urban development based on modern and ecological standards. All these call for changing the development mode and for coordinating industrial development with social, urban, and human development. The comprehensive urban development zone will integrate the knowledge economy, scientific management, and sustainable development all together. To achieve this goal, KETD needs to improve its existing industrial parks and realign them with modern concepts, in compliance with international standards.

### Continue to Be the "Ice-Breaking Ship" for Systematic Innovation

The fundamental changes that happened to KETD during the past 20 years can be attributed mainly to the endless momentum generated through innovation in systems, institutions, and policies. With the success of KETD, however, its management approach is gradually becoming less open and forward looking and more closed and conservative, with its staff lacking aggression and speed in updating knowledge. This change poses serious challenges for KETD's sustained development. For KETD's "second venture," it should continue to encourage system and institutional innovations, continue to play the role of "ice-breaking ship" in many uncharted areas in development, and strive to develop better and faster.

### Continue to Be the "Demonstrator" of Social Harmony

KETD has the noble but difficult mission of being a demonstration model for building a harmonious society, with sound public services and social security system and well-integrated ecological and humanistic functions in the park. KETD, on the one hand, should focus on the expansion of economic functions and the improvement of economic quality to achieve better and faster development. On the other hand, it needs to place people first, faithfully fulfill social responsibilities, improve people's living standards, and emphasize environmental protection and sustainable development.

## Conclusions

As a development zone that started out as a self-financed county-level industrial park, Kunshan benefited from the wave of industrial transfers in East Asia, a very entrepreneurial and probusiness local government, innovative industrial parks, and an effective industrial value chain approach. In the future, continued innovation in institutions and technologies and a sustainable development strategy will be the keys to its continued success.

KETD's experience is unique among special economic zones in China, especially because it did not have direct support from the central or provincial government. But it also shares some commonalities, such as innovation, FDI and diaspora investment, and a strong local government, among others. We hope this case study will shed light on the industrialization process in other developing countries.

## Bibliography

Administrative Committee of KETD. 2009. "The Study of Kunshan Development Zone." *2008 Development Report of Kunshan Economic and Technological Development Zone*, Vol. 4. Unpublished.

————. 2010. "KETD Taking Off in the Course of Reform and Opening Up." Unpublished.

China Executive Leadership Academy, Pudong, Kunshan Branch; Party School of Jiangsu Province, Kunshan Branch; Party School of Kunshan. 2009. *Kunshan Catch-up Strategy of the Private Economy: Scientific Development in Kunshan.* Unpublished.

Gu, Houde. 1996. *Kunshan Mode: The Development Road of the First Self-Supporting State-Level Development Zone.* Beijing: People's Publishing House.

Hu, Ming. 2007. *Fangzheng Collection.* Guangli: Guangli Publishing House.

Lu, Zongyuan. 2009. "Practice and Inspiration of the Development Function of Kunshan Export Processing Zone." In *The Study of Kunshan Development Zone,* Vol. 4 (12). Unpublished.

Nankai University's Multinational Study Center Research Group, Ministry of Commerce, PRC Policy Research Department, Kunshan Bureau of Commerce. 2006. *Utilization of Foreign Investment and the Economic Development of Kunshan.* Shanghai: SDX Joint Publishing Company.

Wang, Chenglong. 2009. *Anthology of the KETD's Leader on the Study and Practice of Scientific Outlook on Development.* Unpublished.

Zhang, Guohua, and Erzhen Zhang. 2007. *Independent Innovation Road of Kunshan under Open Conditions.* Beijing: People's Publishing House.

————. 2008. *Kunshan Road in the Reform and Opening Up.* Beijing: People's Publishing House.

Zhong, Yongyi, and Shucheng Zhang. 2009. *On the First Self-Supporting Development Zone in China—the Impression of Xuan Binlong.* Nanjing: Jiangsu People's Publishing House.

# CHAPTER 5

# Industrial Clustering in China: The Case of the Wenzhou Footwear Sector

## Jici Wang

Developing countries' success in competing in the fast-changing global industrial environment depends on their ability to innovate and learn. To avoid the "low road," multinational corporations (MNCs) must increase outsourcing and the flexibility of the labor market to reduce costs, which is the key challenge for these countries (Pyke and Sengenberger 1992; Humphrey 1995; UNIDO 2002). The fast track to acquiring domestic production capabilities is to participate in global value chains. To do so, though, requires setting basic macroeconomic and social policies and engaging in the collective efforts that are already in place, not just opening up to world market forces and linking with foreign partners.

While research on global value chains has focused mainly on the increasing role of global buyers or global producers in determining local industrial upgrading, the literature on industrial clusters optimistically stresses the role of local actors and their policy network in promoting local upgrading and fostering regional development (Bellandi 2002; Gertler 2003). Mounting evidence shows that local clustering and global production

The author is a professor in the Department of Urban and Economic Geography, Peking University.

networks are not only compatible, but also mutually reinforcing (Humphrey and Schmitz 2000; Bathelt, Malmberg, and Maskell 2002). Latecomer firms in developing countries can be vertically integrated into the global value chain and horizontally integrated into local clusters.

The importance of the links between firms, institutions, and other economic agents located in geographical proximity lies in the generation of external economies of scale (Dicken and Lloyd 1990). Furthermore, geographical proximity and regional agglomeration may greatly facilitate the "learning economy." Some scholars recognize this idea as the territorial process in industrialization and the social process in innovation (Asheim and Cooke 1999). In this sort of agglomeration are the places where the most relational portions of global value chains may be found (Sturgeon 2003).

The framework of global value chains focuses on the nature and content of the interfirm links and concentrates on the power that regulates coordination of the value chain. On the upstream end of the chain, component and equipment suppliers can wield a great deal of power. On the downstream end, highly knowledgeable users can play a significant role in determining the attributes and innovative trajectory of the products and services that global value chains churn out, as they do in many complex service industries. Similarly, lead firms strategies to simultaneously increase outsourcing and consolidate their supply chains have created a set of highly capable suppliers. Those suppliers, in turn, have made outsourcing more attractive for lead firms that have yet to take the outsourcing plunge (Sturgeon and Lee 2001). The evolution of global value chains emanating from one national or local context, especially if successful, provides an example that often generates a reaction in value chains rooted in other places (Gereffi 1994, 1999).

This chapter aims to add new insights to the study of global value chains and local clusters by using the case of the Chinese footwear cluster and citing the representative footwear industry in Wenzhou as a case study. The chapter is divided into five sections: a general review of the development of the Chinese footwear industry, the formation and industrial structure of the Wenzhou footwear manufacturing cluster, the success factors and challenges, a discussion of the strategies for upgrading and sustainable development, and policy recommendations.

## Overview of the Chinese Footwear Industry

The footwear industry, traditionally a low-technology sector, has been viewed as consisting of "sunset activities": that is, it is more difficult to make a technological breakthrough here than in other sectors. For a long time, the sector has been exposed to severe global cost competition, making it plausible for the decline of production sites at "old" locations and the migration of the industry to "young" locations in low-wage regions (Schamp and Main 2003). As a result, labor costs continue to be a dominant factor in the competitiveness of the sector. Entrepreneurs are induced to search for countries and regions with lower wages. More efficient utilization of labor is required even in regions or countries that are generously considered sources of "unlimited cheap wages."

In the 1960s, footwear manufacturing began shifting from developed countries first to Japan, then to the Republic of Korea and Taiwan, China, and in the 1980s to southern China. In the mid-1980s, Korea and Taiwan, China, supplied 45 percent of the world's footwear exports. By 1994, their share of world exports had dropped to 7 percent, while mainland China's share had grown from 8 percent to 50 percent in 1985. In addition, many companies have invested substantially in expanding production lines in China. Since the 1980s, 80 percent of the industry in Hong Kong[1] has shifted a significant part of its shoe production to mainland China, especially to Guangdong Province. More than 90 percent of Taiwan, China's footwear factories (more than 1,000 companies) have set up plants in mainland China, especially in Fujian Province and Guangdong Province.

The demise of mature manufacturing sectors in the developed countries has been foretold by some scholars in recent years. They argue that advances in information and communications technology have paved the way for the emergence of a new knowledge economy where competitive advantage and wealth generation rest increasingly on those economic activities based on learning, innovation, and knowledge creation and less on the processing of physical materials. More recently, however, this narrow interpretation of the knowledge economy has been challenged by the recognition that physical goods also have intangible qualities (or "symbolic forms") and that these qualities increasingly serve as the basis for their economic success (Rantisi 2002).

China has become a key competitor through lower labor costs and more rapid advancement in its shoe production and designs, although it lags slightly in manufacturing value added per capita. Nevertheless, for several reasons the Chinese shoe industry still faces a grim situation. For one thing, it confronts powerful challenges from many competitors in and outside Asia, with its low-grade shoes competing with those made in Indonesia, Thailand, Mexico, and India, and with its high-grade shoes threatened by those made in Italy, Spain, and Portugal. Rigorous competition also exists among the more than 20,000 domestic shoe enterprises, of which most are small firms. In addition, some foreign shoe businesses have established their factories in China to enter the Chinese market, which puts great pressure on the local shoe enterprises.

How did the Chinese footwear industry gain an international competitive advantage in the past 30 years? Discussion has focused on China's cheap labor, even child labor. Labor is a factor, because the Chinese footwear industry is at the low-value-added stage. However, to some extent, demand factors, such as China's huge domestic market and its sophisticated and demanding buyers are ignored. A more important factor is that many local clusters in the footwear industry have built up in China.

The decline of the footwear sector in the high-wage countries opened the opportunity for the value chain to extend into developing countries like China, which has accounted for almost 50 percent of the world's production for five years. China dominates the production scene and serves as both the largest exporter and the largest consumer of footwear products. In 2003, more than 20,000 companies produced more than 6 billion pairs of shoes of various kinds, of which more than 3.87 billion pairs with a value of US$9.47 billion were exported. Sixty percent of the shoes made in China entered the international market, accounting for 25 percent of the total turnover of the shoe industry in the world. In addition, China now produces the highest volume of galosh products in the world and has become the main exporting country of galoshes. China also accounts for about 68.3 percent of all footwear imports into the United States. Because of China's low-cost labor means, it is considered the ideal place for the foreign shoe industry to build factories. Since 1986, U.S. shoe imports from China have increased by a staggering rate of 2,700 percent.

The Chinese will continue to develop their shoe industry for the following reasons:

- *The increasing demand for shoes.* Shoes, together with clothes, have become symbols of fashion for modern Chinese women rather than simply items for keeping warm. With the improvement of living conditions in China, people desire to purchase more shoes with better style; thus, the demand in the domestic shoe market has risen.
- *The labor intensity of the industry.* As a typical labor-intensive industry with a low technology threshold for entry, the shoe industry can help solve the social problem of unemployment. It is especially important

when much of the surplus labor force has been released from state-owned enterprises to search for new jobs.

- *The value of the industry.* The shoe industry is critical to increasing China's domestic income. For example, the export value of shoe products reached US$17.1 billion in 2005.

In China's footwear industry, most of the producers are subcontracted to produce world-class foreign brand names such as Nike, Reebok, Adidas, and so forth, and these products are mainly for export. These producers use modern machinery and technology, consistently developing their production. With the technology assistance provided by the contracted company or the machinery supplier, these producers can manufacture shoes of standard quality acceptable to the world market. Most of them engage in supporting industries such as tanning, shoe mold manufacturing, shoe parts, and others with a view toward enhancing their ability to reduce cost and increase their flexibility in production and quality control.

In the case of Italy, the footwear industry has clustered in the main districts of Lombardy, Veneto, Marche, Emilia-Romagna, Tuscany, Campania, and Puglia. Likewise, the major footwear produces in India are clustered in Chennai, Ranipet, Ambur in Tamil Nadu, Mumbai in Maharastra, Kanpur in Uttar Pradesh, Jalandhar in Punjab, Agra, and Delhi. Similarly, most of the shoe-related enterprises of China have clustered mainly in the eastern coastal provinces of Guangdong, Fujian, Zhejiang, and Shandong (in south-north order), with a few scattered in the western region. At present, the volume of leather shoe production in the eastern region accounts for about 80 percent of the whole of China, while the volume of sports shoe production accounts for more than 90 percent. The output of cloth shoes and plastic shoes is also high in the eastern coastal region.

Only a few companies specializing in shoemaking lie outside of clusters. Qingdao Double Star Group Haijiang Shoes Co., Ltd., in Shandong Province, is an example. This large manufacturer of sports shoes originated from the state-owned ninth rubber factory in Qingdao, which was established in 1955 and was converted into a multilocation and diversified business enterprise group in 1990. At present, it has 90 subsidiary and branch companies with about 20,000 employees and fixed assets of more than RMB 200 million. The Double Star brand has won the National Famous Trademark prize. However, the main business of Double Star in shoemaking is as an original equipment manufacturer (OEM). As one of the Payless shoe sources, the company exports almost 9.98 million pairs of shoes to the United States each year. Double Star learns a great deal from global buyers—Payless Shoe Source—about how to improve its product quality and increase its speed of response to customer orders.

## The Formation of the Wenzhou Footwear Industry

The city of Wenzhou has had a shoe manufacturing industry for hundreds of years, providing a fertile environment for new entrepreneurs rising and responding to the global challenge. In China, the first pair of pigskin shoes, the first vulcanized shoes, and the first press molding shoes all came from Wenzhou. In other words, Wenzhou is one of the seedbeds of the Chinese shoe manufacturing industry and represents the history of China's shoemaking industry. Its industry size, the number of enterprises, its production value, its quality, and the completeness of its production chain have made it the footwear capital of China. Not only are the prices competitive, but also the shoes are world-class commodities in design and quality. Wenzhou has won three of 10 "kings of genuine leather shoes" awards in China in 1998–2000. Having grown from family workshops into modern enterprises, the shoe industry in Wenzhou is moving up the global value chain.

In 2005, Wenzhou had 4,000 shoemaking firms, 2,500 of which were specialists in chemical materials and metal hardware, shoe-adorning material, leather production, sole production, and shoemaking machines. Accommodating more than 400,000 workers, these firms produced more than 1 billion pairs of shoes in that year, one-fourth of the gross domestic footwear output and one-eighth of the total footwear production of the world. The production of shoes in Wenzhou was valued at US$3.8 billion; the value of exports reached US$837 million, and its share of the domestic market and global market is also expanding. The footwear manufacturing cluster in Wenzhou has followed a successful development path, has promoted the upgrading of local industry, has cultivated many well-known brands, and can boast many more success stories. However, the footwear manufacturing cluster in Wenzhou has also confronted the bulk of antidumping claims in the global market.

### The Formation of the Wenzhou Footwear Manufacturing Cluster

Wenzhou, birthplace of the shoemaking industry in China, has a long history dating back to 422 AD and over time has built local production and capabilities for innovation. Since the reform and opening up of China, the shoemaking industry in Wenzhou has experienced rapid growth in industrialization and clustering, a process of development that can be divided into three phases (see figure 5.1).

***The "family workshop" stage, from the 1970s to the 1980s.*** In the 1980s, the shoemaking industry in Wenzhou boomed as a rural cluster. Taking advantage of the reforms and opening up policy, local families with specialties in shoemaking started low-end businesses. The industry featured family workshops that had the advantages of low costs and low risks.

However, several problems came along with the prosperity of the shoe-manufacturing industry. Before 1987, the market with its thousands of workshops was expanding rapidly in Wenzhou, but inferior shoes were being made by profiteers who substituted leatherette for real leather or even used cardboard for soles and shoe supports. Soon footwear products from Wenzhou gained the reputation as having a "one-week life expectancy" in the industry, and shoe retailers all over China refused to sell the footwear products from Wenzhou. The most serious negative occurrence was the so-called Wulinmen incident. In August 1987, a number of people who bought fake and inferior shoe products from Wenzhou gathered at the Hangzhou Wulin Plaza, where they angrily burned more than 50,000 pairs of inferior shoes, announcing their boycott of the fake shoe products from Wenzhou. The incident was noted by the relevant regulatory authority, and, as a result, the former Ministry of Light Industry united with five other ministries and listed Wenzhou footwear products as the major target for remediation and imposed strict regulation. That regulation made significant progress in improving the quality

**Figure 5.1    Formation of the Wenzhou Footwear Manufacturing Cluster, 1970s–Present**

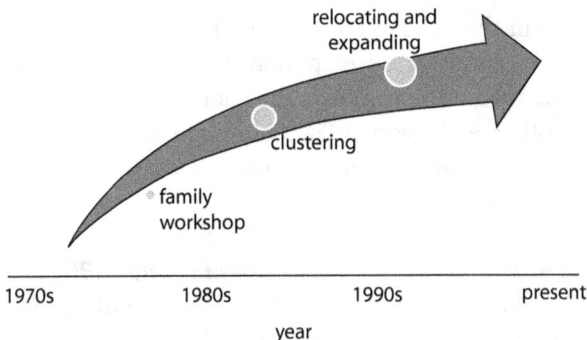

*Source:* Author.

of the shoes manufactured in Wenzhou. In the later 1990s, Wenzhou footwear products regained their reputation for high quality and were received in markets all over the nation.

***The "clustering" stage, from the late 1980s to the late 1990s.*** The "clustering" stage has two separate phases: spontaneous clustering and government-induced clustering. Over time, the "local" mode faced the disadvantage of distance from the market, inconvenient transportation, and inadequate information and communication. The small family workshops then spontaneously relocated in or close to the town. In addition, professional retailers started their own manufacturing business according to a new mode of "factory and shop." Meanwhile, several shoe production sites formed, where families sold their goods in the local market or at transportation sites. These gathering sites further attracted the shoemaking and cluster-support firms, generated the network of specialized family workshops, and later formed the rudimentary shoe manufacturing cluster in Wenzhou.

However, the development of Wenzhou's shoemaking cluster was stagnant in the 1990s, calling for further government regulation. Low quality was one threat to its growth. Since the Wulinmen incident in 1987, footwear products from Wenzhou had faced stricter quality controls, but the industry still needed the involvement of the local government for guidance on quality standardization. Moreover, the need for land with abundant infrastructure was increasing. The well-developed firms with strong market expansion and innovative capabilities particularly needed a better infrastructure environment for scaling up production, more convenient transportation for reducing cost, and more advanced channels of communication, all of which relied on the efforts of the local administration. Since the 1990s, the local administration of Wenzhou has played an active role in the development of the footwear manufacturing cluster: it instituted industry development policy and planning, improved local infrastructure, and promoted the standardized shoe-product market, among other endeavors. (The role of local administration is discussed in more detail in the section titled "Dynamics: The Local Production Network.")

***The relocation and expansion stage, from the late 1990s to the present.*** In the late 1990s, the firms in the footwear manufacturing cluster in Wenzhou began moving out: some firms relocated or expanded to other cities. Several factors contributed to this relocation and expansion, namely, the tension among the supply of local industrial land, the increase in labor costs, and the investment attraction of other cities in China, among others. The footwear industry in Wenzhou was also experiencing a phase of relocation and expansion both domestically and overseas.

On the domestic scene, the Wenzhou footwear industry has expanded to such cities as Lishui and Taizhou in the nearby areas of Zhejiang Province. In 2003, more than 10 shoe leather production firms invested in Lishui, a city close to Wenzhou. Shoemaking firms also moved to the western part of China. Bishan Town (in the western part of Chongqing City) government actively worked to attract leading shoemaking firms from Wenzhou to invest and set up streamline manufacturing in the local industrial areas. In 2003, Aokang Corporation invested RMB 1 billion (approximately US$130 million) in Bishan, building up the West Footwear Industry Development Zone with an output of 100 million pairs of shoes per year and attracting investment from many supporting firms.

Compared to the eastern parts of China, western China enjoys the comparative advantage of low costs. For example, the cost of electricity in the town of Bishan is only 80 percent of that in the city of Wenzhou, the average wage for the frontline workers is RMB 200–300 lower in Bishan, and the average material cost for soles is RMB 4 lower per pair, or 30 percent. In addition, the Aokang Group has a strong domestic market and sells some 7 million pairs of shoes from Bishan to markets in western China, which helps the company balance its loss of international market share.

The attraction of western China is one part of the story. The other part is the two endogenous problems of the Wenzhou footwear manufacturing cluster—the high cost of land and the shortage of skilled labor. The conflict between the urgent need for industrial land and the policy of protecting farmland is becoming an obstacle to the development of local firms. For instance, the average land price per mu$^2$ is approximately RMB 250,000 in Wenzhou City and towns nearby, while it is only RMB 30,000 per mu in the Shanghai suburbs. The price of land is far too high for small and medium enterprises; therefore, they choose to locate their firms in cheaper provinces with preferable policies. Another major problem for firms relocating in other cities is the lack of specialized skills, as the high real estate prices and low quality of local research institutions make Wenzhou less attractive to the talented workforce needed by most footwear manufacturing firms compared to cities such as Shanghai, Guangzhou, and Shenzhen. In Aokang's footsteps, Hongqingting Group invested RMB 200 million (approximately

US$26 million) in the Chongqin Tongliang Industry Development Zone and formed an association with more than a hundred commercial and service firms. Hence, more and more footwear manufacturing firms in Wenzhou are preparing to leave the area.

As for overseas expansion, several corporations have developed distribution channels overseas on the basis of exports. In 2001, Kangnai Group set up franchise stores in Paris and New York, and later the number of overseas franchises grew to 83. The average export price for a pair of shoes was US$15, and the average retail price was US$60. Kangnai is a successful example for the whole shoemaking industry dealing with the challenge of antidumping in overseas markets. Besides Kangkai's expansion of its franchise stores, Aokang followed a strategy of cooperation with Italy's GEOX Corp. to sell through GEOX's sales network. In addition, the footwear manufacturing firms in Wenzhou began to set up overseas research centers and production sites. In 2004, the Wenzhou Hazan Shoes Company set up the Hazan-Wilson Footwear Research Center in Italy and merged with Italy Wilson Footwear Manufacturing Corporation and Lijiang Commerce Firm in Taiwan, China. Meanwhile, Hazan invested in a production factory in Nigeria, making Hazan the first MNC in the Wenzhou footwear industry. Aokang is also preparing for a manufacturing industrial development zone in Ethiopia.

## The Structure of the Wenzhou Footwear Cluster

Over the past three decades, the footwear industry in Wenzhou has developed from isolated family workshops to a cluster with the advantages of external economies, specialization, and brand effect.

### The Rapid Growth of the Local Cluster

Wenzhou is home to more than 4,000 footwear manufacturing firms and is the largest footwear manufacturing city in China. Firms in the cluster have achieved an interorganizational division of labor, cooperation, and intensive interconnections and have shared the rapid growth of the industry. In an illustration of their success, more than 30 firms in Wenzhou have an output of more than RMB 100 million per year; 70 percent of the top 30 domestic highest-selling footwear firms are from Wenzhou. The output of the footwear industry in Wenzhou in 2007 reached more than 890 million pairs (574 million leather shoes and 318 million rubber shoes), which accounted for approximately 25 percent of domestic output in 2007.

Output data of the Wenzhou shoe and leather industry is presented in table 5.1 and figure 5.2. The compound annual growth rate (CAGR) of shoe and leather production and the CAGR of shoe product manufacturing are 25.00 percent and 15.29 percent, respectively, indicating a rapid growth of the industry in the five years from 2001 to 2005. Meanwhile, the CAGR of export value was 36.08 percent, two times that of shoe-product manufacturing in Wenzhou (which was 15.29 percent), suggesting the expansion of overseas markets.

**Table 5.1    Annual Output and Growth Rate of Wenzhou Footwear Industry, Selected Years, 1990–2005**

|  | Shoe and leather | | Shoe products | | | |
|---|---|---|---|---|---|---|
|  | Output (million pairs) | Growth rate (%) | Output (RMB 1 billion) | Growth rate (%) | Export value (US$ millions) | Growth rate (%) |
| 1990 | 60.87 | — | — | — | — | — |
| 1995 | 115.07 | — | — | — | — | — |
| 1997 | 118.13 | — | — | — | — | — |
| 1998 | 388.48 | 229 | — | — | — | — |
| 1999 | 330.92 | −15 | — | — | — | — |
| 2000 | 371.92 | 12 | — | — | 316.9 | — |
| 2001 | 464.37 | 25 | 24.9 | — | 461.79 | — |
| 2002 | 556.15 | 20 | 26.3 | 5.62 | 667.23 | 44.37 |
| 2003 | 562.63 | 1 | 30.7 | 16.73 | 837.46 | 25.49 |
| 2004 | 835.05 | 48 | 34.6 | 12.70 | 1149.03 | 37.28 |
| 2005 | 822.11 | −2 | 44.0 | 27.17 | 1583.99 | 37.86 |
| CAGR (%) | 25.00 | | 15.29 | | 36.08 | |

*Source:* Wenzhou Shoe Association and Statistical Yearbook of Wenzhou, various years.
*Note:* — = not available.

**Figure 5.2    Annual Output of the Wenzhou Footwear Industry, 1990–2005**

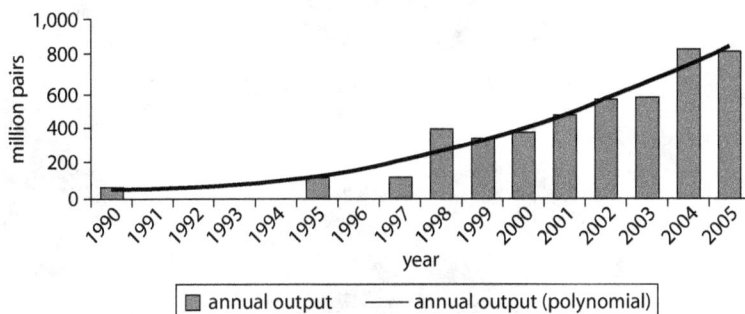

*Source:* Wenzhou Shoe Association and Statistic Year Book of Wenzhou, various years.

### The Structure of the Wenzhou Footwear Cluster

Nowadays, Wenzhou's footwear products account for one-fourth of China's and one-eighth of the world's footwear products, and the footwear sector is becoming a vibrant manufacturing cluster with more than 300,000 employees. An analysis of the cluster structure can help reveal the dynamics of the booming industry (figure 5.3). The industrial manufacturing structure of the Wenzhou footwear cluster has four integral parts: a labor-division network, a specialized supplier market, a solid sales network of domestic and foreign markets, supporting institutions, and industrial associations.

*The clustering effects.* Because the production process is technically divisible, each small and medium enterprise (SME) tends to cover an individual phase of production and is connected by specialized transaction networks coordinated by more or less explicit forms of cooperation. The cooperation among small and medium-sized firms generates the effect of the external economy. A Chinese economist calls the vigorous SME-dominated Wenzhou economy a "small dog economy," that is, a mode of development characterized by a clear division of labor and close cooperation. In fact, the economy of Wenzhou is better described as a "swarm effect."

Shoemaking consists of five key factors: leather production, sole production, shoe adorning, last production, and shoemaking machinery. The

**Figure 5.3    Structure of the Wenzhou Footwear Cluster**

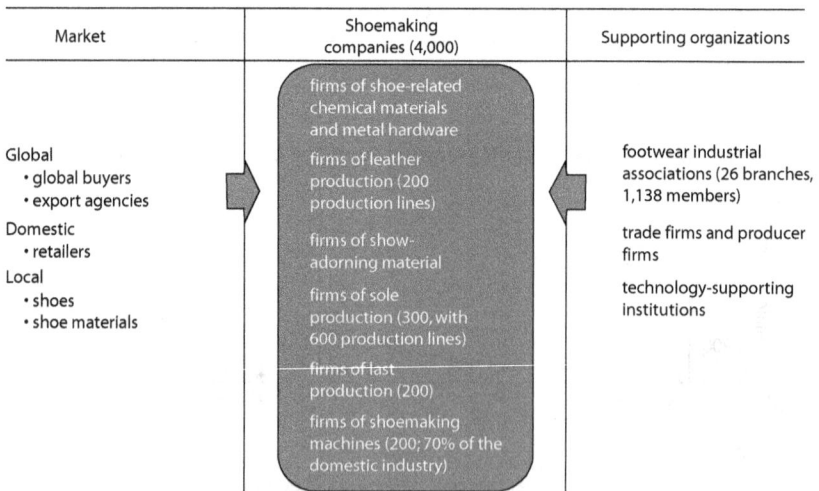

| Market | Shoemaking companies (4,000) | Supporting organizations |
|---|---|---|
| Global<br>• global buyers<br>• export agencies<br><br>Domestic<br>• retailers<br><br>Local<br>• shoes<br>• shoe materials | firms of shoe-related chemical materials and metal hardware<br><br>firms of leather production (200 production lines)<br><br>firms of show-adorning material<br><br>firms of sole production (300, with 600 production lines)<br><br>firms of last production (200)<br><br>firms of shoemaking machines (200; 70% of the domestic industry) | footwear industrial associations (26 branches, 1,138 members)<br><br>trade firms and producer firms<br><br>technology-supporting institutions |

*Source:* Author.

localized clustering of shoemaking firms in Wenzhou has produced a network based on the local division of labor: more than 200 firms of shoe-making machines (70 percent of the domestic firms), more than 200 last-producing firms, more than 300 sole-producing firms with 600 production lines, more than 200 leather-producing firms, and more than 100 shoe-adorning firms. The cluster offers the advantage of cutting the cost of production and complementarity (map 5.1). In the meantime, the labor-division network positively stimulates the diffusion of knowledge and information in the local industry.

***Specialized supplier market.*** The specialized markets in the urban and rural areas of Wenzhou provide abundant raw materials for the local footwear manufacturing firms at short notice and serve as a significant channel for the wholesaling and retailing of local footwear products. The large number of stalls and annual transaction value of the North Zhejiang Shoe-Material Market and the Wenzhou Shoe-Material Market indicate the important role of specialized supplier markets in the manufacturing structure of the Wenzhou footwear cluster.

The Wenzhou Shoe-Material Market is located in the town of Quxi, 7 kilometers from the Wenzhou freight train station. Built in 1991, the market specializes in leather trade and now has 235 leather trading rooms, 60 stores with sufficient support facilities, and an annual turnover of RMB 1.3–2 billion, placing it at the top of the domestic leather trade markets (table 5.2). The market organizes a professional leather whole-sale network for a number of countries and areas.

***Sales network of domestic and overseas markets.*** The businesspeople and entrepreneurs in Wenzhou have developed a sensitivity to the changing market of shoe products and have formed a solid network of domestic and foreign markets. On the basis of the personal connections of domestic and overseas Wenzhou entrepreneurs, the footwear industry in Wenzhou has built up a global sales network consisting of global buyers, export agencies, and retailers. These connections explain the continuous success of Wenzhou's export in past years. The sales network encourages firms in Wenzhou to cooperate with each other to expand into the mature market and enter new ones.

This solid sales network has made a great contribution to the rapid growth in value of Wenzhou's shoe exports in recent years. In the international footwear market, the shoe products from Wenzhou can be found in the markets of Italy, Germany, Portugal, the Czech Republic, the Arab

**Map 5.1   Shoemaking Companies in Wenzhou**

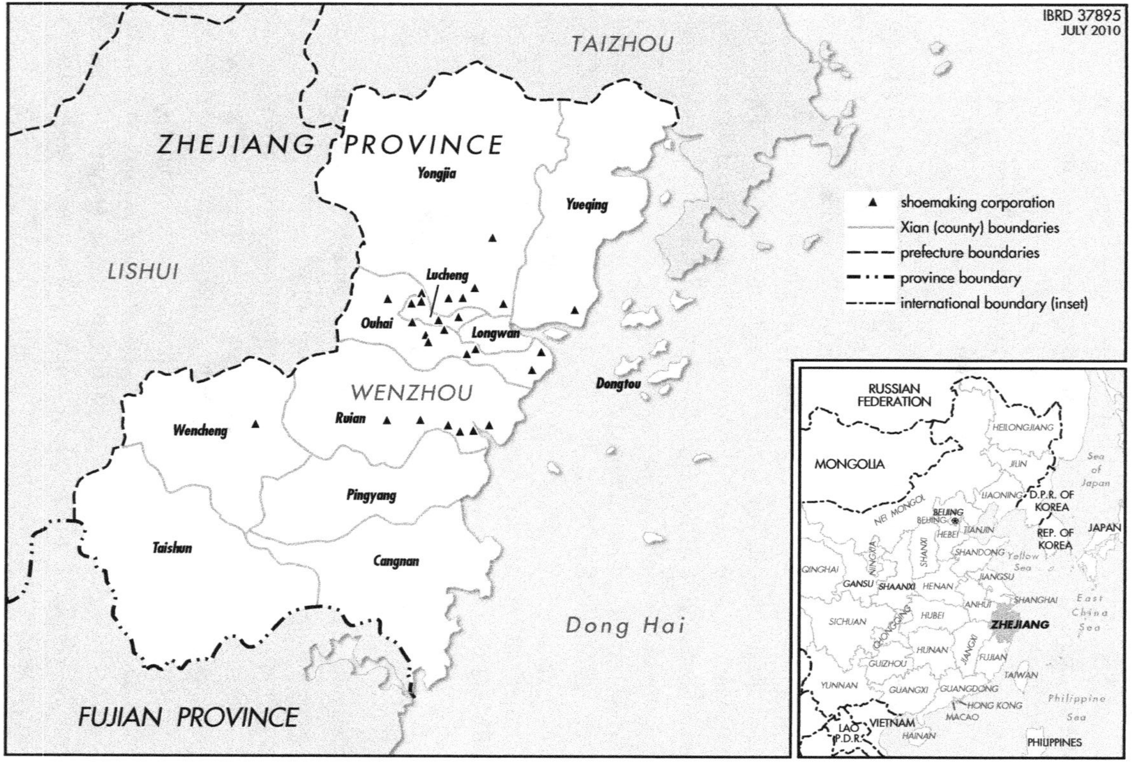

Legend:
- ▲ shoemaking corporation
- — Xian (county) boundaries
- —·— prefecture boundaries
- —··— province boundary
- —·—·— international boundary (inset)

IBRD 37895
JULY 2010

ZHEJIANG PROVINCE

TAIZHOU

LISHUI

WENZHOU

Yueqing

Yongjia

Longwan

Lucheng

Oujhai

Ruian

Pingyang

Cangnan

Wencheng

Taishun

FUJIAN PROVINCE

Dong Hai

Dongtou

Inset:
RUSSIAN FEDERATION, MONGOLIA, NEI MONGGOL, HEILONGJIANG, JILIN, LIAONING, D.P.R. OF KOREA, REP. OF KOREA, JAPAN, Sea of Japan, BEIJING, TIANJIN, HEBEI, SHANDONG, Yellow Sea, SHANXI, SHAANXI, GANSU, QINGHAI, NINGXIA, HENAN, JIANGSU, SHANGHAI, ANHUI, HUBEI, ZHEJIANG, East China Sea, JIANGXI, HUNAN, FUJIAN, TAIWAN, SICHUAN, GUIZHOU, GUANGXI, GUANGDONG, HONG KONG, MACAO, HAINAN, YUNNAN, VIETNAM, LAO P.D.R., Philippine Sea, PHILIPPINES

*Source:* Author's research.

**Table 5.2    Number of Stalls and Annual Transaction Value of the Shoe-Material Market in Wenzhou, 2000–07**

| | Commodity exchange markets | | | |
| | North Zhejiang Shoe-Material Market | | Wenzhou Shoe-Material Market | |
| | Stalls (number) | Annual transaction value (RMB 1 million) | Stalls (number) | Annual transaction value (RMB 1 million) |
|---|---|---|---|---|
| 2000 | 596 | 50.00 | 570 | 45.50 |
| 2001 | 596 | 50.00 | 500 | 49.00 |
| 2002 | 442 | 24.00 | 658 | 45.00 |
| 2003 | 442 | 23.35 | 658 | 44.54 |
| 2004 | 675 | 26.34 | 658 | 27.33 |
| 2005 | 675 | 50.11 | 564 | 28.48 |
| 2006 | 675 | 76.19 | 658 | 23.39 |
| 2007 | 979 | 73.29 | 658 | 20.66 |

Source: *Statistical Yearbook of Wenzhou*, various years.

Republic of Egypt, and other countries. Some leading firms in Wenzhou, such as the Kangnai Group, have even set up franchise stores in foreign markets.

***Support institutions and the industry association.*** With the development of the local footwear zone, some support institutions were introduced into the cluster: the Footwear Testing Center of China, China Shoes Library, China Shoes InfoCenter, China Shoes Museum, Institution of Shoemaking Technology of China, the *China Shoes Journal* editorial board, and China Shoes Tech-Center. These supporting institutions have strengthened the competence of the Wenzhou footwear cluster in technology innovation, sales, and product quality control.

In addition, universities and research institutions play an important role in supporting technology innovation in footwear manufacturing in Wenzhou. In recent years, Wenzhou University has put much effort into research on innovations in leather production and cooperated with several firms in the industry to set up the Leather Production Technology Research Center of Wenzhou in 2004. The center concentrated on green industrial product development, clean leather production technology, and other high-tech research in leather production. In 2006, the center became the Key Leather Project Laboratory of Zhejiang Province and established the Service Platform for Leather Production Innovation of Zhejiang Province to strengthen research capabilities. The Key Leather Project Laboratory of Zhejiang Province and the Leather Industry Technology

Research Center of Wenzhou are the only leading professional and high-end leather research institutions in eastern China. In cooperation with Wenzhou University, the laboratory has concentrated on producing and testing leather chemicals, genuine and synthetic leather-processing technology and performance testing, and the environmental management of leather production and pollutant treatment.

Besides the supporting institutions, the shoemaking firms in Wenzhou formed an association with 1,138 members and 26 association branches. In recent years, it has made a great effort to improve shoe quality, help the member enterprises enter and expand in the domestic and overseas markets, set up enterprise groups, and build and strengthen electronic information networks. Connected by the association, the firms in the Wenzhou footwear industry formed a highly competent and dynamic group.

## Success Factors and Challenges of the Wenzhou Footwear Manufacturing Cluster

Wenzhou's success could be attributed to its highly developed local production network and its very capable industrial association and local government, as well as the very dynamic local entrepreneurs. However, in recent years, the Wenzhou cluster also faces challenges of antidumping, higher eco-standards, low technology, and lack of indigenous innovation.

### The Success Factors

***Dynamics: the local production network.*** The footwear industry in Wenzhou has formed a large local production network with thousands of independent small and medium enterprises covering independent but related phases of production. Referring to the previous research on the development of clustering, the following characteristics are identified as prerequisites for the success of an industrial cluster (Schmitz 1995):

- The division of labor and specialization among firms
- The provision of specialized products and services at short notice
- The emergence of suppliers to provide raw materials and components
- The growth of suppliers of secondhand machinery and spare parts
- The emergence of agents who sell to distant national and international markets

- The growth of specialized producer services in technical, financial, and accounting matters
- The formation of associations providing services and lobbying for members

The Wenzhou footwear industrial cluster of the local production network meets all these prerequisites. Currently, there are shoe enterprises that specialize in three industrial activities (tanning, leather shoes, and leather articles) and footwear-related industries including leather chemical engineering, leather mechanical engineering, leather hardware, footwear material, and so on. The footwear industrial cluster of Wenzhou is noted for the large size of its industry, the cooperative industrial system, the highly concentrated shoe brand names, the strong marketing network, and the local industrial association. Besides, the Wenzhou footwear industrial cluster has a mature specialized market that supplies raw materials, a well-developed domestic and overseas sales network, and industrial associations that provide up-to-date information to the companies and facilitate their communication with each other.

An analysis of the footwear industry in the Lucheng District, the most centralized shoe manufacturing zone in Wenzhou, reveals further features of the dynamics of the local production network. Lucheng is located in the center of Wenzhou and has an area of 104 square kilometers. It has a population of 875,000, of whom more than 344,800 come from outside the city for work. There are 905 industries in the footwear industry with an annual output of more than 300 million pairs of shoe products, amounting to one-eighth of the total output of shoe products in China. There are more than 300 million square meters of factory buildings and more than 550 advanced production lines for manufacturing. The value of the annual output of shoe products is RMB 25 billion (US$3 billion), accounting for 20 percent of China's domestic shoe market. Besides dominating the domestic market, the shoe products from Lucheng are sold in a multinational market of more than 20 countries and regions, including North America, Europe, South America, and the Middle East. In the domestic and overseas markets, these products are well-known brands that have been extremely successful in the past few years.

In the Lucheng District, a local division of labor among suppliers, including shoemaking machines, lasts, soles, shoe-related chemical materials, and metal hardware, has emerged. The production districts and trade markets are colocated around the Lucheng shoe production zones: the production zone in Baishi of Yueqing Town; the district of shoe-adorning materials in Yongjia of Huangtian Town; the shoe material market with an annual transaction value of RMB 3 billion in Hetongqiao; and the raw leather market, leather machine market, and leather chemicals market, with an annual transaction value of RMB 2 billion in Shuitou Town. Clustering brings a close and convenient connection among the firms in different parts of the value chain. However, as the products are mainly homogeneous, clustering also generates the problem of brutal competition among materials suppliers, pushing them to use and develop their resources fully. Furthermore, the low labor cost in local zones helps cut the price of the products.

With its specialized manufacturing network, the Lucheng District has attracted both big brand-name companies in China and multinational firms from Italy, Germany, Japan, Brazil, and Taiwan, China, to build factories or set up agencies. To illustrate, Nike has now been purchasing leather material from the Far-East Company in Shutou since 1998.

***Connecting: the local industrial association.*** Since the reform and opening up of China, the SMEs in Wenzhou have grown at an amazing rate, generating an economy of agglomeration. However, clustering alone without an association to connect firms to each other would not lead to breakthroughs in industry upgrades. In the process of cluster development, the first Chinese shoemakers' association in Wenzhou has played an important role. The formation of the industry association was closely related to the development of the industry. As mentioned earlier, the footwear industry of Wenzhou developed from local family workshops. These family workshops had little encouragement as well as little impediment from the planned economic system that existed in China before 1978 (the year of the implementation of the reform and opening up policy). The local entrepreneurs created the initial shoemaking industry in Wenzhou with their wisdom, diligence, bravery, broad vision, and great creativity. They created the various prevailing and attracting commodities at a low price.

However, in the 1980s, the period of excess demand for shoes in the domestic market, the shoemaking cluster in Wenzhou suffered a serious crisis of trust: the low quality of its products at that period severely damaged the reputation of Wenzhou-made footwear products. For one thing, large numbers of replica shoes came from unlicensed factories; for another, some enterprises with poor management went for high profits by cutting costs and producing shoes with low quality, which finally led to the Wulinmen incident. Since then, the shoemakers in Wenzhou have realized that products should meet quality standards. In 1991, the firms spontaneously founded the Wenzhou Lucheng Shoe Industrial Association. Acting as the bridge between the government and its member enterprises, the association started standardizing quality and played an important role in enlarging the influence and enhancing the reputation of Wenzhou shoe products.

At present, the association has 1,138 member enterprises and 26 branches. According to interviews with the entrepreneurs of local shoe-making firms and the leader of the association, the role of the footwear association can be summarized as follows:

- *Connecting the local administration and the industry.* The association acts as the bridge between the local administration and the enterprises. It passes the regulatory policy pertaining to enterprises and also transmits the requirements of the enterprises to the administration.
- *Serving members of shoemaking firms.* The association serves the enterprises in every aspect and helps them strengthen their brands.
- *Promoting the industry.* The association often holds exhibitions of high-quality shoes in other cities in China and introduces Wenzhou shoes to other buyers. It also invites the local commerce bureau and reporters to Wenzhou to extend their understanding and impression of the shoe products in Wenzhou.
- *Exchanging information.* The association holds lectures on learning techniques and new equipment and provides information.
- *Introducing new technology.* The association encourages the shoe companies to introduce advanced production lines and organizes them to visit companies in other countries, such as the United States, Italy, and Korea.
- *Promoting trade.* The association keeps in close touch with the trade association of Italy and invites experts to give lectures on using new equipment and materials.
- *Training.* To enhance the design level, the association offers training classes given by the national footwear institution and Beijing Leather College. These activities greatly help upgrade the Wenzhou shoe industry.

China's entrance into the World Trade Organization created opportunities and challenges for the shoemaking industry in Wenzhou. The association focuses on how to call global attention to Wenzhou and how to promote the Wenzhou footwear industry so that it can prosper in the international market. To illustrate, the association has held international exhibitions to help expand the influence of the Wenzhou footwear industry in the international market and has introduced advanced technology as well as recent market information to its members. In addition, since 1996, the association has held an annual exhibition of advanced equipment, material, and techniques, which has become one of the most influential professional shoemaking exhibitions in Asia.

***Promoting: the local administration.*** The local government of Wenzhou has played an active role in the development of the footwear manufacturing cluster. It constituted the industry's development policy and planning, improved local infrastructure, and promoted a standardized shoe product market, as well as providing other assistance. The main contributions of the local administration are as follows:

- *Encouraging the development of the shoe industry.* As early as 1978, when China began implementing its significant economic reforms and opening up policy, the local administration in the towns of Wenzhou became the leading force. It instructed the local people to conduct any legal privately or publicly owned business to help them solve the problems of poverty and become prosperous. In that laissez-faire institutional environment, the privately owned township firms in the rural areas of Wenzhou experienced an unprecedented boom.

- *Setting regulations.* The local administration also played an important role in quality control. Due to the low quality of the shoe products in the 1980s during the development of the shoe business, Wenzhou-made shoes had the advantage of low prices but the disadvantage of a bad reputation. Since the Hangzhou Wulin–Gate incident, the administration has called on enterprises to improve their standards of shoe quality. This governmental instruction has not only regulated the shoemaking industry, but also prompted shoe companies to develop into branded corporations. Since then, some brands have risen to among the top 10 in China's shoemaking industry and have expanded the national market.

- *Promoting technology learning and innovation.* The local administration encourages entrepreneurs in Wenzhou to build learning institutions. Moreover, it has persuaded the shoe manufacturing business in Italy to set up a footwear design center in Wenzhou, marking its transition from an industry solely concentrated in manufacturing into a cluster with internal innovation capability. It also built up or introduced professional shoe leather majors in the local colleges and schools and educated thousands of young professional graduates in the sustainable development of the industry.

- *Improving the local infrastructure.* Infrastructure is a principal factor in the development of an industry cluster, because it is the key to site location, cost of transportation, and ease of access to business partners for face-to-face communications. The government of Wenzhou City is investing RMB 557 million in setting up an industrial zone called the "Chinese shoe metropolis" in Shuangyu Town, Lucheng District (see figure 5.4). The zone covers an area of 6.5 square kilometers, with a building area of 697,000 square meters. It is planned as a large industrial complex of shoe development that integrates technological training, trading, testing, and information provision and production. The zone will be divided into four separate functional sectors of shoemaking, shoe machinery, shoe service, and shoe culture. A museum of shoe culture, an exhibition hall for shoe transactions, and a park based on shoe culture are to be built. This complex combines a manufacturing specialty with a focus on tourist and consumer services. Visitors will enjoy learning about both the new technology of shoemaking and the traditional culture of Wenzhou. It is anticipated that the annual output value of the zone may be more than RMB 20 billion after it has reached full manufacturing capacity.

**Figure 5.4    The Development of the "Chinese Shoe Metropolis," 1999–2008**

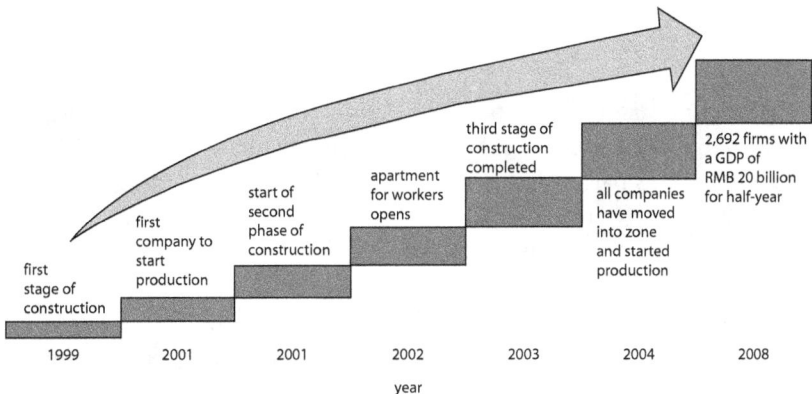

*Source:* Author.

The establishment of the Wenzhou China Shoe Capital (WCSC) project is a good example that illustrates how the local government implements significant strategy for the industry. The WCSC is a large shoemaking base that integrates production with scientific research, testing, information, and trade.

***Venturing: the local entrepreneurship.*** Local entrepreneurship in Wenzhou has a long and prosperous history in the development of the local economy. The network of entrepreneurs from Wenzhou extends to every part of the world market, through dynamic information sharing, learning, market expansion, and capital accumulation. The entrepreneurs are a key driving force in the development of the Wenzhou shoe industry. Their role in Wenzhou is summarized as follows:

- *The spirit of venturing.* The history of the SME boom in Wenzhou exemplifies the spirit of venturing. The development of privately owned businesses in Wenzhou required entrepreneurs to make a breakthrough in the existing market system and develop an economy suitable for SMEs. Through trial and error, SMEs in Wenzhou prospered, evolving from small-scale enterprises into a variety of clusters and going from doubt to hope. The venturing spirit was therefore essential to the success of the industry.

- *Building a global network.* There are more than 2 million people in the shoemaking industry; they live or work in every part of the world and form an invisible but powerful global network of information, knowledge, and markets. The entrepreneurs in Wenzhou have been active in setting up various overseas markets in light industry and expanding demand for local products.

- *A keen understanding of the global value chain.* Thousands of SMEs in Wenzhou concentrate on a single specialized phase of production and thus serve as part of the global value chain. The specialization of production contributes to the SMEs' keen understanding of cooperation in the global division of labor.

### The Challenges to a Sustainable and Upgraded Cluster

Generally, to maintain sustainability and perform upgrades, firms in clusters need to gain additional value from innovation in new products, a larger scale effect, and a bigger share of the domestic and overseas markets. All these can help maintain and improve the competence of local industry and lead the upgrading from the bottom to the top in the global value chain.

In the development environment of the international and domestic shoe product market, several factors create challenges to the sustainability and upgrading of the footwear manufacturing cluster in Wenzhou, particularly dumping, eco-standards, and low technology and lack of independent innovation and concerted action among the enterprises.

*Antidumping.* There are two essential prerequisites for charging an industry with "dumping": the price of the item is lower than the cost of production and disrupts the local market. Foreign countries set up antidumping barriers against Chinese goods for three main reasons:

- *"Dumping" activities by Chinese firms in the European and American markets.* The firms in Wenzhou are willing to export their products at a price under their costs to the overseas markets, because they can gain back the export taxes through subsidies. That strategy, however, actually constitutes dumping the goods in overseas markets.
- *Unilateral policies for protecting the local industry.* The combination of low price and desirable quality in Chinese products severely threatens local industry in other countries. To protect local markets and industries, countries take unilateral actions such as antidumping measures and punitive tariffs to restrict the entrance of Chinese products.
- *Low added value of Chinese products.* Due to the weakness in innovation and technology development, Chinese products can easily be supplemented with homogeneous products from other countries. For whatever reason, governments of the developed overseas markets generally take "antidumping" actions to benefit local firms and industries.

At present, the average export price for a pair of shoes from China is no more than €3, while the average sales price for shoes in the European markets is €35–70. Chinese shoe products, therefore, are vulnerable to investigations of dumping. If the export prices for shoe products from China were to reach the average sales price in the European market, it would not only increase revenues 10 times for the shoe-exporting firms in Wenzhou, but also would avoid the deep suspicion of illegal dumping. If that were the case, though, it would raise the question of how the footwear manufacturing firms in Wenzhou could reach the threshold of €35.

*Eco-standards.* Eco-standards are an issue in the context of environmental protection and sustainable development. Various such barriers exist in the international market, specifically, the RoHS (Restrictions on the Use of Certain Hazardous Substances) in Europe, the WEEE (Waste Electrical and Electronic Equipment) system, REACH (Registration, Evaluation, and Authorization of Chemicals), and EuP (Energy-using Products). These restrictions will significantly affect manufactured products exported from the developing countries to the European markets.

REACH is the regulation directly restricting the materials used in the process of shoemaking. At the end of 2005, for example, Chinese shoe products exported to Italy were charged with containing excessive nickel, azo dyes, cadmium, and pentachlorophenol. In addition, a shipment of rubber shoes sent back from Germany was charged with containing excessive formaldehyde. These experiences with eco-standards suggest that Wenzhou should change its practices to meet the requirements of overseas markets.

*Low technology.* Compared to shoe production techniques in Italy, Spain, and Taiwan, China, production methods in Wenzhou rely on lower-level technology. Few shoemaking firms in Wenzhou have mastered advanced technology in nanomaterials, solvents, and surface treatment agents. Generally, shoe manufacturing industries in developed countries take advantage of computer-aided design (CAD), computer-aided manufacturing, (CAM), and product data management (PDM) for their designs. They also use streamlines, automatic control systems, and lasers to increase the efficiency and quality of the products. These advanced technologies significantly improve design capability, R&D capability, and manufacturing. Although streamlines are prevalent in Wenzhou, the application of these other advanced technologies is rare, indicating a lack of industrial innovation capability. Meanwhile, the footwear industry in Wenzhou depends heavily on assistance from developed countries such as Italy, which restricts the improvement of local innovation.

*Lack of independent innovation.* At present, many outstanding firms have strong, independent innovation capabilities in Wenzhou; they have developed many new functional products with excellent sales records. These products—such as the Goodyear Shoe by Kangnai, the Antibacterial Shoe by August, and the Nanomaterial Shoe by Gierda—were developed through a combination of foreign advanced shoe manufacturing and domestic needs. These examples demonstrate that leading firms in the Wenzhou shoe industry have been aware of the significance of independent innovation. More than 80 percent of the SMEs in the shoe industry in Wenzhou, however, specialize in processing and manufacturing OEM products for other firms; lack of awareness of the importance of independent innovation has impeded the further development of the whole industry.

*The call for collective action.* Because antidumping restrictions affect the interests of the whole industry rather than just individual firms, shoemaking firms need to take collective action and cooperate with each other to respond to the challenges. The firms in the architectural ceramics industry in Guangdong Province, for example, learned the lessons of the punitive tariff of 247 percent in the Indian market when no Chinese firm responded to the unreasonable antidumping restrictions. Fortunately, awareness is increasing within the footwear industry of the need to unite in collective action. For example, on March 8, 2006, members of the footwear association in Wenzhou, Quanzhou, and Guangdong founded a union to respond to charges of dumping in the European market. Such collective action will help the footwear industry in Wenzhou preserve its rights in the global market.

## Independent Innovation: The Road to Upgrading

As discussed in this chapter, challenges exist to the future development of the footwear industry in Wenzhou. But responses like collective action and mastering international market regulations are not enough to solve the fundamental problem of upgrading. The most essential point for the sustainable development of the footwear industry in Wenzhou is to improve the capacity for independent innovation to help the industry reach a higher place along the global value chain. In the development of China's industries, specialized OEM manufacturing has brought prosperity to millions of SMEs. OEM, however, can only help China become the mass production factory for the global market; it cannot transform China into an innovative industrialized country.

Independent innovation is a multifaceted concept. It contains the four patterns of innovation proposed by the United Nations Industrial Development Organization—product innovation, production innovation, function innovation, and interdepartmental innovation—and emphasizes the role of interorganizational R&D departments, research centers with outputs of new technology, other firms with advanced technology, and universities. It is a process of imitation, digestion, assimilation, and re-creation; it even requires firms to improve their business mode, sales mode, service mode, brand operations, and other value-added capabilities.

A brief review of the developmental history of the Kangnai Company illustrates how independent innovation helps the firm thrive and succeed. Figure 5.5 illustrates the process of Kangnai's transition from family workshop to leading firm in the Wenzhou footwear industry. In each phase of development, Kangnai was a pioneer in introducing new technologies and independent innovation. Because of its roots in the footwear industry, Kangnai has been one of the most active participants in the Shoe and Allied Trade Research Association (SATRA). However, it has since diversified to become a specialist in testing consumer products. It is also one of the largest research and certification institution in China, with pervasive influence, and it is the first Chinese footwear manufacturing firm to participate in setting regulations. Kangnai has invested RMB 10 million in building a world-class R&D center in Wenzhou to work on the latest footwear manufacturing technology, materials, processing, and environmental standards. It has set an example for other shoemaking firms in Wenzhou to improve their capacity for independent innovation and increase their competence.

## Policy Suggestions for Upgrading the Footwear Industry in Wenzhou

Basically, the development and upgrading of the industry depend on the strategies of firms within the cluster, and the most effective method is to

**Figure 5.5    Development Stages of the Kangnai Company, Selected Years, 1980–2004**

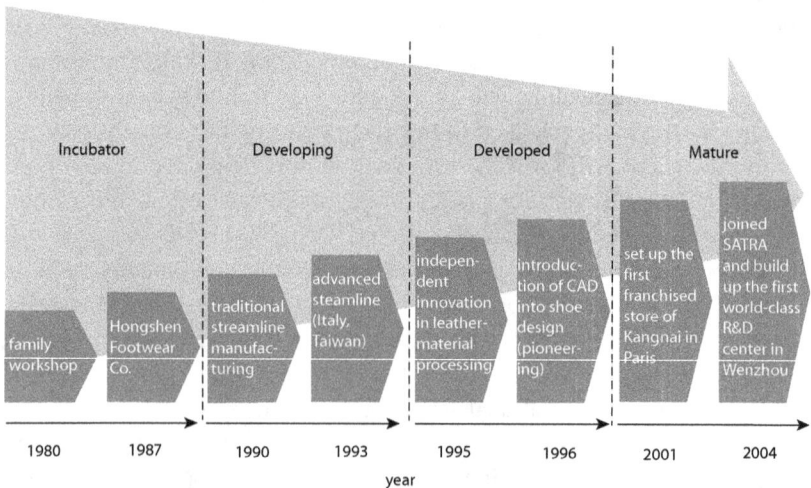

*Source:* Author.

improve the independent innovation capability of the firms to respond to the challenge of antidumping barriers. Meanwhile, the significance of the role of local government, associations, research centers, and universities must be emphasized, because they are all involved in the development process. To meet the challenges to further development of the sector, this chapter offers the following policy recommendations for the footwear manufacturing sector in Wenzhou:

- *Provide a better environment for further development.* The high price for land use is becoming a major obstacle to the further development of most footwear manufacturing firms. The local administration should improve land-use and transference policies and put some effort into creating better infrastructure in the industrial zone to help the footwear firms. The administration of Jinjiang may serve as one good reference point for Wenzhou in making land-use policy: the local administration provides a two-thirds discount off the land price for those firms designated as a Famous Brand of China and provides preferable policy support for the development of local firms.

- *Establish a professional training center for footwear manufacturing.* The lack of technology talent is another threshold for the labor-intense footwear manufacturing industry, which closely relates to the capability of technology innovation and research. The establishment of a training center would provide professional labor to the local firms and help increase the innovation capabilities of local industry. In the town of Shiling of Guangzhou City, for example, the Professional Training Center of China Light Industry and the Shiling Base of the China Leather Industry Training Center have proved helpful in making the local professional labor market successful and have provided a sufficient supply of technology talent for the firms.

- *Encourage firms in the footwear industry cluster in Wenzhou to improve their independent innovation capabilities.* To increase investment in independent research and new-product innovation, firms should receive support in their effort to enter the global value chain system through innovation in product, function, brand, and sales mode. By learning from successful foreign corporations, local firms can increase and accumulate independent innovation experience. The development of Kangnai's innovation capability mentioned earlier is one successful case study for other footwear manufacturing firms to emulate.

- *Promote cooperation and pursue collective action.* Promoting cooperation and pursuing collective action by using overseas networks can help the people of Wenzhou gain and transmit information and strengthen individual firms as well as clusters. For local enterprises, the footwear industry association is an essential way of connecting firms; in the domestic realm, the governmental departments can serve as nodes linking the firms, research centers, universities, and the other institutions.

- *Regulate domestic eco-standards to meet the requirements of the global market.* Firms, the administration, and the industry association should develop an agreement on eco-standards for footwear products; then domestic regulations should enforce the quality of local products for the global market.

## Notes

1. The historical name *Hong Kong* refers to the period before July 1, 1997, when the former British colony was restored to China.

2. 1 mu is equal to 1/15th of a hectare. A square mile has about 3,885 mu.

## Bibliography

Asheim, B. T., and P. Cooke. 1999. "Local Learning and Interactive Innovation Networks in a Global Economy." In *Making Connections*, ed. E. Malecki and P. Oinäs, 145–78. Ashgate: Aldershot.

Bathelt, H., A. Malmberg, and P. Maskell. 2002. "Clusters and Knowledge: Local Buzz, Global Pipelines and the Process of Knowledge Creation." Working Paper 02-12, Danish Research Unit for Industrial Dynamics (DRUID), Copenhagen.

Bellandi, M. 2002. "Italian Industrial Districts: An Industrial Economics, Interpretation." *European Planning Studies* 10 (4): 425–37.

Dicken, P., and P. Lloyd. 1990. *Location in Space: Theoretical Perspectives in Economic Geography.* London: Harper and Row.

Gereffi, G. 1994. "The Organization of Buyer-Driven Global Commodity Chains: How U.S. Retailers Shape Overseas Production Networks," in *Commodity Chains and Global Capitalism*, ed. G. Gereffi and M. Korzeniewicz, 95–122. Westport: Praeger.

———. 1999. "International Trade and Industrial Upgrading in the Apparel Commodity Chain." *Journal of International Economics* 48: 37–70.

Gertler, M. 2003. "Tacit Knowledge and the Economic Geography of Context, or the Undefinable Tacitness of Being (There)." *Journal of Economic Geography* 3 (1): 75–99.

Humphrey, J. 1995. "Industrial Reorganization in Developing Countries: From Models to Trajectories." *World Development* 23 (1): 149–62.

Humphrey, J., and H. Schmitz. 2000. "Governance and Upgrading: Linking Industrial Cluster and Global Value Chains Research." IDS Working Paper 12, Institute of Development Studies, University of Sussex, Brighton.

Pyke, F., and W. Sengenberger, eds. 1992. *Industrial Districts and Local Economic Regeneration.* Geneva: International Institute for Labour Studies.

Rantisi, N. 2002. "The Local Innovation System as a Source of 'Variety': Openness and Adaptability in New York City's Garment District." *Regional Studies* 36 (6): 587–602.

Schamp, E., and F. Main. 2003. "Decline of the District, Renewal of Firms: The Case of Footwear Production in a German Border Area." Paper presented at the workshop "The Restructuring of Old Industrial Areas in Europe and Asia," Department of Geography, University of Bonn, Germany, August.

Schmitz, H. 1995. "Small Shoemakers and Fordist Giants: Tale of a Supercluster." *World Development* 23 (1): 9–28.

Sturgeon, T. 2003. "What Really Goes On in Silicon Valley? Spatial Clustering Dispersal in Modular Production Networks." *Journal of Economic Geography* 3: 199–225.

Sturgeon, T. and Ji-Ren Lee. 2001. "Industry Co-Evolution and the Rise of a Shared Supply-Base for Electronics Manufacturing." Paper presented at Nelson and Winter Conference, Aalborg, June.

UNIDO. 2002. *Industrial Development Report 2002/2003: Competing through Innovation and Learning.* Vienna: United Nations Industrial Development Organization.

*Wenzhou Shoe Association and Statistical Yearbook of Wenzhou.* Various years.

# CHAPTER 6

# Cluster Development and the Role of Government: The Case of Xiqiao Textile Cluster in Guangdong

## Jun Wang and Fangmin Yue

Since China's reform and opening up in 1978, Chinese products have been increasingly exported all over the world. Buyers, both domestic and foreign, would be surprised to find that hundreds of suppliers in one town, county, or municipality are producing the same products. Along the eastern coast of China, especially in Guangdong and Zhejiang provinces, a "world factory" for various products has rapidly emerged, creating the "China miracle" that puzzles the world's experts: how did China build such a competitive advantage during a short 30-year span? Lower labor cost is only one of the reasons; another critical factor, the industry cluster—a form of industrial organization—has played a very important role.

This cluster-based development pattern is suitable to China's level of industry, which greatly benefited from such advantages as the availability of a labor pool, technology and knowledge transfer, lower transportation costs, easy supply of intermediate inputs, lower transaction costs due to a high degree of social trust, high-level specialization, and shared public

Dr. Jun Wang is professor of economics at Lingnan College, Sun Yat-Sen University. Dr. Fangmin Yue is professor in the Economics Department of Guangdong Institute of Public Administration.

infrastructure with geographical proximity. Besides these general factors, how did China's clusters develop so successfully? What lessons can be learned from that development? What role does policy play? A case study might help us gain insight and lead to some answers.

This study takes one typical case, a textile industry cluster in Xiqiao Town in Guangdong Province, as the epitome of traditional industry cluster development in China. To give a clear picture, a brief introduction to the background of cluster development in China and Guangdong Province is presented first.

## An Overview of Industrial Cluster Development in China

Based on the formation and development mechanisms of clusters over different periods, we can divide the evolution of China's cluster development into three phases: formation, consolidation, and upgrading or transfer. Because different mechanisms operate in each of these three phases, it is difficult to specify exactly the time frame of cluster development. In addition, differences exist among clusters in eastern, central, and western China with respect to formation mechanisms. For the currently emerging clusters in central and western China, industry transfer and expansion from eastern China and policy encouragement over recent years are the main factors, for example, the formation of the Chengdu footwear cluster in Sichuan Province. This kind of cluster will not be analyzed here. We shall focus only on clusters in eastern and southern China, particularly those in the Pearl River Delta in Guangdong and in the Yangtze River Delta.[1] (See map 6.1.)

### Formation, Early 1980s through Mid-1990s

Early in the transformation of the planned economy into a market-oriented one, China suffered from product shortages; an enterprise could sell almost everything it manufactured. After a few enterprises had demonstrated some financial success, more and more peasants, workers, and even officials and scholars began to run businesses or enterprises. Hence, clusters of small and medium enterprises (SMEs) emerged in Guangdong and Zhejiang provinces, mostly in traditional industries such as textiles, garments and apparel, metalwork, household electrical goods, furniture, and leatherwear. The phenomenon of "one town, one industry—one village, one product" was widely evident in the Pearl River Delta area of Guangdong and Zhejiang. In Guangdong, this phenomenon came

**Map 6.1    Provinces, Autonomous Regions, and Municipalities**

Source: Authors' research.

to be called the "specialized town," while in Zhejiang it was referred to as the "block economy." Some of these clusters were derived from specialized product markets. Around these markets, related producers came together, and gradually a particular cluster formed.

At the initial stage of the reform and Open Door policy, quite a number of businessmen from Hong Kong[2] and Taiwan, China moved their factories or investments into Guangdong to manufacture clothing, electronic goods, toys, and footwear. The information technology (IT) cluster in Dongguan City, Guangdong Province, is a typical case. In that area, 84.3 percent of the IT enterprises were foreign investments by the end of 1998, while only 15.7 percent were enterprises with domestic investment. Then, more and more foreign direct investment (FDI) entered China, of which 85 percent was concentrated in Guangdong, Jiangsu, and Zhejiang provinces. Business enterprises from Japan and Taiwan, China were often clustered together: when the core enterprise moved, its suppliers—that is, those enterprises providing parts or materials for the core business—moved along with it. Most of them were involved in export-oriented processing activities.

The formation of those clusters was driven by market demand, both at home and overseas. The cooperation of enterprises in the supply chain is usually frequent and strong, while horizontal cooperation—that is, cooperation among similar enterprises—is less so. These clusters, especially the endogenous ones, were characterized by small scale, extensive imitation, lower innovation capacity, and rapid expansion with low quality. Low-cost production was their main advantage. Some high-tech industry parks with capacity for innovation were set up too, however, such as the Zhongguancun High-Tech Park in Beijing.

### Adjustment and Consolidation, Mid- and Late 1990s to 2000

Since the mid-1990s, after an initial period of fast development, domestic markets became buyers' markets, that is, the supply of a commodity exceeded the demand. In addition, competition inside and outside the cluster became more and more fierce as the size of the cluster increased. Most of China's clusters declined for some time because of low innovation dynamics, inadequate innovation capacity of SMEs, and strong market competition, and experienced an adjustment and consolidation development period. For example, after such a decline, the Wenzhou footwear cluster in Zhejiang Province began to pay attention to quality, consumer trust, and regional brands, and Xiqiao textile cluster in Guangdong began to raise its innovation capacity with the support of local government. From this period onward, local government began to intervene in cluster development, following the central government's reform of the tax distribution system in 1994, which allowed local government to share a certain proportion of taxation (Zhang et al. 2007; Fu 2008).

Because clusters were recognized as the growth engine of the regional economy, local government—including provincial, municipal, county, and town governments, especially the latter three—began to support cluster development through taxation, loans, and direct support such as infrastructure and innovation services. Meanwhile, enterprises, businessmen, and local governments in the cluster set up industry and commerce associations. Innovation for development and for improving competitiveness was the main theme of this period. As a result, eastern China gradually developed into the "world factory." Various new clusters—such as those in IT, software, biomedicine, and new energy—emerged to replace most of the traditional industry clusters of the former period. Although these changes indicated an adjustment in the structure of Chinese industry, overall clusters in China were still "driving on the low road," meaning that they were positioned at the lower end of the global manufacturing value chain, based on their low-cost advantage. How to move up the global value chain, how to make growth more efficient, how to move the cluster from the "low road" to the "high road," and how to maintain sustainable development are now China's main challenges for cluster development.

### Upgrading Development since 2001

After more than 20 years of development, most of the clusters in China are mature or relatively mature; they typically have large-scale industry, complete industry chains, and high market share. At the same time, however, since the start of the new century, cluster development in China has confronted new challenges, such as increasing costs of production, limited development space, resource depletion for the time being and more vigorous competition. Therefore, labor-intensive and resource-based industry clusters, such as textile, garment, footwear, and ceramics manufacturing clusters, have begun to move or spread into central and western China. Other clusters have begun to enter international markets and invest more in research and development (R&D) and innovation, while some creative industry clusters have emerged in Shanghai, Beijing, Hang Zhou, and elsewhere.

Upgrading and transforming have been the outstanding features of this period. Some clusters whose advantages had been lost in eastern China have tried to relocate to other provinces, even to other countries like Vietnam. In central and western China, provinces such as Jiangxi, Hunan, Hubei, Sichuan, Anhui, and Guangxi began to attract these industries, with some new clusters being gradually formed. For example, the footwear manufacturing cluster in Chengdu in Sichuan Province has benefited greatly from this cluster diffusion and has developed rapidly during recent years. By the end of 2005, this region in western China had agglomerated more than 1,200 footwear enterprises, and more than 3,000 related enterprises, producing more than 10 million pairs of leather shoes and accounting for more than 50 percent of the total footwear export volume of western China (Yuan and Li 2008).

### Types of Clusters in China

Based on different formation dynamics, China's clusters can be divided into two categories, endogenous and exogenous.[3] The endogenous type is driven by local factors, including local natural resources, industry history, entrepreneurial culture, large-scale enterprises, universities or colleges, specialized markets, and an enabling local policy environment. Examples are the textile, metalware, and household electronics clusters in Guangdong, Zhejiang, and Jiangsu provinces; the Puer tea industry cluster in Yunnan; and the coal cluster in Shanxi Province.

Certain high-tech clusters have been formed on the basis of local universities, for example, the Zhongguancun cluster in Beijing. At the end of 2006, more than 16,000 firms in Zhongguancun Science Park were involved in software, integrated circuits, network communications, biomedicine, and new environmental resource industries. Some clusters have taken shape through the incubation of large and medium stated-owned and private enterprises, such as the automobile industry in Changchun City, the household electronics cluster in Qingdao in Shandong Province, the motorcycle cluster in Jiangmen in Guangdong Province, and so forth.

As noted earlier, the footwear industry cluster in Chengdu was formed by industrial relocation from eastern China. Since 2000, the increasing costs of land, labor, and energy resources have forced some labor-intensive industries to relocate their production base from southern and eastern China to the inner provinces to form new clusters. More and more such clusters will emerge in China.

The exogenous cluster comes into being through foreign direct investment. At the end of the 1970s, with rapid economic development, increasing costs forced some businesses from Hong Kong and Taiwan, China to move elsewhere. With the proximity of the neighboring Guangdong and Fujian provinces, some enterprises first ventured into these regions, and their success led others to follow. Encouraged by local government, more and more related enterprises gathered together and formed a cluster. An example is the IT cluster in Dongguan, Guangdong Province, where 83.4 percent of the enterprises have FDI, such as those from Japan. Another example is the IT and electronics cluster in Suzhou in Jiangsu Province, in which some investors are from Singapore.

### Main Features of China's Cluster Development

By the end of 2007, China's clusters were located mainly in the southeast coastal region, especially in Jiangsu, Zhejiang, Shandong, and Guangdong, where the manufacturing clusters accounted for 54.5 percent of the national total. The distribution ratio of industry clusters in eastern, central, and western China was approximately 79:12:9,[4] with actual numbers being 3,630, 557, and 418, respectively (Yuan and Li 2008, 1–12). The textile clusters and transportation equipment clusters are distributed over the three regions, while the electrical and communication equipment and facilities clusters are mainly in eastern China. However, clusters in central and western China are mostly in the process of forming. Clusters in eastern China are fairly advanced in terms of agglomeration, export ratio, innovation, and growth ratio, while those in central China have higher profits and development potential; most of the clusters in western China are resource dependent, focused mainly on basic processing.

China's clusters came into being gradually during China's opening up and reform process, a development promoted by both the central and the local government. Policies have played an important role in China's cluster development. Enterprises in China's clusters are mostly SMEs, with low innovation ability and competitiveness. As China's enterprises are gradually losing their low-cost labor, cluster upgrading and transfer have become the key tasks of current cluster development.

## Outline of Industrial Cluster Development in Guangdong

As a coastal province of China, Guangdong has played an important role in China's economic development since the 1980s. It was the frontier of China's opening up and reforms and the earliest developed area to benefit from the national reform policy. After more than 30 years of development, Guangdong has basically completed its industrialization and urbanization process and become an industrial province rather than an agricultural one. In 2008, with a growth rate of 10.1 percent, higher than that for the previous year, Guangdong's gross domestic product (GDP) was US$509.884 billion, accounting for 11.87 percent of China's total GDP. The per capita GDP of the province reached US$5,369, much higher than China's average level (US$3,097). Although Guangdong was affected by the current financial crisis, it was still ranked first in China in total imports and exports in 2008 (see table 6.1).

As the growth pole of Guangdong, the Pearl River Delta area has become the world's factory.[5] Here, clusters have played an important role in the rapid economic development in the province. Particularly after the 1990s, in some counties with an active market, sound transportation, and telecommunication and information services, many towns established industries with output values ranging from RMB 1 billion up to RMB 10 billion. In those towns that are more or less concentrated on one industry, specialized divisions of labor and business networks have become key factors in economic development. These industrial clusters are located within the township administrative boundary and hence are known as specialized towns.[6]

The clustering industries in these towns are called *specialized industries* and have developed with integrated production, supply, and sales chains

**Table 6.1  Key Economic Indicators for Guangdong Province and China, 2008**

| | Area (sq. km) | Population (millions) | GDP (billions) | GDP per capita | Primary industry (%) | Secondary industry (%) | Tertiary industry (%) | Growth rate 1980–2008 (%) | Import (billions) | Export (billion) | FDI inflow (billion) |
|---|---|---|---|---|---|---|---|---|---|---|---|
| Guangdong Province | 179,757 | 94.49 | 509.88 | 5,369 | 5.5 | 51.6 | 42.9 | 13.15 | 279.2 | 404.1 | 19.2 |
| China | 9,600,000 | 1,386.28 | 4,294.73 | 3,097 | 11.0 | 49.0 | 40.0 | 10.25 | 1,133.1 | 1,428.5 | 92.4 |
| %[a] | 1.87 | 6.82 | 11.87 | n.a. | n.a. | n.a. | n.a. | n.a. | 24.64 | 32.29 | 28.29 |

*Sources:* China data are from China Monthly Economic Indicators, February 2009. Guangdong data are from Guangdong Provincial Government Report, February 13, 2009, and other reports.

*Note:* The population is 2008 data. n.a. = not applicable.

a. % = to the % of Guangdong accounting for China's total.

and are usually privately owned. These towns are located mainly in the inland regions and east bank of the Pearl River Delta, some are in the eastern Guangdong. By 2008, there were a total of 277 such specialized towns or industrial clusters.

By 2007, 228 clusters in Guangdong, with a GDP of RMB 765.049 billion, accounting for 24.9 percent of the total provincial GDP, had become the key force driving the development of the provincial economy. As the growth engine of the local region, the 104 industry clusters in the relatively developed Pearl River Delta region contributed 28.4 percent of the regional GDP, within which 33 clusters in Foshan, with an industrial and agricultural output value of RMB 294.225 billion, contributed 81.6 percent of the GDP of Foshan (Provincial Science and Technology Bureau of Guangdong 2008). Table 6.2 gives some basic information on the clusters in Guangdong.

Cluster development in Guangdong has greatly accelerated the process of industrialization and urbanization. Currently, the Pearl River Delta has reached the middle-to-advanced stage of industrialization and the middle stage of urbanization, with a 72.8 percent level of urbanization in 2003 compared to an average of 55 percent for the province as a whole. During recent years, with current industry transfers and development, clusters newly formed in the peripheral area of the Pearl River Delta have contributed 44.3–67.6 percent of local economic growth. Therefore, industry clusters are regarded as the key policy instruments for developing underdeveloped areas.

The clusters that are scattered primarily through the Pearl River Delta and eastern areas are now relatively mature and involve not only labor-intensive industries, such as textiles and garments, foodstuffs, construction ceramics, and metalware clusters, but also communication equipment, automobiles, the IT industry, household electronics, and high-tech industries. In the western and northern parts of Guangdong, clusters focus on natural resource industries, such as water and sea products, aquaculture, fruit, masonry materials, farming, and some small household electronics. And in the eastern areas, such as Shantou, Chaozhou, and Jieyang, industrial clusters specialize in stainless steel products, toys, wedding and knitted garments, foodstuffs, ceramics, and the like (see map 6.2).

Guangdong's industrial clusters can be classified into endogenous and exogenous types. The exogenous clusters, mainly driven by overseas Chinese firms and foreign investments, are concentrated on the eastern side of the Pearl River in the Shenzhen, Dongguan, and Huizhou areas. These clusters developed because of their proximity to Hong Kong, China,

**Table 6.2  Key Economic Indicators of Guangdong's Clusters, 2001–07**

| | 2001 | 2002 | 2003 | 2004 | 2005 | 2006 | 2007 |
|---|---|---|---|---|---|---|---|
| Clusters (number) | 21 | 50 | 71 | 103 | 159 | 201 | 228 |
| Total GDP of specialized towns[a] (RMB billions) | 44.069 | 97.610 | 146.712 | 228.015 | 465.832 | 609.115 | 765.049 |
| Proportion of provincial GDP (%) | 4.14 | 8.32 | 10.77 | 14.22 | 20.83 | 23.25 | 24.94 |
| Total population of specialized towns (10,000) | 148.0 | 351.5 | 549.9 | 850.3 | 1,358.1 | 1,708.6 | 2,037.2 |
| Total S&T personnel in towns (10,000) | 10.69 | 18.78 | 26.01 | 48.16 | 42.24 | — | 42.23 |
| Number of enterprises in towns (10,000) | 3.92 | 9.79 | 13.47 | 16.40 | 23.94 | 36.66 | 41.39 |
| Number of high-tech enterprises (unit) | 68 | 257 | 336 | 513 | 688 | 971 | 1,222 |
| S&T investment by township governments (RMB millions) | 135.27 | 29.525 | 41.132 | 60.004 | 61.283 | — | 65.544 |
| Accumulated patents granted (number) | 2,852 | 16,289 | 23,006 | 46,101 | 49,285 | 68,964 | 108,416 |
| Number of enterprises engaged in industrial cluster (10,000 units) | 1.48 | 3.39 | 4.32 | 4.81 | 10.07 | — | 10.33 |
| Output value of cluster (RMB billions) | 42.245 | 127.138 | 178.027 | 269.365 | 468.313 | — | 973.136 |
| Taxes contributed by clusters (RMB billions) | 1.181 | 4.039 | 6.319 | 7.230 | 11.635 | — | 26.423 |
| Total employees in clusters (10,000) | 52.95 | 182.29 | 241.74 | 266.47 | 370.71 | — | 431.48 |
| S&T personnel in clusters (10,000) | 3.36 | 11.78 | 14.94 | 18.71 | 24.11 | — | 26.30 |

*Sources:* Lu, Lin, and Guan 2008, 217. Data of 2007 are updated by authors according to the survey and report of the Development and Planning Department of the Provincial Science and Technology Bureau of Guangdong.

*Note:* — = not available. S&T = science and technology.

a. Specialized towns are towns where clusters are located.

# Map 6.2 Industrial Clusters in Guangdong Province, 2004

*Province names:* FUJIAN, JIANGXI, HUNAN, GUANGXI, HONG KONG, MACAO

**FOSHAN**
Nanzhuang (ceramics)
Shiwan (ceramics)
Zhangcha (knitting)
Lunshi (stainless steel)
Pingzhou (footwear)
Shishan (electronics)
Dali (nonferrous metal)
Guanyao (toy)
Jiunan (gems)
Beijiao (electronics)
Lecong (furniture)
Longjiang (furniture)
Lalu (hardware, electronics, machinery)
Jinsha (knitting)
Xiqiao (textile)
Yanbu (underwear)
Lunjiao (machinery)
Gongluo (breading)
Renhe (metal materials)
Datang (vegetable)

**YUNFU**
Hekou (stone materials)
Xincheng (stainless steel)
Tiantang (vegetable, flower, agricultural product processing)
Jiancheng (wampee, orange)
Mancheng (fruit)
Fucheng (electronics)
Luocheng (textile, apparel)

**ZHOAQING**
Jinli (hardware)
Dongcheng (jade processing)
Huanggang (jackstone)
Xiangang (vegetable)

**MAOMING**
Shange (porcelain clay)
Ganzi (litchi)
Bohe (litchi)
Huazicheng (bamboo weaving)

**ZHANJIANG**
Mazhang (food, aquatic product)
Yingli (pineapple)
Lanzhou (rice cooker)
Shijing (orange)
Bopu (plastic shoes)
Tangwei (down products)

**YANGJIANG**
Dongcheng (hardware)
Pingang (aquaculture)

**JIANGMEN**
Pengjiang (motorcycle and accessory)
Duruan (hardware, bathroom accessory)
Jianghai (electronic materials)
Da'ao (container)
Siqian (hardware, stainless steel products)
Shuangshuican (fishery)
Shuikou (water supply and heating equipment)
Shagang (chemical fiber)
Shaping (footwear)
Encheng (microphone and accessory)

**ZHUHAI**
Baijiao (aquaculture)

**ZHONGSHAN**
Huangpu (food processing)
Nantou (electronics)
Xiaolan (hardware)
Guzhen (lighting)
Shaxi (casual wear)
Dayong (rosewood furniture)
Minzhong (fruit, vegetable)
Dongfeng (electronics)

**DONGGUAN**
Shilong (electronics, medicines)
Shijie (electronics, information products)
Changping (logistics)
Houjie (furniture)
Chang'an (hardware, electronics)
Humen (apparel)
Dalang (wool weaving)

**GUANGZHOU**
Shiling (leather products)

**SHAOGUAN**
Lishi (hoggery, plantation)

**HEYUAN**
Zhongxin (peanut, garlic)
Chuanhang (Dongyuan chestnuts)

**HUIZHOU**
Huidongbu (footwear)

**SHANWEI**
Kutang (jewelry)
Gongping (apparel)

**JIEYANG**
Dongshan (stainless steel products)
Xichang (food, food machinery)
Yuhu (Huraishan taro)
Hepo (electronic piano)

**MEIZHOU**
Gaopo (ceramics)
Yanyang (golden-pomelo)
Tongkeng (electronic sound devices)
Xinwei (handicraft)

**CHAOZHOU**
Guxiang (ceramic bathroom products)
Anbu (food product, printing)
Fenghuang (tea, tourism)
Guihong (stainless steel products)
Huanggang (aquarium equipment, apparel)
Jinshi (flower)
Fengxi (ceramics)

**SHANTOU**
Guroa (textile, apparel)
Waisha (knitting handicraft)
Yongsheng (package printing)
Dahao (handicraft packaging)
Shipaozhai (light machinery)
Chaoyahao (wool apparel)
Liangying (knitted garments)
Xinjin (package printing)
Xiezhan (fine chemical engineering)
Heping (music, video products)

*Cities labeled:* Shaoguan, Qingyuan, Meizhou, Chaozhou, Shantou, Jieyang, Shanwei, Heyuan, Huizhou, Shenzhen, Dongguan, Guangzhou, Foshan, Zhaoqing, Yunfu, Jiangmen, Zhongshan, Zhuhai, Yangjiang, Maoming, Zhanjiang

**Legend**
- industry clusters
- prefecture capitals
- province capital
- prefecture boundaries
- province boundaries

*Source:* Authors' research.

and the preferential development policy for coastal regions in effect since the 1980s. Dongguan is regarded as a major center. Among these clusters, both well-known foreign personal computer–related companies, including IBM, Compaq, Dell, and Acer, and domestic companies, such as Legend and Founder, have established plants in this area. More than 20,000 firms are engaged in parts and components processing for personal computers.

The endogenous clusters mainly consist of domestic firms, mostly SMEs, and engage in traditional industries, such as shoes, textiles, garments, aluminum alloys, toys, foods and beverages, construction materials, paper, auto parts, arts and crafts, leather goods, metalwork, plastics, furniture, apparatus manufacturing, nonferrous metals, and so on. These clusters can be found in many regions and are anchored to a network of small and medium towns somewhere between the large cities and the interior countryside (Wang and Mao 2005). In 2006, among the 201 clusters in Guangdong, about 83 percent belonged to this type (see figure 6.1). Among the 103,300 enterprises in these clusters, some have grown up

**Figure 6.1    Distribution of Industrial Clusters in Guangdong, 2006**

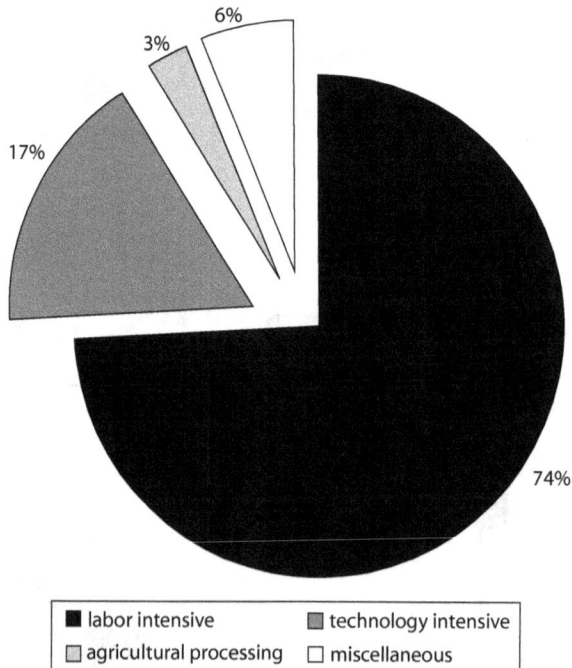

*Source:* Guangdong Bureau of Science and Technology, 2006.

and become leaders in local clusters and have played a key role in cluster innovation and development upgrades.

Three features of endogenous clusters can be observed in their processes of emergence and development:

- First, almost all endogenous clusters consist mainly of family-owned SMEs, which result in the importance of family ties, traditions, and a sort of "path dependence," which means that these are minor SMEs operated and managed by families at a low level and that it would be difficult to develop most of them into modern firms.

- Second, SME clusters are mainly labor intensive and focus on products with lower added value. These characteristics reflect the history of their establishment, in which they started with simple products, such as food, clothes, and shoes, and clustered in the neighborhoods surrounding a marketplace for selling their products.

- Third, the low price of the products, linked with the low cost of labor, is their most important basis for competitiveness. For example, at the beginning of the 1990s, the price of a pair of sports shoes made by state-owned enterprises in Guangzhou City was nearly twice as much as those made by private enterprise in rural areas only some 50 kilometers away. However, low price is often associated with the low quality and old technologies of SMEs. With the increase in competition and cost of labor, product quality and technological capability have become more important factors in improving competitiveness.

In recent years, labor costs in Guangdong have already become higher than in Vietnam and India. Competition from domestic and foreign companies is increasing rapidly. Low price alone is no longer a sustainable long-term strategy. Growth characterized by quantity with low quality, low productivity, and high pollution cannot be sustainable. Because of increasing labor costs, since 2000 some enterprises have begun to move their production to areas outside the Pearl River Delta and into neighboring provinces. To keep these enterprises and facilitate development of other regions in Guangdong, since 2005 the provincial government has worked out a series of policies to encourage local governments in the Pearl River Delta and other areas to jointly construct industry transfer parks in underdeveloped areas.

So far, there are 29 provincial-level industry transfer parks in eastern, western, and northern Guangdong. In 2008, under the new industrial development policy, the province appropriated a total of RMB 7.5 billion to develop 15 industry-transfer demonstration parks to induce industries to move from the Pearl River Delta area to the underdeveloped areas in Guangdong. It is required that all industries accepted by these parks be developed into one or more clusters, with one dominant sector and several supporting sectors.

Because most of the clusters are producing low value-added products and lack innovation capability, the Guangdong Science and Technology (S&T) Bureau initiated a program to address these issues and to advance the S&T progress of the specialized towns. In 1999, the bureau launched the Guangdong Specialized Town Technology Innovation Pilots and provided RMB 300,000 for each pilot to set up technology innovation platforms. The city and township governments were asked to invest matching funds in the proportions of 1 (province):10 (city): 50 (town) by 2007, a total of 153 such platforms had been established. These platforms provide product identification and other information services, facilitate innovation, help commercialize R&D results, and facilitate cooperation among industry, university, and research institutes (see the sections "Implementing an S&T Strategy" and "Giving Impetus to Cluster Upgrading" later in the chapter for details). Among these, most of the platforms operate as quasi-public institutes or as public organizations. These account for 75.8 percent of the total; 11 of them, accounting for 7.2 percent of the total, operate as private enterprises.

By the end of 2007, these platforms had facilitated 856 projects in total. The focus of these platforms has gradually shifted toward R&D, and local governments have increased their R&D investment. Some of the platforms have become demonstration projects in the province, even in the country, such as the Xiaolan productivity promotion center in Zhongshan City and the Xiqiao textile technology innovation center in Nanhai, Foshan City. Through the support of these innovation platforms, Guangdong's cluster development has entered the upgrading stage.

How did these clusters develop? What are the roles of local government? What are the challenges these clusters face? How can they best respond to those challenges? What are the policy implications for cluster development in other regions? To answer these questions, we need to explore particular clusters. The following section takes one textile industry cluster in Guangdong as a case study.

## A Typical Textile Cluster in Xiqiao Town

Xiqiao Town is located in the inland region of the Pearl River Delta in Guangdong Province, southwest of the Nanhai District of Foshan City, covering an area of 177 square kilometers. Xiqiao Town covers four jurisdictions and 26 administrative villages, with a resident population of 140,000 and a floating population of 70,000. With convenient sea and land transportation, and located only 45 kilometers from Guangzhou, Xiqiao has a unique geographical advantage. Since 2000, Xiqiao has made great economic strides. In 2006, the total value of local industrial output amounted to RMB 21.4 billion, up 22 percent from the previous year. The output of the textile industry was valued at RMB 5.62 billion, accounting for 60.1 percent of the value of Xiqiao's total industrial output (see table 6.3) and 30 percent of the total market share of textile fabrics in Guangdong Province, 11 percent of the China market, and 6 percent of the international market. The production volume of textile fabrics reached 1.2 billion meters, out of which 0.11 billion meters were for export, with a value of US$87.52 million. This volume accounted for 15 percent of the total domestic exports of fabrics and 6.5 percent of the global market.

### China's Famous Town of Textile Fabrics and the
### First Textile Industry Upgrading Demonstration Pilot

In 2002, Xiqiao was awarded the title China's Most Famous Town of Textile Fabrics by the Textile Industry Association of China (TIAC); it was the second-largest production and sales base for textile fabrics after Shaoxing in Zhejiang Province. In May 2004, TIAC launched the first Textile Industry Upgrading Demonstration Pilot program in Xiqiao. The local specialized market, Xiqiao Textile City, is one of the three largest textile wholesale markets in China and is the number-one textile production and distribution base in southern China.

Such titles have laid a foundation for further development of the Xiqiao textile cluster and are attracting more related enterprises to join. As a typical endogenous SME cluster, among the current 741 textile enterprises,[7] only a few have investments from Hong Kong, China or Taiwan, China; more than 90 percent are privately owned, and more than half are operated by local people. Among the first-generation entrepreneurs in Xiqiao, almost none had graduated from any textile university or college of science and technology. Most of them had worked in the processing line in the plants and picked up their professional knowledge and skills and their market information on textile fabrics through learning by doing.

**Table 6.3　Key Statistics on the Textile Industry in Xiqiao Town, 2000–06**

| | 2000 | 2001 | 2002 | 2003 | 2004 | 2005 | 2006 |
|---|---|---|---|---|---|---|---|
| Gross industrial and agricultural output value (RMB billions) | 6.97 | 9.78 (industry: 9.017) | 11.37 (industry: 10.434) | 13.262 (industry: 12.41) | 154.05 (industry: 12.434) | 17.228 (industry: 14.156) | 21.4 (industry: 17.982) |
| Total output value of textile industry (RMB billions) | 2.66 | 4.33 | 4.98 | 4.91 | 5.039 | 9.09 | 10.8 |
| Output value of textile industry as % of gross industrial output | — | 43.6 | 47.7 | 39.6 | 40.5 | 64.2 | 60.1 |
| Number of textile enterprises | 1,600 | 1,636 | 1,265 | 1,259 | 1,100 | 1,102 | 800[a] |
| Number of employees in textile industry (thousands) | 40.61 | 44.481 | 49.405 | 62.905 | 60.0 | 62.9 | 60.0 |

*Sources:* Yue, Cai, and Liang 2008. All data are based on the report "Briefing of Xiqiao Textile Industry" made by Nanhai District Policy Research Office, September 2007. Other data (that is, the textile proportion of the total industrial output value data) are based on the research and calculations by the authors.

*Note:* The number of textile enterprises in this table contains enterprises as legal entities, industrial units, and the like. The number of employees includes those who work in positions associated with the textile industry. — = not available.

a. Approximate number.

As part of the industry upgrading demonstration pilot, some well-known large enterprises in the industry chain have invested in the Xiqiao textile industrial base, which helps extend the local industry chain from the weaving of specialized fabrics at one end of the chain to a complete textile cluster with textile machinery, weaving, printing, dyeing, and finishing of various fabrics for garments and furnishings, as well as garment manufacturing, at the other end. With a contribution of 60.1 percent to local GDP in 2006, the textile industry has become an important pillar of Xiqiao's economic development.

## The Formation of the Xiqiao Textile Cluster

Although Xiqiao has a thousand-year history in the textile industry, it began to emerge as a cluster only after China's reform and opening up. Its development has gone through three phases: the formation phase from the 1980s to the early 1990s, the innovation and expansion phase from the mid-1990s to the early years of the 21st century, and the comprehensive upgrading phase since 2004.

*History of the textile industry in Xiqiao.* The textile industry in Xiqiao first prospered during the Tang Dynasty (618–907 AD) and reached its peak in the Ming Dynasty (1368–1644 AD), benefiting from Guangzhou's reputation as a source of superior-quality silk and yarn. During the Tang and Song dynasties, China's economic center gradually moved south. In the process of exploring and developing the Pearl River Delta area, people created the traditional production pattern of "combining fish farming with mulberry cultivation,"[8] which provided the raw materials needed for the development of the silk textile industry.

After the Opium War in 1840, stimulated by world demand, large quantities of raw silk were exported, boosting the industry. In 1872, Chen Qiyuan, well known as the Father of Textiles, established the Ji Chang Long Silk-Reeling Factory and opened a new era in which machines were used to reel silk, greatly stimulating local industrial development. By 1924, Xiqiao owned 12,000 sets of silk machines, accounting for one-third of the total silk operations in the Pearl River Delta area. During China's War of Resistance against Japan (1937–45), the textile industry in Nanhai County was nearly destroyed. On the eve of liberation, the textile industry began to recover, with 982 textile enterprises in 1949 and 2,562 manually operated textile machines. Only 1,963 silk looms remained, and the annual output was valued at RMB 2.53 million, accounting for only 6.04 percent of Nanhai County's annual gross industrial output.

After 1949, the textile industry in Xiqiao Town and Nanhai County began to be developed by state operation through merging the privately owned and the government-owned enterprises. At the end of 1957, local enterprises began to manufacture artificial silk products. Three state-owned silk factories in Xiqiao Town were set up in 1973 and 1974, on the basis of several silk enterprises owned by towns or villages. They belonged to the Nanhai County government and were named Nanhai Silk Factory, Nanhai Silk Factory II, and Nanhai Silk Factory III. By 1972, all manual looms had been replaced by machinery and electrical equipment, speeding up the development of the silk industry. The principal local products included silk fabrics, silk yarn, rayon woven products, and the like, which were sold at home and abroad. In 1978, the textile industry output of Nanhai was valued at RMB 47.37 million, accounting for 12.98 percent of the county's total GDP (Nanhai County Textile Group 1992).

***Formation of the Xiqiao textile cluster.*** During the 1980s, the reform and opening up policy had significantly driven forward the development of Xiqiao's textile industry. More and more local farmers set up factories rather than farming in the fields, and private textile mills emerged rapidly. Simultaneously, with the deepening of the market-oriented reforms during the late 1980s, the business of the three state-owned silk factories in Xiqiao started to decline. The reasons included serious shortages of raw silk supplies, lack of incentives, and the low efficiency of state-owned enterprises. Many skilled employees left these factories to run their own businesses. At the same time, local private businesses were experiencing rapid development. Minle Village, for example, had more than 400 individual textile mills, with nearly 5,000 looms. Many individual plants only had three or four machines, and others were run by partnerships of local farmers, with an investment of several thousand yuan each and no more than 10 machines. The textile industry supported almost 60–70 percent of villagers.

In the late 1980s, when the three state-owned enterprises underwent restructuring, a large number of laid-off workers moved to private enterprises as skilled laborers. With a rapid increase in domestic demand for textile goods, a production and marketing system with more than one thousand factories, ten thousand looms, and more than 10 million meters of textile production was formed in Xiqiao Town, which then became one of the major production and sales bases for textile products in China. The embryonic form of the Xiqiao textile cluster emerged.

In 1986, to address the backlog of several tons of cloth, the town government coordinated the stakeholders and established the Southern

Textile Market (also called the Southern Cloth Wholesale Market) on Jiangpu Dong Road in the Guanshan District, based on the original market formed by the local producers. Some 400 wholesale stores with various types of cloth attracted both domestic and foreign textile fabric manufacturers and retailers, who subsequently set up businesses there. By 1995, the Xiqiao Southern Textile Market had become one of the largest professional wholesale markets in the world, with 1,338 fabric stores in an area of 50,000 square meters. The expansion of this professional market also contributed to the prosperity of the surrounding industries that offered related services.

With a production base of more than 2,000 small and medium enterprises and a well-developed professional market, a prosperous textile industrial cluster finally emerged in Xiqiao Town. By the mid-1990s, there were 2,234 textile factories, 13,432 looms, and more than 20,000 employees. The textile industry had become an important pillar of Xiqiao's economy.

The development of the Xiqiao textile cluster during this period, however, was a simple expansion of low-quality production (Wang and Yue 2008). Many textile looms were outdated, and some had been abandoned by the former state-owned plants. Obsolete equipment led to low-grade products and low efficiency, creating a great challenge for the cluster. On the one hand, the launch of a large number of textile projects across the country led to a rapid increase in the capacity for textile production and caused heated competition in the domestic market. Meanwhile, along with rising income, domestic consumer demand began to shift toward new raw materials and fashion designs, resulting in an overstock of low-grade textile products.

At the same time, local SMEs lacked the technical capacity for innovation. First, most of the workers were from other provinces and had low skills. Being located in townships and far away from the center of the city, local SMEs found it difficult to attract high-quality talent. In addition, according to one questionnaire given out to 32 enterprises (Wang et al. 2008), the educational level of the workers and staff in these enterprises was generally low: 65.2 percent had a high school education or below, 25.02 percent were from secondary professional schools, 8.86 percent had three or four years of university or college education, and 0.92 percent had master's degrees. Technicians accounted for less than 10 percent of the total labor force in many small enterprises, and senior technicians and departmental managers accounted for even less. Moreover, it is very difficult for SMEs in China to obtain finance from commercial banks.

Lacking innovation resources, these SMEs chose to imitate. By relying simply on imitation, however, the SMEs in the Xiqiao textile industry ended up with a serious shortage of innovation dynamics and capacity (see table 6.4).

***Innovation for development of the Xiqiao textile cluster.*** Facing the structural imbalance of the textile market in the mid-1990s—that is, with low-grade fabrics in excessive supply and some 30–50 percent of mid- and high-grade fabrics being imported—the Xiqiao Town government realized that it was necessary to enhance the overall quality of its textile products through technology innovation. The town government thus implemented a strategy of revitalizing the textile industry through science and technology.

From 1995 onward, the town government implemented three main measures under this strategy: building a textile city, establishing a fabric sample manufacturing company, and invigorating large enterprises while relaxing control over small ones, an approach that was to help large enterprises gain bank loans to buy advanced equipment. In view of local enterprises' lack of innovation dynamics and ability, the government decided to assist them through a technology service organization that would offer public services aimed at innovation and upgrading for the textile industry, including, for example, product testing, certification, protection of intellectual property rights, and professional training.

Through these measures, a large number of enterprises have now updated their equipments and attained broader capabilities for producing new products on their own or with the help of the technology innovation center (TIC). Within a decade, local textile enterprises had invested a total of RMB 4 billion in upgrading equipments and machines. As a result,

**Table 6.4    Innovation Methods Used by SMEs in the Xiqiao Textile Industry, 2004**

|  | New sample or design supplied by clients (OEM) | Imitation and innovation | Independent R&D |
|---|---|---|---|
| Enterprises | 9 | 21 | 8 |
| Percentage | 28 | 66 | 25 |
| Sequencing of the largest percentage[a] | 2 | 1 | 3 |

*Source:* Wang et al. 2008, 99.
*Note:* Number of SMEs is 32.
a. Sequencing refers to the percentage of innovation methods used by SMEs, ranging from 1 to 3; 1 refers to the most frequently used method.

the Xiqiao textile cluster has gradually passed through the difficult times and made some substantial progress in technology upgrading.

*Upgrading the development of the Xiqiao textile cluster.* At the beginning of 2004, China's textile industry experienced three "cold fronts": the shortage of electrical power and pressure for saving energy; increasing costs of raw materials; and a price war that was getting more intense in the textile industry, especially in the low- and medium-quality product markets. Meanwhile, some overseas trade protection measures created friction in export markets. The traditional growth path of Chinese textile industry, that is, to win by sheer quantity with low prices, had come to an end. The Xiqiao textile cluster faced not only domestic competition from Jiangsu and Zhejiang, but also international competition from India, Pakistan, and other countries. Under such circumstances, the textile cluster had to upgrade, that is, to increase the added value of products through innovation (Pietrobelli and Rabellotti 2004).

To promote the restructuring and upgrading of the textile industry, in 2004 TIAC chose Xiqiao as the first national textile industry upgrading pilot. Since then, the Xiqiao textile cluster has entered an upgrading era. A technology innovation center was constructed to offer more effective services to SMEs and to enhance the overall innovation ability of the textile cluster.

## Role of Government, Policy Instruments, and Their Implementation

The administrative decentralization brought on by the 1994 fiscal reform of the tax-sharing system allowed local government to share tax revenues to a certain extent with the central government. Under this system, local governments bear certain responsibilities for providing public goods. And because their fiscal revenues are derived mainly from enterprise income tax, value-added tax, sales tax, and land transfer fees, the more developed the local economy is, the more revenue the local government collects. This arrangement has provided strong institutional incentives for local governments to participate actively in developing the local economy.

### The Role of Local Government in Cluster Development

Along with the deepening of China's reform, however, the role of local government began to change. Qiu and Xu (2004) point out that during the transition to a market economy, the role of local government evolved

from "local state corporatism"—that is, local government directly partici-
pated in setting up enterprises to gain profit and assumed the characteristics of a "corporation," while its officials played the role of entrepreneurs
(Oi 1992, 1995, 1998,1999; Walder 1995)—to "post–local state corporatism," in which local government withdrew from owning and operating
all kinds of enterprises and focused on levying taxes and providing a full
range of services for local economic development. State government then
moved into "post–post–local corporatism," in which the government supported intermediary organizations and enabled them to replace part of
local government's functions so that government could govern the local
society and economy more effectively. With this evolution, a market-
oriented economic system gradually developed. Such a path can be
clearly observed in the case of Xiqiao.

Under China's old system of the planned economy, all sectors and
industries were owned and operated by the state government, and state-
owned enterprises in China have played key roles in local cluster development. For example, the Xiqiao textile cluster was formed from three
state-owned silk enterprises. Most of the private enterprises routinely
obtained their raw material, technology, and market information from
them. Many managers, technicians, and workers in private enterprises had
formerly worked for those state-owned textile factories. Along with the
system transition, local government's roles also changed at different stages
of cluster development as shown in table 6.5.[9]

### Policy Instruments and Their Implementation

*Facilitating the formation of local clusters.* Since the early 1980s,
town governments have implemented a series of policies and measures
to support the development of the local textile industry: (a) encouraging and supporting local farmers in setting up textile enterprises indi-
vidually or with other farmers; (b) coordinating four trade companies
with related government agencies and setting up a professional team to
assist local enterprises in purchasing raw materials and selling fabric
products; (c) in the early 1990s, targeting the most outdated looms and
equipment that produce low-quality products and providing financing
guarantees to help SMEs gain bank loans to update their machines;
(d) establishing the specialized Southern Textile Market in 1985 to
regulate the local trading market and stimulate mass production and
sales. These policies and measures have proved fairly effective in promoting the development of local SMEs and facilitating the formation
of the Xiqiao textile cluster.

**Table 6.5  Evolution of Local Government Role in Xiqiao Cluster Development**

| Stage | Formation (1980–95) | Innovation for development (1996–2003) | Upgrading (2004–present) |
|---|---|---|---|
| State of cluster and enterprises IC | Cluster already formed | Maturing cluster | Cluster being upgraded |
| | State-operated silk enterprises, local family mills, and private SMEs; lack of advanced looms and IC; mainly depending on imitation | Some SMEs were set up by people from other provinces; some private SMEs began to emerge; certain IC in product and process became available | 1/7 of firms are large enterprises with some IC; SMEs still rely on TIC to innovate; became textile industry upgrading demonstration region based on TIC and textile industrial base and Xiqiao Textile City; more strong agglomeration effects |
| Challenges in cluster development | Buyers' market emerging, facing fierce competition; cannot meet market demand in new products due to shortage of IC; local cluster stepped into predicament | Fiercer competition; IC constraint; more variability in technology and market demand; more innovation pressure; more difficult to keep competitive advantage | Increasing production costs; labor shortage; influenced by RMB appreciation and financial crisis; shrinking international and domestic market; low IC; cluster upgrading |
| Local government's role | • Encourage and support local textile industry development | Implement this strategy to break out of the predicament: | To facilitate local cluster upgrading: |
| Public policy and its objective | • Set up Southern Cloth Wholesale Market to facilitate sales of local products, and to accelerate local cluster development | • Build Xiqiao Textile City to promote specialized market | • Enrich the functions and raise the efficiency of TIC |
| | • Provide financial guarantee for local enterprises to gain bank loan and buy new looms | • Set up the Fabric Sample Manufacturing Company and TIC as industry public innovation service platform to enhance cluster IC and local competitiveness; transform TIC into private operation to make it more effective and sustainable | • Encourage e-innovation through specific measures to enhance local cluster competitiveness |
| | • Formulate the strategy of revitalizing the textile industry through science and technology | | • Construct eco-textile industry park to reduce production cost and protect environment and to attract more investment and to extend local industrial chain |

*(continued)*

**Table 6.5** Evolution of Local Government Role in Xiqiao Cluster Development *(continued)*

| Stage | Formation (1980–95) | Innovation for development (1996–2003) | Upgrading (2004–present) |
|---|---|---|---|
| Evolution of local government's role | Owner and operator of enterprises; both player and administrator in local economy development; dual roles: both public servants and entrepreneurs | • Provide guarantee for large local enterprises to get bank loans for equipment upgrading to raise production efficiency<br>• Construct textile industrial base from player to referee; transform from direct supplier of new products to administrator of local innovation service public platform; supplier of better infrastructure, production and marketing environment; public servants | • Widely brand "Xiqiao Fabrics" Regulator to set rules for TIC; designer for local cluster upgrading; supporter of local industrial association; promoter of regional brand; strategists for local development |

*Sources:* Authors, based on data and materials in Yue, Cai, and Liang 2008, Yue 2009.
*Note:* IC = innovation capacity.

***Implementing a "science and technology" strategy to support cluster development.*** A large number of similar small and medium enterprises in the cluster compete intensely through low prices. As a result, some enterprises in Xiqiao eventually had to move away, change to other businesses, or go bankrupt. Consequently, the number of enterprises fell dramatically from more than 2,200 in the mid-1990s to just over 1,300 in 2000.

Under such circumstances, the Xiqiao Town government decided to focus on the development of large enterprises to sustain the growth of local industry. By offering bank credit guarantees to some promising enterprises, local government helped them buy advanced equipment to produce new fabrics of better quality. With limited R&D and manufacturing ability, local fabric producers usually purchased advanced equipment to achieve process innovations. At the same time, government reduced some taxes and administrative fees to support enterprise development.

Another key policy instrument, the Fabrics Sample–Manufacturing Corporation (FSMC) backed by town governments, was set up in 1998 specifically to address local enterprises' lack of innovation capabilities. The FSMC was composed of three departments—the Solid Colored Fabric Design Department, the Jacquard Fabrics Computer Design Department, and the Printing Color Separating Design Department, which specialized in developing new fabrics, new dyeing processes, and new printing and dyeing formulas and in analyzing new weaving processes using information technology. The Xiqiao government invested more than RMB 4 million, mostly to buy systems for computer-aided design (CAD), computer-aided manufacturing (CAM), and computer-integrated manufacturing systems (CIMS). This equipment was beyond the purchasing power of most small enterprises at that time. Later on, the FSMC, using its own intellectual property, developed a small-sample loom that was able to produce small fabric samples, which greatly reduced the cost of product innovation for SMEs.

Before the FSMC, one private firm specialized in manufacturing fabric samples for other enterprises. But its new products were sold at higher prices. For example, one piece of new sample fabric made by the private company sold for RMB 1,000, which was beyond what the SMEs could afford. Now, with FSMC, a sample similar to that made by the private firm sold for only RMB 300.[10] Those who had bought new samples to weave new fabrics could earn more profit from the new product. Such a move encouraged local enterprises to innovate either through setting up their own R&D departments or through buying new products from FSMC.

At the end of 1999, encouraged by the example of Xiqiao's FSMC, Guangdong Provincial Science and Technology Bureau began to construct technology innovation platforms in all selected towns for innovation piloting. Since 2000, on the basis of the FSMC and with the support of the provincial government and the Nanhai government, Xiqiao Town established the Southern Technology Innovation Center (TIC), with a total investment of RMB 0.2 billion. Since its completion in 2001, the TIC has attracted more professional technological institutions and intermediary agencies to provide comprehensive services. By 2007, there were 11 agencies specializing in or related to technology innovation services.

By providing enterprises with newly designed products, the FSMC stimulated their innovation activities and helped clusters make significant progress from "weaving cloth by scissors," which means imitating other enterprises' cloth through cutting their new cloth with scissors to "weaving cloth by computers," which means Xiqiao enterprises can weave cloth based on technology innovation through CAD and CAM. Meanwhile, the TIC provided not only new products, but also innovation services, including information, technical consultation, professional textile training, testing and certification, and so on. To supply all these services in a market-based way, all departments and agencies inside the TIC are now owned and operated privately as independent legal entities. After its withdrawal, local government has acted solely as an administrator. The TIC has now become a platform for cooperation among government, industry, and research institutes and a facilitator for enterprise innovations.

***Giving impetus to cluster upgrading.*** To upgrade the local cluster, Xiqiao Town has focused on five goals, called the "five ones":

- *One system*. To construct a textile industrial system by introducing textile machinery enterprises upstream and garment enterprises downstream to build a complete textile industry chain
- *One platform*. To strengthen the functions and efficiency of the TIC, the public innovation platform, to offer better services
- *One base:* To further improve the infrastructure of the local textile industrial base
- *One market*. To build a Xiqiao Textile City to provide a communication bridge and an interactive link between the textile enterprises and the trade market (*China Economic Weekly* 2006)
- *One brand*. To establish one regional brand, Xiqiao Fabrics, under the guidance of the Nanhai district government[11]

Local government has also hosted fairs and public activities on several occasions to promote the reputation of Xiqiao Fabrics and has set up relevant testing institutes to ensure the quality of the fabrics. Following are details of two of the policy instruments that have been implemented.

*Investment attraction activities.* To extend the textile industry chain by attracting more upstream and downstream enterprises into the Xiqiao Textile Industrial Base, the local government has carried out a new round of investment attraction activities since 2002. The Foshan and Nanhai governments have implemented a series of preferential policies. For example, for the high-tech enterprises established in the industrial park, according to the Nanhai government, enterprise income tax can be exempted in the first two years and paid at a reduced rate of 15 percent in the following three years.

Meanwhile, the government is now setting up entry barriers to foreign direct investment, so that only those high-tech enterprises and textile enterprises that are in accord with requirements can be admitted, in an attempt to emphasize the quality and efficiency of the investment. Due to increasingly heated competition among districts and the shortages of land and electricity resources, local government needs to increase the output value of investment per unit of area while decreasing potential pollution problems. According to the 2006 policy, the minimum investment intensity has to be more than RMB 1 million for an area of about 670 square meters, and all newly invested projects have to be set up inside the industrial park. To attract the new enterprises it needs, Xiqiao Town has created an award to encourage those who successfully introduce an enterprise accepted by the government.

Within this first eco-industrial park, the Xiqiao government has tried to supply complete infrastructure and quality services to foster a better development environment, and has taken the lead in unifying the supplies of water, steam, and sewage treatment for enterprises in the park. Here, sewage can be recycled through a thorough treatment in the plant and further deep treatment in a stretch of artificial wetland. In this way, enterprises do not have to invest separately in building their own boilers, sewage treatment facilities, and sewage pipeline. Furthermore, an effective system of sewage treatment enables printing and dyeing enterprises to be licensed to operate in the park, businesses that have been subject to sanctions in Xiqiao because of heavy pollution.

*"One platform, five pillars."* To promote the upgrading of the local textile cluster, the Xiqiao textile TIC has now been extended further, with its "one platform, and five pillars" (see figure 6.2) (Wang and Yue 2008). The five pillars of the TIC are meant to supply product innovation and technical services for those local enterprises that have their own R&D departments and mainly supply new products to local and regional SMEs. Many of these are large local enterprises that occasionally buy new products from the TIC but mainly have a need for technical services, such as product testing and certification and professional training in textiles. Operated by the Information Department of the TIAC, the Textile Industry (Southern) Fabric Testing Center with the TIC has been accredited by the China National Accreditation Board for Laboratories under its testing and quality authentication system. Its functions cover normal testing, eco-testing, and functional testing for guaranteeing the quality of textile

**Figure 6.2    Public Platform of "One Platform and Five Pillars" for Upgrading the Innovation of the Textile Cluster**

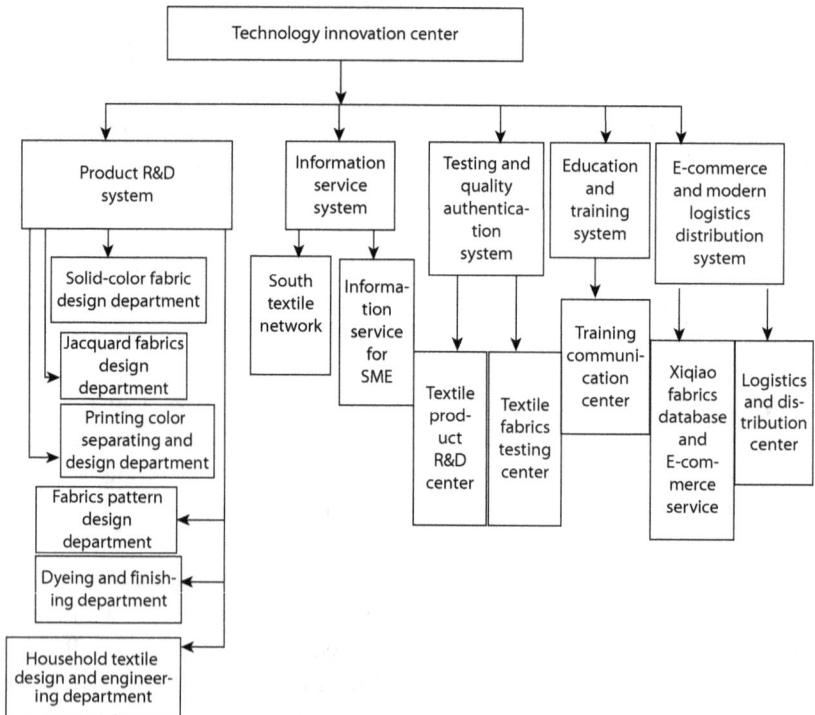

*Source:* Authors' research.

products for sale in both domestic and overseas markets. Fabrics with test certificates issued by this center are accepted by more than 40 countries and regions including Europe, the United States, the Republic of Korea, Japan, and Southeast Asia. To introduce this system, early in 2003, Nanhai District and Xiqiao Town governments reached an agreement with TIAC that they would invest in physical assets, such as equipment and offices, while TIAC would supply human resources and other intangible assets. It is the first testing and quality authentication system to be located in a town in China and has played an important role in raising the image of Xiqiao Fabrics.

For local SMEs, the town government requires that all R&D and service organizations supply them services at a 70–80 percent discount as a kind of support measure, and, as compensation, their rents are set at a much lower price of RMB 10–15 per square meter, while the rent is RMB 20–28 per square meter for other companies inside the TIC building. As the administrator of the TIC, the Xiqiao Textile City Administrative Committee acts only as a building property manager and a monitor to ensure that these privately owned and operated organizations perform their public service functions.

## Evaluation of Government Policy and the Xiqiao Textile Cluster

Through the constant efforts of local enterprises and with the support of local government and the TIC, the innovation ability and competitiveness of Xiqiao's textile cluster are continuously increasing. One survey shows that more than 60 percent of the total of 56 enterprises have accepted product design and R&D services, nearly 20 percent of the enterprises have accepted services on patents, and about 34 percent have used information services from the TIC (see table 6.6) (Wang et al.

**Table 6.6    Technical Services Accepted by Textile Enterprises from Xiqiao's Technology Innovation Center, 2004**

|  | Product design | Service for patent | Process improvement | Quality control | Information service | Training service | Others |
|---|---|---|---|---|---|---|---|
| Enterprises | 34 | 11 | 13 | 10 | 19 | 16 | 14 |
| Percentage | 60.7 | 19.6 | 23.2 | 17.9 | 33.9 | 28.6 | 25 |
| Ranking | 1 | 6 | 5 | 7 | 2 | 3 | 4 |

*Source:* Sun Yat-Sen University 2008.
*Note:* N = 56.

2008). The Xiqiao TIC has greatly reduced the production cost of enterprises and has facilitated local innovation.

### Effectiveness of the Technology Innovation Center

Among the 153 public innovation platforms in Guangdong's specialized towns, by 2007 not all of them operated smoothly, some had already disappeared, and some had been replaced by a local innovation network dominated by a large enterprise in the cluster. So far, however, Xiqiao's Technology Innovation Center is working well and playing a critical role in cluster upgrading. Since 2008, TIAC has begun to replicate its experiences in 133 textile cluster pilots throughout China. Xiqiao's TIC has now been designated the Guangdong Provincial Textile Fabrics Engineering and R&D Center and has become the first textile technology and engineering center in China.

Table 6.7 shows the changes from before the establishment of the TIC in 1998 up to 2003, in which we can see that the sales value of textiles rose from US$342.2 million in 1998 to US$788.8 million in 2003, although the number of enterprises fell from 1,590 to 1,380; the average R&D investment of enterprises increased from US$140 to US$4,280; and the total number of patents rose from zero to 188, while the number of employees increased by more than 10,000.

Fabrics made in the Xiqiao cluster already have a certain competitive advantage. Up to 2007, more than 20,000 new products were developed by the TIC, more than 20 new fabrics were qualified as "China Popular Fabrics," and more than 70 new products developed by more than 30 enterprises shared the title "China Popular Fabrics." So far the Xiqiao cluster has obtained more than 300 national patents for the appearance and practical design of its products and owns 24 provincial and national brands. The regional brand, Xiqiao Fabrics, has already been established (Nanhai District Government 2006).

With the support of the TIC and through the efforts of the large enterprises themselves, the development cycle of new fabrics in Xiqiao has been shortened from 20–30 days to 1–5 days, while development costs have dropped more than 50 percent. Inside Xiqiao Textile City, some 30–40 percent of new products were developed by the TIC, and about 30 percent were independently developed by local enterprises. Although the average unit price of new fabrics made in Xiqiao is 15–20 percent higher than those made in other regions, their better quality has won an increasing market share. For example, one meter of jean cloth made in Xiqiao can be sold for RMB 23, while the same sells for RMB 16–17 when made

**Table 6.7 Xiqiao's Clusters Before and After the Establishment of the Technology Innovation Center, 1998 and 2003**

| Employees | 1998 | | | | | 2003 | | | | |
|---|---|---|---|---|---|---|---|---|---|---|
| | Firms | Employees | Output (US$ millions) | R&D (US$ thousands) | Patents | Firms | Employees | Output (US$ millions) | R&D (US$ thousands) | Patents |
| <10 | 795 | 7,055 | 44.6 | 0 | 0 | 465 | 3,715 | 31.9 | 0 | 0 |
| 11–50 | 583 | 26,235 | 130.1 | 0 | 0 | 534 | 25,299 | 94.5 | 0 | 0 |
| 51–100 | 205 | 19,475 | 106.1 | 0 | 0 | 359 | 33,387 | 323.2 | 2,256.7 | 22 |
| >100 | 7 | 1,094 | 61.5 | 230 | 0 | 22 | 6,445 | 339.2 | 3,648.2 | 166 |
| Total | 1,590 | 53,859 | 342.3 | 230 | 0 | 1,380 | 68,846 | 788.8 | 5,904.9 | 188 |
| Firm average | 32.28 | | 0.21 | 0.14 | 0 | 49.86 | | 0.58 | 4.28 | 0.14 |

*Source:* Sun Yat-Sen University 2008.

in Zhejiang. Some large enterprises have also supported their suppliers in making innovations in raw materials distributed in other provinces. Nowadays, the fabrics of many nationally known garment brands are made in Xiqiao, including Jaquer, HuBao, Shanshan, Baoxiniao, Hongdou, and Busen.[12]

Through the TIC's promotion, local textile enterprises have begun to use information technology more widely. According to local government statistics, 10 percent of the enterprises have already applied CAD and CAM systems; 25 percent of the enterprises have used office automatic systems; and about 15 percent of the local enterprises have established Management Information Systems (MIS) and Enterprise Resource Planning (ERP) systems, which have greatly improved management, efficiency, and productivity.

### Achievements in Implementing Cluster Upgrades

In its innovation and upgrading policy, the Xiqiao cluster has achieved great success. The good local development environment has attracted both upstream and downstream enterprises. Since 2003, more than 100 textile enterprises have been established in Xiqiao's textile industrial base. The scale of enterprise has been expanded, although the number has been reduced from 1,259 in 2003 to 741 in 2008. The larger local enterprises own 200–300 weaving machines, while the number of weaving machines owned by the typical smaller enterprises has increased from 4 up to at least 30, illustrating that these smaller enterprises are growing, too. By 2008, there were more than 20,000 spinning machines, about half of them shuttleless, which is a much higher percentage than the corresponding 10 percent average countrywide. Private enterprises account for more than 90 percent; 9 enterprises have an annual output of RMB 100 million, and more than 50 have an annual output of RMB 5 million. With a more complete industry chain, the Xiqiao textile industrial cluster will have an even greater agglomeration effect.

In 2007, the transaction amount of Xiqiao Textile City reached RMB 25 billion, an increase of RMB 7.2 billion over 2006. More than 5,000 new products are released into the market every year, and many of them lead new fashions. Specialized cowboy cloth, casual fabrics, and fabrics for household decor have become the most competitive products. Xiqiao fabrics are not only sold in the domestic market, but also in Japan, Canada, the Russian Federation, Europe, and other countries and regions. It is estimated that the value of Xiqiao's trade accounts for 10 percent of China's total and 40 percent of Guangdong's total. Even during the 2008 global crisis, the output value of the textile industry still reached RMB 7.885 billion, an increase of about 40 percent from 2003. With about 60,000 employees, the textile industry is still an important pillar of the local economy.

### Key Success Factors of the Xiqiao Cluster
Several key factors are responsible for the success of Xiqiao's endogenous textile cluster. The cluster's spirit of entrepreneurship, its social network, its capacity for innovation, and the role of government are the primary reasons for its continued prosperity.

*The spirit of entrepreneurship and social networks.* The informal institutional environment created by the social culture and local customs—namely, entrepreneurship, the probusiness atmosphere, and the industrial foundation—provided the necessary soil for enterprise growth. In Xiqiao Town, with its long history of the textile industry, its traditional entrepreneurial culture, and its venturing spirit, drove local farmers one by one to stop farming and set up enterprises in the early 1980s. At that time, the sound of looms could be heard everywhere in the villages. Xiqiao's people have had an innovative spirit ever since ancient times. Early in 1872 in the Qing Dynasty, for example, Chen Qiyuan, a citizen of Xiqiao, opened a new era of reeling silk by machine. A daring spirit of venturing and an atmosphere encouraging innovation shaped the necessary environment for Xiqiao's textile industry.

With the emergence of the private economy, more and more skilled workers left local state-operated silk enterprises and set up their own factories or worked for private enterprises. Through a network of colleagues, friends, relatives, and people from the same village, the techniques, raw materials, and market information formerly in the state-owned enterprises were transferred to private enterprises. Within a village or town, the demonstration effect is strong, and it is very easy for residents to learn from each other. In addition, many officials in town government had close connections with local firms. When these private enterprises met difficulties in raw material purchasing or sale of products, for example, local government was willing to actively help them to resolve the problem. This kind of social network facilitated local cluster formation and development as well.

*Innovative capability and the role of government.* After cluster formation, innovation is a very important source of competitiveness for sustaining cluster development. To increase the added value of products and to upgrade local clusters from the low end to the high end of the value chain, clustering enterprises must have innovation capability. And even under dual challenges, internal and external, only about 30 enterprises disappeared from the Xiqiao cluster in 2008. One important reason is that Xiqiao enterprises have obtained certain innovation capabilities.

Another factor is that the enterprises have benefited from the services of local government. In addition to the measures mentioned above, including the TIC, in 2008, the Nanhai government implemented a scheme called the Eagle Plan to upgrade eight local clusters and strengthen the competitiveness of local enterprises through financing, technology innovation, and regional brand support. Local government supplied RMB 80 million in credit guarantees so that local enterprises could apply for bank loans. These funds were to go toward helping them obtain loans from local commercial banks worth 10 times the loan guarantees. In the first batch of more than 70 enterprises selected in this scheme, more than 20 were from the Xiqiao cluster. At the same time, the costs of raw material and energy had dropped because of the crisis. Therefore, for those enterprises that were competitive, the opportunity for development outweighed the challenges caused by the crisis. In any case, however, the drop in market demand at home and abroad was really a great challenge in general, and only those with innovation capability could come out winners in such fierce competition.

### Main Challenges for Cluster Sustainability

Despite its great success, given the current worldwide financial crisis, the Xiqiao textile cluster continues to confront both external and internal challenges, the former coming from weak demand from the global market and enhanced competition. Meanwhile, with the appreciation of the RMB, garment exporters' profits have been greatly reduced; as their fabric suppliers, Xiqiao producers are directly affected, although not as seriously as other regions. In addition, domestic and overseas competition is becoming increasingly stronger. This situation is especially difficult for small enterprises.

Inside the cluster, despite many successful firms, a number of textile enterprises are still not competitive, have low innovation capability and low managerial skills, and lack any well-known brands. In addition, horizontal linkages between similar textile enterprises are missing, which lowers the collective efficiency of the cluster.

From the global perspective, the Xiqiao cluster, along with most clusters in China, is still counting on low costs for its competitive advantage rather than R&D, innovation, and branding. Without sufficient technical and managerial personnel in the cluster, some development opportunities might be missed, such as new applications of textile materials in agriculture, medicine, building, aerospace, and state defense, among others.

In addition, as an accelerator of cluster development, the efficiency of the TIC, the public innovation platform, needs to be enhanced as well. Most important, the innovation ability of each design department needs to be improved. More specialized R&D and technical personnel also need to be hired. Some particular training services required by the enterprises cannot be supplied by the TIC, which now offers only the generalized training required by the industry.

## Discussion, Conclusion, and Policy Implications

Hereinafter are the discussion, conclusion, and policy implications of the role of government and technology service organizations in clusters, especially in traditional industrial cluster development.

### The Role of Government in Cluster Development

In conclusion, some policy implications can be drawn about the development experience of Guangdong and Xiqiao:

- The role of policy is different at different phases of cluster development and should be adjusted accordingly as the cluster develops. At the stage of cluster formation, policy needs to focus more on strategic sectors. A strategic industry plan involving the whole province should be in place before specific cluster policies are issued. Otherwise, intense competition among local governments will cause duplication of efforts and waste of resources, as well as a high level of fragmentation.

- After the cluster has come into being, support for the cluster should focus on helping build its innovation ability. Most SMEs in a traditional industry cluster do not have enough innovative resources, such as technical and R&D personnel, or funds to carry out product and process innovations. In such a situation, the establishment of public innovation platforms by local governments is a viable choice.

- A production service industry is critical for cluster upgrading, including technology service institutes, logistical services, and intellectual property protection services that can support enterprises' innovation activities.

- Human resources are very important for cluster development at any time, especially during the process of upgrading. The education, training, and recruitment of personnel are quasi-public responsibilities from the perspective of knowledge and technology spillover. Each different level of government can play its own role, such as working out policies for attracting R&D talent and setting up colleges and schools to educate and train technicians and professional personnel for local cluster development. Moreover, local government should supply complete infrastructure and good living and commercial environments to attract talent and investment.

- A cluster needs to keep innovating and upgrading; otherwise, it will go into decline and may eventually disappear and become an empty shell. Enterprises should enhance their technology innovation capabilities and try to upgrade their competitiveness through R&D and branding. A single internationally famous regional brand is helpful in raising the added value of the product and enhancing the competitiveness of the cluster.

- Local government must support enterprises in setting up their professional associations to enable the enterprises to be self-governed and at the same time to build a bridge between government and market.

Generally speaking, the role of government is indispensable in cluster development. However, government should only do what it needs to do to avoid market failure. On the stage of a market-oriented economy, enterprises are the main actors. As the regulator of the market, however, the government must intervene appropriately and offer necessary support. It is difficult for government to know when and how to intervene, but to build a good institutional environment and to provide sound public or quasi-public services are always the top priority of government.

### Technology Services in the Cluster
The view that an industry cluster is helpful for enterprise innovation is widely accepted, but clusters alone are no guarantee that such innovation will happen naturally. Many scholars point out that SMEs in clusters have

difficulties in innovation for many reasons (Bellandi 1994; Glasmeier 2005), which are difficult for SMEs to overcome by relying on their own technology and funds. Therefore, it is necessary to introduce an innovation-support organization as a way of breaking out of this plight (Bianchi 1996). Guangdong's cluster development experiences and those of other counties in Zhejiang and other provinces show the necessity for local government's provision of support for SME innovations in clusters, such as working out a subsidy policy, building an industry innovation fund, establishing an innovation service organization, and the like. (Brusco 1990; Asheim et al. 2003; Wang and Yue 2008). However, even when technology service organizations (TSOs) are set up under quite similar situations, the results may differ. Some of them are successful in leading and supporting local cluster innovations (for example, the TIC in Xiqiao), while others have disappeared or been run with lower efficiency in the development process or have been replaced by an innovation network established by local core enterprises. Why? Wang and Yue (2008) point out that a TSO's success is critically dependent on whether it can adapt to the demands of enterprise innovation in the cluster.

In the Xiqiao experience, the TIC ensured that most SMEs would have innovation capability, thus bolstering the sustainability of the local cluster. While engaged in this process, the roles of both the TIC and the local government have had to evolve to adapt to changing demands. Through an analysis of the successful experience of Xiqiao's TIC, four conclusions can be drawn on ways that a TSO can work more effectively:

- In the process of cluster development, a TSO, as an innovation service platform, needs to be built. Because of its quasi-public nature and the technology and knowledge spillovers generated from it, it is necessary and reasonable that the TSO be sponsored by local government.

- The function of a TSO depends on the innovation ability of the enterprises it serves. In developed countries, the enterprises in a cluster already have their own innovation capability; therefore, the TSO's main function is to supply technical consultation, product testing, information, training, and other technical services. In developing countries, though, because most of the enterprises in traditional industrial clusters lack innovation ability, the TSO needs to focus on specialized functions first, such as introducing new designs, materials, and products. With the development of a cluster, the function of a TSO will inevitably evolve and will need to adapt constantly to the needs of the enterprises.

- For a TSO to supply better innovation services, it is necessary to mobilize social resources and, at a certain point, to transform the TSO into a market-oriented operation. Local government should not withdraw from supporting the TSO until many enterprises can make new products by themselves instead of buying from the TSO. To ensure that the public innovation platform operates in a market-oriented way and can effectively provide public functions, local government needs to provide guiding regulations and to work out some evaluation indicators to measure its services.

- The interactive innovation mechanism between a TSO (which is located at the TIC) and the enterprises it serves is based on the transaction, that is, on the commercialized operation. The enterprises are to buy the new products or innovation services supplied by the TSO, even though the initial equipment and facilities for innovation in the TSO are financed totally or partially by the government. For that reason, it is critical, even mandatory, for the TSO to be operated effectively and efficiently. As for the process of interactive innovation, besides the evolution of the TIC's function, the interactive patterns of innovation have evolved from the beginning when the enterprise's innovation capability derived mainly from the TSO itself to the point at which innovation has become a cooperative activity between the TSO and the enterprise in two ways: one in which SMEs supply the sample and the TSO assists them in improving and designing new ones and the another in which the SMEs describe their ideas and concepts for the new product and the TSO helps them develop it into a tangible new product (Yue 2009).

## Notes

1. Yangtze River Delta refers to Zhejiang Province, Jiangsu Province, and Shanghai.
2. The historical name *Hong Kong* refers to the period before July 1, 1997, when the former British colony was restored to China; *Hong Kong, China* refers to any time after that date.
3. Jun Wang (2005) points out that three kinds of clusters can be observed in China, that is, endogenous, FDI-driven, and market derivative, according to the forming mechanism. Yuan and Li (2008) divided China's clusters into six types: resource-driven, trade-driven, science-tech resource driven, large enterprise-hatching cluster, industry transferring-driven, and FDI-driven clusters. Here, we merge the former five types into the endogenous, and regard the FDI-driven one as the exogenous cluster.

4. The eastern China region includes Beijing, Tianjin, Hebei, Liaoning, Shanghai, Jiangsu, Zhejiang, Fujian, Shandong, Guangdong, and Hainan. The central part includes Shanxi, Jilin, Helongjiang, Anhui, Jiangxi, Henan, Hubei, and Hunan Provinces. The others belong to western China.

5. The Pearl River Delta includes nine cities: Zhuhai, Zhongshan, Guangzhou, Foshan, Dongguan, Huizhou, Shenzhen, Zhaoqing, and Jiangmen, in which there are 42 counties. The industrial and agricultural output value of clusters in the former six cities accounted for 70.6 percent of the total clusters in 2007.

6. This concept of "specialized town" was proposed by several experts: Jun Wang, Ping Lu, Xinchun Li, et al., August 1999, *GD with Its New Economic Development Pattern*. This was also proposed in their report entitled *The Specialization Town Innovation Pilot in GD*, which was approved by the provincial Science and Technology Committee.

   In 2005, there were a total of 1,117 towns in Guangdong, out of which 159 were specialized towns. There are two main indicators for measuring a specialized town: the first is that the output value of the local dominant industry and its related industries accounts for more than 30 percent of the town's total output; the second is that more than 30 percent of the employees are from this industry (Wang 1999).

7. In 2007, the number of textile enterprises was less than 800; in 2008, it was 741. Although the number of enterprises is falling, the size of the remaining enterprises and the output value of this cluster have grown (see table 6.3).

8. The production mode refers to the use of silkworm excrement to feed fish and pond mud to fertilize mulberry trees. Mulberry trees, silkworms, and fish are linked together in an eco-production circle.

9. Local government in this case refers mainly to Nanhai District and Xiqiao Town. Nanhai County has been one of the districts of Foshan City since 2003.

10. The data are based on a research interview with the Xiqiao government on August 15, 2002.

11. Based on an interview with Nanhai District government, September 2007.

12. Data and materials are supplied by the TIC.

## Bibliography

Asheim, Bjorn T., Arne Isaksen, Claire Nauwelaers, and Franz Todtling, eds. 2003. *Regional Innovation Policy for Small-Medium Enterprises*. Cheltenham: Edward Elgar.

Bellandi, M., 1994. *Decentralized Industrial Creativity in Dynamic Industrial Districts in Technological Dynamism in Industrial Districts: An Alternative*

*Approach to Industrialization in Developing Countries?* New York: United Nations Conference on Trade and Development.

Bianchi, P. 1996. "New Approaches to Industrial Policy at the Local Level." In *Local and Regional Response to Global Pressure: The Case of Italy and Its Industrial Districts,* ed. F. Cossentino, F. Pyke, and W. Sensenberger, 195–206. Geneva: International Institute for Labour Studies.

Brusco, S. 1990. "The Idea of the Industrial District: Its Genesis." In *Industrial Districts and Inter-firm Co-operation in Italy,* ed. F. Pyke, G. Becattini, and W. Sengenberger, 10–19. Geneva: International Institute for Labor Studies.

*China Economic Weekly,* 2006. "The Breakthrough of Textile Enterprises in the Upper-Level Chain of Guangdong Textile Industry." February 23.

Fu, Yong. 2008. "Does Fiscal Taxation Power Separation Reform Rise Local Government's Fiscal Incentive Strength?" *Finance & Trade Economics* 7: 35–41.

Gereffi, G. 1999. "International Trade and Industrial Upgrading in the Apparel Commodity Chain." *Journal of International Economics* 48.

Glasmeier, A. K. 2005. "Economic Geography in Practice: Policy on Local Economic Development." In *Oxford Economic Geography Handbook,* ed. G. L. Clark, M. P. Feldman, and M. S. Gertler, 565–84. Translated by Weidong Liu et al. Beijing: Guangdong Bureau of Science and Technology. 2006. Internal Reports. The Commerce Press.

Guangdong Bureau of Science and Technology. 2006. Internal reports.

Humphrey, J., and Hubert Schmitz. 2003. *Governance in Global Value Chains.* http://www.globalvaluechains.org.

Kaplinsky, R., Olga Memedovic, Mike Morris, and J. F. Readman. 2003. *The Global Wood Furniture Value Chain: What Prospects for Upgrading by Developing Countries: The Case of South Africa.* Vienna: United Nations Industrial Development Organization.

Lu, Ping, Ping Lin, and Chunhua Guan. 2008. *The Rising and Innovation of Specialization Industrial Towns in Guangdong Province.* Guangzhou: Guangdong Science-Tech Press. Updated by authors with new 2007 data from Development and Planning Department of Guangdong Provincial Science-Tech Bureau's survey and report.

Nanhai County Textile Co. (Group) et al., eds. 1992. *Nanhai County Textile Industry History/Records:*1–40.

Nanhai District Government, Policy Research Department. 2006. *Report on Xiqiao Town Pushing Textile Industry Upgrading through Technology Innovation.*

Oi, Jean. 1992. "Fiscal Reform and the Economic Foundation of Local State Corporatism in China." *World Politics* 45 (1).

———.1995. "The Role of the Local State in China's Transitional Economy." *China Quarterly* 144.

————. 1998. "The Evolution of Local State Corporatism." In *Zouping in Transition: The Process of Reform in Rural North China*, ed. Andrew Walder, 35–61. Cambridge: Harvard University Press.

————. 1999. "Local State Corporatism." In *Rural China Takes Off: Institutional Foundations of Economic Reform*, ed. Jean C. Oi 95–138. Berkeley: University of California Press.

Pietrobelli, C. 2004. "Upgrading and Technological Regimes in Industrial Clusters in Italy and Taiwan." In *Linking Local and Global Economies: The Ties That Bind*, ed. C. Pietrobelli and A. Sverrisson, 133–59. London: Routledge.

Pietrobelli, C., and R. Rabellotti. 2004. *Upgrading in Clusters and Value Chains in Latin America: The Role of Policies*. Washington, DC: Inter-American Development Bank.

Provincial Science and Technology Bureau of Guangdong, Development Department. 2008. *Statistical Investigation Report of GD Specialization Towns in 2007*.

Qiu, Haixiong, and Jianniu Xu. 2004. "The Behavior Analyses of Local Government in Regional Innovation." *Management World* 10: 36–46.

Sun Yat-Sen University. 2008. *Xiqiao Town Surveys*. Guangzhou, China.

Walder, Andrew. 1995. "Local Governments as Industrial Firms." *American Journal of Sociology* 101(2).

————. 1997. "The State as an Ensemble of Economic Actors: Some Inferences from China's Trajectory of Change." In *Transforming Post-Communist Political Economics*, ed. Joan M. Nelson, Charles Tilly, and Lee Walker, 432–52. Washington, D.C.: National Academies Press.

Wang, Jici. 2005. "Chinese Industry Clusters." *Interpreting Industry Clusters* 1: 11–15.

Wang, Jici, and Tong Xin. 2005. "Industrial Clusters in China: Embedded or Disembedded?" In *Linking Industries across the World*, ed. Claes G. Alvstam and Eike W. Schamp, 223–42. Hants: Ashgate Publishing Company.

Wang, Jun. 1999. "SMEs Specialization Development and Network." *Academic Research* 9: 16–20.

————. 2005. "The Emergence and Evolution of Specific Market Based Clusters in Guangdong Province, China." *Management World* 8: 80–86.

Wang, Jun, Ping Lu, and Xinchun Li. 1999. "The Specialization Town Innovation Pilot in Guangdong." In *The Rising and Innovation of Specialization Industrial Towns in Guangdong Province*, ed. P. Lu, P. Lin, and C. Guan, 60–65.

Wang, Jun, and Yanhua Mao. 2005. "On the Technology Innovation Mechanism of Specialization Town in Guangdong Province." Research project report for Provincial Science and Technology Bureau of Guangdong.

Wang, Jun, and Fangmin Yue. 2008. "Technology Service Organization and the Formation of Innovation Capabilities of Clustering Enterprises—A Case Study of Xiqiao Textile Cluster." In *China Institutional Change Case Study*, Guangdong volume, ed. Shugang Zhang et al. Beijing: China Finance and Economy Press.

Wang, Jun, et al. 2008. *Technology Innovation and Cluster Development in China: On Technology Innovation Mechanics in China's Specialized Town Economy*. Beijing: Economy and Science Press.

Xiqiao Town Government. 2003. "The Pilot Scheme of Xiqiao Town Principal Agent for Investment-Attraction." *The Award Scheme of Xiqiao Town Encouraging Attraction of Investment, 2003*. http://info.textile.hc360.com/2005/05/16144521995.shtml; http://www.xh108.com/thj_view.asp?id=624. Accessed April 10, 2008.

Xu, Jianniu. 2010. "Post Local State Corporatism: A Case Study of Local Government's Role in the Development of Industrial Cluster after Privatisation." In *Asian Industrial Clusters, Global Competitiveness and New Policy Initiatives*, ed. Bernard Ganne and Yveline Lecler, 307–24. Beijing: World Scientific Publishing.

Yuan, Dongmin, and Zuojun Li. 2008. "Introduction." In *China Cluster Developing Report (2007–2008)*, ed. Liu Shijin, 2–8. Beijing: China Development Press.

Yue, Fangmin. 2007. "On Cluster Enterprises Innovative Dynamics and Path: Based on Guangdong Traditional Industrial Clusters." *Academic Research* 7: 42–48.

———. 2009. "Interactive Innovation Mechanism Based on Transaction of Industrial Cluster: Case Study on Interaction between Technology Service Organization and Enterprises in Xiqiao Textile Cluster." PhD dissertation, Sun Yat-Sen University.

Yue, Fangmin, Jinbing Cai, and Ying Liang. 2008. *The Path of Innovation and Upgrading: Research on Development Pattern of Xiqiao Textile Cluster*. Guangzhou: Guangdong Renmin Press.

Zhang, Jun, Yuan Gao, Yong Fu, and Hong Zhang. 2007. "Why Has China Had Good Infrastructure?" *Economy Research* 3: 1–19.

# Index

Figures and tables are indicated by *f* and *t* following the page number.